The Challenge of Diversity

Industrial Policy in the Canadian Federation

August 1983

Science Council of Canada
100 Metcalfe Street
17th Floor
Ottawa, Ontario
K1P 5M1

© Minister of Supply and Services, 1983

Available in Canada through

Authorized bookstore agents
and other bookstores
or by mail from

Canadian Government Publishing Centre
Supply and Services Canada
Hull, Québec, Canada K1A 0S9

Vous pouvez également
vous procurer la version française,
à l'adresse ci-dessus

Catalogue No. SS21-1/50E
ISBN 0-660-11400-3

Price: Canada: $8.95
Other countries: $10.75

Price subject to change without notice.

HD
3616
.C23
J46 / 57,007
1983

The Challenge of Diversity

Industrial Policy in the Canadian Federation

by Michael Jenkin

CAMROSE LUTHERAN COLLEGE
LIBRARY

Michael Jenkin

Michael Jenkin was born in Redruth, England in 1948 and attended elementary and secondary schools in Toronto and Newmarket, Ontario. He obtained his Honours BA at Trent University in history, politics and economics in 1972. After serving as research coordinator for the Commission on Canadian Studies (sponsored by AUCC and the Canada Council), he pursued postgraduate studies at the University of Manchester on a Commonwealth Scholarship, obtaining an MA in economics and PhD in politics and economics.

In 1977, he joined the staff of the Science Council's Industrial Policies Study as a science adviser and has contributed to a number of Council publications. His current research interests centre on the institutional and political problems of industrial policy formulation. He is the author of several articles and a book, *British Industry and the North Sea: State Intervention in a Developing Industrial Sector.* Dr. Jenkin recently joined the federal public service.

Contents

CAMROSE LUTHERAN COLLEGE
LIBRARY

List of Figures

List of Tables

Foreword

Science and technology policies are key components in the broader industrial policies of any country. The political environment crucially influences how such policies are developed and implemented. Without a clear understanding of this political environment, it is often difficult to make sensible recommendations about the type of industrial studies which are appropriate and likely to succeed. In its latest report on industrial policy, *Forging the Links: A Technology Policy for Canada*, Council stressed the importance of the country's system of federal-provincial relations for industrial policy. Subsequently, it explored aspects of the issue in two of its occasional publications, *The Politics of an Industrial Strategy*, issued in March 1979, and *The Limits of Consultation*, published in May 1981.

In *The Challenge of Diversity*, Dr. Michael Jenkin investigates more fully the severe problems posed by distinctive regional economies, and their representation by provincial governments, for the development of coherent national industrial and technology policies. By examining the various attempts at interprovincial and federal-provincial cooperation over such policies, the author assesses the prospects for cooperation to produce an effective response to the country's industrial problems. In the process, he makes a number of interesting and constructive recommendations about how both levels of government, but particularly the federal government, can adapt to what seems to be an increasingly decentralized and regionalized industrial policy environment.

In publishing this background study, the Science Council hopes to stimulate debate on the various ways Canada can help overcome its regional divisions and build a stronger public policy response to the problem of industrial change. As with all background studies published by the Science Council, this study represents the views of the author and not necessarily those of Council.

Maurice L'Abbé
Executive Director
Science Council of Canada

Preface

Canada faces a major challenge during the 1980s – how to restructure the industrial base to adapt to rapid technological change and a hostile, and increasingly competitive, world trade environment. Developing coherent industrial policies that address this new environment, however, will be far from easy. Canada confronts a number of difficulties in forging a consensus on industrial policy, not the least of which is a pronounced growth of regional economic awareness, and the advocacy of that awareness by provincial governments. In many ways, therefore, the problem of developing an effective industrial strategy in Canada has become a problem of intergovernmental bargaining (and conflict) over the direction and content of the country's industrial policies. This study examines the problems that the growing awareness of regional economic interests pose for industrial policy makers and how these problems have become enmeshed in our federal system. The study emphasizes, therefore, the character of intergovernmental relations with respect to industrial policy and how these relations could be changed to promote a more effective response to the challenge of structural change in Canada.

Another important aspect of the problem of industrial policy, however, is the generation of a consensus, or at least an effective working relationship, between the functional actors involved in industrial policy: business, labour and government. The introductory chapter explains that the construction of effective links among these actors has been an important element in the success of industrial policy in other countries. Regrettably, Canada faces particularly difficult problems in this area, partly because the highly regionalized nature of the country's economy works against the creation of coherent national interest groups. Surprisingly, therefore, the amount of academic research which has been carried out on the role and function of industrial interest groups in Canada and their relationship to government is pitifully small, although a few interesting studies are now helping to improve our knowledge of the area. Hopefully, a sufficient level of research will be carried out in the near future to allow an indepth study on this important topic.

One final point. This study is concerned with the problem of how to create a consensus on industrial policy in the *intergovernmental* context. As such, it is not directly concerned with the content of that policy, but rather with the process of developing an industrial policy. It is, however, very difficult to totally dissociate questions of process from those concerning the content of an industrial policy, and, of course, the study does contain a number of assumptions about the character of industrial policy. Perhaps the most notable are the following: that governments will continue to be deeply involved in leading structural change; that such change often requires very detailed and specific modifications to the structure and conduct of industrial activity at the level of the firm; and that such government involvement must frequently stress the innovative and technological capability of firms, be they in manufacturing, the resource sector or the service industry. That, however, is as far as this study takes the issue of the *content* of industrial policy. The issue is a broad subject, examined in some detail in other reports by both the Science Council and other organizations and individuals. This study concentrates on the broader political economy constraints facing industrial policy makers in Canada and how these constraints manifest themselves in the process of federal-provincial relations. With a clearer understanding of the limits placed by the regional structure of our economy and our federal system on the development and implementation of industrial policy, we can deal more intelligently with the issue of content.

Because federal-provincial relations is a very broad area of public policy, often shrouded in secrecy, it would have been impossible to have written this study without generous assistance from a great number of people. Both in Ottawa and the provinces, many individuals were kind enough to spend a great deal of time with me discussing the issues addressed here. Civil servants and officials in intergovernmental organizations were also kind enough to comment on various parts of the manuscript. I am grateful for their efforts.

I would also like to thank my colleagues at the Science Council for their support, encouragement and the time they took to discuss the study's progress with me: Guy Steed, Bill Forward, Jim Gilmour and Paul Dufour commented at length on several drafts of the manuscript and provided many helpful suggestions. I also benefitted from a commentary from Professor Donald Smiley of York University. In the long and tedious process of carrying on the research for this study, three very able assistants, Anne Smith, David Phillips and Nicholas Sidor worked long and hard hours ferreting out much of the information presented here. More important, they also contributed very substantially to the study's insights and analyses, and without their help this would have been a less substantial research effort.

A researcher is only as good as the information at his disposal; and I was lucky to have access to the Science Council library. Special thanks to Frances Bonney, Faye Borden and Francine Benoit for being able to obtain even the most obscure documents within frequently unrealistic deadlines. The charts and diagrams in the study were drafted by Leo Fahey, who was also an adviser on the graphical presentation of much of the statistical information. David Morel capably assisted in checking and assembling a wide variety of statistical information.

My secretary, Cher Daley, provided invaluable assistance with the organization and management of the study from its inception, and typed, and retyped, drafts of the manuscript with skill and patience; her good humour helped to make a long period of research more enjoyable. Patricia Teskey and Colleen Gray edited the manuscript and saved me from a number of grammatical and stylistic faux pas.

Finally, I would like to thank my wife Phyllis for putting up with a frequently preoccupied husband, and for injecting a lot of common sense and analytical judgement into the process of the study. Naturally, any remaining weaknesses or errors are my responsibility.

Michael Jenkin
January 1983

Part One

Introduction

I. The International Imperative and Canadian Industrial Policy

The Canadian Dilemma

With the possible exception of the Constitution, more time has been spent debating industrial strategy than any other issue in Canadian public policy. The potential for unending balance-of-payments deficits, increased isolation from world-trading blocs and a weakening position in international economic forums are just some of the undesirable trends that have brought to the fore the question: "What kind of industrial policy should Canada follow?"[1]

Raising this question is, however, as far as we have come. At present we seem unable to decide which actions and strategies would pull the country out of its present economic predicament. The current debate over the future direction of Canadian industrial policy is, in itself, one of the most powerful symbols of this impasse, caught as it is (perhaps oversimplistically) between the two major competing schools of thought, continentalist free trade[2] and economic nationalism.[3]

The spectacle of Canadian policy makers indulging in a Hamlet-like debate over whether to have or not to have an industrial policy while other countries move ahead to restructure their economies is exceeded only by the irrelevancy of the debate itself. Partly due to significant changes in the international trading system, the battle for "tariff-free" trade has been largely won. However, as tariff barriers have been lowered throughout the industrialized world, nontariff barriers to trade have grown significantly. Industrialized countries now deploy what are called "positive and defensive adjustment policies," designed both to prop up ailing industries threatened by foreign competition and to encourage the growth of new industries.[4] Even the former champion of world free trade, the United States, now talks not of "free trade," but of "fair trade."[5] Thus, what we saw in the 1970s was a resurgence of industrial policies designed both to insulate national economies from the effects of greater trade liberalization and to organize and restructure domestic firms to exploit new markets and technological advances. The liberalization of trade relations and the growing international mobility of capital and technology are forcing many countries to explore new ways of controlling their domestic economies and, in the process, they are being pushed to adopt more direct and forceful industrial strategies.

Our hand-wringing over whether we need a strong industrial policy, similar to those being implemented abroad, is worrying. This problem is, however, compounded by the growing confusion about which level of government is responsible for fashioning Canada's response to the changing world trade environment. Provincial governments are increasingly deploying industrial policies to serve their own specific needs, as part of a larger exercise in "province building." At the same time, the federal government is under attack for the regional bias of its policies, and seems uncertain about its own role, or in what direction its policies should move. Indeed, we present a confused and incoherent picture to those outside Canada, and frequently to ourselves.

Whereas political systems in other countries tend to emphasize the traditional divisions between business and labour on economic issues, in Canada *territorial* divisions predominate, and find expression most frequently in federal-provincial, or interprovincial, conflict. It is doubtful, therefore, that we will ever develop an effective approach to industrial policy making in Canada until the impact of intergovernmental relations on economic policy issues is fully addressed. In a country where, historically, deep regional economic divisions have found effective expression through provincial governments, it could hardly be otherwise.

This study explores the problems of developing an industrial strategy in the federal-provincial milieu. By examining the structure of regional economic conflicts in Canada, and by analyzing the attempts made in the past to overcome some of these conflicts, we can obtain a sense of the opportunities and limits for industrial policy formulation in a highly decentralized federal state. Before we can do this, however, it is important to outline the nature of industrial policy as it is practised both in Canada and abroad in order to understand the political demands that industrial policy formulation and implementation place on governments.

The Deep Roots of Intervention

In many countries, the link between the economy and an interventionist state is deeply rooted. One has only to cite France's traditional use of the economy as a tool of foreign policy,[6] or the role state intervention played in unifying and consolidating the economies of the German principalities into the German Empire during the last century to illustrate this point. And where the state has played a lesser role in economic development, it was usually because the countries involved so effectively dominated international markets that the "night watchman" state was seen to be all that was required. This is evident, for example, in Britain's commitment to free trade in the 19th century and a similar commitment to free trade in the United States following World War II.[7]

The tendency for industrialized states to intervene in their economies has been reinforced by the economic, social and political problems of recent decades. In the postwar period, most industrialized countries have been unable to rely solely on market forces to rationalize their economies. Tremendous efforts on the part of governments were required after 1945 to rebuild the war-torn economies of Germany and Japan. In Britain, government intervention grew rapidly after World War II because of the large number of declining and uncompetitive industries. In other countries, for example France under de Gaulle, a desire to restore the nations' place in the international economic system and to challenge the technological and economic pre-eminence of the United States motivated government action.[8]

Although state intervention in the postwar era began as a response to the problems of reconstruction, it often continued as governments grappled with such long-term structural issues as lack of competitiveness in traditional industries, employment maintenance, and regional development, to the point where in many countries intervention became the norm rather than the exception. During the 1950s and 1960s, government responsibility for the direction and shape of economic affairs reached its most explicit form with attempts at indicative economic planning in France, Belgium, the Netherlands and Britain.

In recent years, problems posed by these long-term structural issues have been complicated by a number of significant changes in the international economic system. The rise of new industrializing countries (NICs), rapid increases in energy costs, and the growing importance of technology in determining comparative advantage in world trade[9] have forced a number of countries to re-evaluate their industrial structures. Faced with domestic industrial decline – in part because of increased competitive pressure from both lower-cost producers[10] and the more technologically advanced countries – governments have been steadily forced to intervene to alleviate the effects of import competition upon declining industries and to build up high-technology industrial capacity.

The nature and scope of industrial policies now deployed by most western countries range from a variety of industrial support services to outright nationalization.[11] These policies often involve quite novel institutional innovations, such as the National Enterprise Board (NEB) in Britain, which combined the roles of state holding company and venture capitalist to assist in the restructuring of existing manufacturing firms and the creation of new, high-technology businesses. A common thread in the recent evolution of industrial policy has been its tendency to become more focussed and specific. This reflects the disenchantment in many countries with the effectiveness of macroeconomic policy in promoting industrial development. A number of countries, notably Britain and France, had unsatisfactory experiences with Keynesian demand management techniques in the 1950s, and with more specific, but still macroeconomic instruments such as indicative economic planning in the 1960s.[12] These macroeconomic policies, because they are aimed at broadly based economic phenomena, have often been ineffective and inappropriate for the rapidly changing and sectorally specific problems faced by industry in the 1960s and 1970s. Indeed, much industrial policy today is based on highly discriminatory measures that distinguish not only between industrial sectors, but also between firms.[13]

This tendency has been reinforced as governments have been obliged to come to terms with growing corporate concentration resulting from domestic mergers and the presence of multinationals in many strategic economic sectors. Large firms, domestic or multinational, can frequently have a disproportionate impact on areas of traditional government interest such as export promotion, capital investment and employment,[14] especially in high-technology industries, where a specific firm, or group of firms, may be uniquely capable of developing or marketing products or processes of strategic importance to a country's position in world markets.[15] Frequently, this results in governments trying to back existing winners with various types of tax, financial and technical assistance, or to pick winners from a group of enterprising, smaller firms.

In many cases, owing to the rapidly changing nature of industrial activity, governments are endeavouring to *anticipate* change by ensuring that a specific firm, or group of firms, is capable of meeting a new technological opportunity. In some instances, governments accomplish this by requiring firms to merge to create either a single firm, or a few firms capable of taking on the challenge (as the Japanese did in the case of automobiles and electronics).[16] In other instances, a government may enter into a joint venture with a promising firm, or even create a firm to meet a specific technological opportunity. Once established or chosen, these firms frequently receive not only selective financial assistance (for example, targeted R&D grants and tax breaks for capital investment), but also assistance on the demand side. Governments organize markets to create a demand for a favoured firm's product either by erecting nontariff barriers to imports, or by using public procurement (for example, of new telecommunications devices for state-owned telecommunications utilities) to launch a product or to get it to a critical level of domestic market penetration, which can assure export success. In doing this, governments may appear to be ignoring markets, but they are actually trying to anticipate market opportunities and formulate government and private sector strategies accordingly.

Thus, over the past 20 years, the character of industrial policy has changed as governments have attempted to come to terms with the social, political and economic implications of industrial change. Industrial policy has become more complex and microeconomic in focus as governments increasingly seek influence at the level of the industrial sector and now even at the level of the firm. However, it is important to remember, as well, that in industrial policy more than any other area of government activity, the rhetoric usually differs somewhat from the practice. Even governments that claim to follow the market in their economic policies can usually be found intervening in a highly selective manner in one industrial sector or another. The Conservative government in Britain, while espousing a free market approach to industrial policy, has engaged heavily in interventionist policies in the microelectronics field. The present US administration's approach to industrial policy in the automotive field has also been contradictory. Despite its claims to support the "magic of the market" and the beneficial effects of international free trade, it has continued the rescue of the Chrysler corporation and has attempted to restrict the flow of automobile imports into the United States in the interests of "fair trade".

A final element in the evolution of industrial policy making abroad has been the close association in most countries between industry, government and, on occasion, labour. In some cases, tripartite institutions, such as social and economic councils, which involve both industry and labour, have been created. These councils have been used in the economic policy process in such countries as Belgium, France and the Netherlands, while in other countries, like West Germany, labour has been included less formally – mainly through codetermination arrangements on individual boards of directors.[17]

Relations between industry and government have generally been much closer and more informal when they have not involved labour. In most advanced industrial economies, there are large, integrated, central business organizations, such as Japan's *Keidanren* or the French *Conseil nationale du patronat français*, that interact continuously with government. In addition, there is usually a wide variety of relationships between government and individual trade associations or single large firms. Indeed, because of the level of corporate concentration in Europe and Japan, single large firms often have a special relationship with their governments. These firms can become, in effect, "national champions" and are frequently the focus of specific policies. Examples include Philips and Shell in the Netherlands, Renault in France and IRI in Italy.

The Canadian Imperative

Industrial policies are as necessary in Canada as elsewhere. Canada has a very open economy and the changes now occurring in the international economic system will have a great impact on it. Further, the need for significant structural change in the Canadian economy is incontrovertible. Even studies published by organizations which once simply advocated trade liberalization to make Canadian industry more productive are now proposing at least some restructuring before embarking on further liberalization measures.[18] The Canadian economy's small size, and the growing uncertainty of resource markets (and, indeed, the future competitiveness of many of Canada's resource sectors) have placed our traditional reliance on resource exports in doubt. As well, the structural weakness of Canadian manufacturing and the trend towards continental production and marketing arrangements[19] suggest that our manufacturing sector will fare poorly in a more open world economy. Canada, like other countries, will have to embark on a restructuring of its industrial base, and the government will play a leading role. This does not necessitate elaborating a highly detailed national plan. Rather, it means a systematic attempt to assist successful firms and to identify and support those new industrial opportunities that have the most promising growth potential.

Despite our poor prospects if we continue without restructuring, the federal government has been, at best, a reluctant supporter of the industrial strategy concept, and has usually avoided commitments to systematic industrial restructuring, except for isolated *ad hoc* projects.[20] Part of the government's current reluctance is due to misgivings about the efficiency of intervention in social and economic affairs. As well, the development of an industrial strategy requires governments to make explicit choices about what sectors and firms to assist. Choices of this kind raise the prospect of failure as much as success. Under any interventionist regime, policy options become more stark and their potential for controversy increases – a situation most politicians and civil servants wish to avoid.

The federal government has usually preferred macroeconomic policies that reinforce the industrial status quo and do not discriminate between firms or sectors. These policies, while having the advantage of being less explicit and less politically visible, are, however, increasingly ineffective in managing economic change.

The Price of Policy Sophistication

What demands does industrial policy place on a political system? What do the Japanese and Europeans do that we might emulate? To start with, Japan and Europe have a much greater range of policy instruments, which enables their governments to work at both the micro and macroeconomic levels. Some of these policies are highly innovative in coping with new industrial problems or opportunities. Like Canada, the Japanese and Europeans finance various forms of R&D, regional location and other types of assistance to industry. However, the amount of monetary support in these countries is frequently larger than in Canada, and is applied in a much more varied manner.[21]

But the greatest differences between the Canadian and the Japanese and European forms of industrial policy relate more to institutional and political factors than to the scale of national resources directed to industrial support policies. In Japan and Europe, effective industrial policies have emerged from industrially partisan governments possessing specific relationships with individual companies and industrial sectors. Experience in these countries also indicates that extensive intervention in the economy carries with it a need for some central policy direction, through either a planning ministry or well-established interdepartmental cooperation. Most countries have gained considerable experience in this area, partly as a result of planning experiments in the 1950s and 1960s, and partly because of the volume of industrial restructuring since World War II.

The political structures supporting industrial policy formulation in Europe and Japan are also well developed. Continuous links with trade associations and large firms allow governments to keep in touch with industrial problems and communicate policy objectives effectively . These relationships also make it easier for governments and industries to agree on sectoral restructuring. Furthermore, it is clear that industrial policy is more effectively formulated in economies which are highly reliant on manufacturing. Clear national interests on issues relating to industrial development tend to come into focus more readily when this is the case.

Ultimately, however, what is essential for the effective implementation of industrial policy is that the central government have the authority and capacity to influence companies and industries. The ability of the state to do this is primarily a function of its historical role in nation building. It is also the result of it being forced, for reasons of industrial collapse or crises, to become deeply involved in the workings of industry.

The Canadian Case
Compared to Japan and Europe, Canada seems a relative novice in the area of industrial policy. This is ironic because, historically, the Canadian government has probably played as significant a role in economic development as governments in Europe or Japan. Government involvement in the Canadian economy has ranged from support for canal building in colonial times to the construction of railways following Confederation, and the creation of manufacturing enterprises during two world wars.[22] At both the federal and provincial levels, government has played a large role in the creation of transportation, energy, communication and other industrial infrastructures. Whether this significant level of government involvement contributed to Canada's transition to an industrial economy or simply reinforced its role as an exporter of staples is debatable.[23] Yet Ottawa's capacity to promote significant economic change has never been in doubt. Indeed, the existence of a Canadian national economy can in some measure be viewed as a triumph of political will – one which maintained an east-west pattern of trade when economic forces became increasingly north-south in orientation.[24] Still, our economic history has severely limited our ability to implement industrial policy in the manner of the Europeans or the Japanese in two ways. First, industrial interest groups have been highly diversified and have had little in common. Second, these groups have had an uncertain commitment to policies supporting manufacturing. The reasons for this reflect Canada's historical emphasis on the export of raw materials and agricultural products and the concomitant development of an economic infrastructure necessary to support those exports.[25] Industrial and commercial interest-group activity aimed at supporting government measures which broadly benefited a resource-based production system. This included the construction of an efficient transportation network and the support of a commercial system (for example, banking and retailing) to facilitate trade. To a large extent, Canada is still a staples economy. Questions concerning resource policy and transportation remain central political issues. We still have heated debates over the construction of natural gas pipelines, the setting of rail freight rates and the ability of our rail system to carry grain exports to port.

Since the beginning of this century, secondary manufacturing has grown in importance. But even at its peak in the late 1940s and early 1950s, manufacturing never accounted for more than a quarter of the country's gross domestic product (GDP) and has never been the predominant sector in terms of output.[26] In fact, manufacturing has played a far less significant role in Canada than in virtually any other industrialized country (see Table I.1). Moreover, the growth of manufacturing was not based on domestically owned firms as much as on foreign-owned branch plants. Between 1926 and 1970, foreign control of manufacturing rose to a peak of 61 per cent from 38 per cent.[27]

Table I.1 – **Gross Domestic Product Accounted for by Manufacturing Activity, 1979**

Country	Percentage of GDP
Germany	37.6
Japan	29.7
France	27.1
Netherlands	27.4*
Belgium	26.2
United Kingdom	24.0
United States	24.0
Sweden	22.9
Canada	19.5
Norway	17.5
Turkey	12.3

* 1977 Figures
Source: OECD *National Accounts*, vol. II, Paris, 1981.

The consequences for industry-government relations are clear. Even in the relatively homogenous economies of Europe and Japan, building a consensus on industrial issues is never easy. But at least in these countries the structure of traditional industry-government relations, and the bias towards manufacturing, allows the development of a consensus on specific issues. In Canada, manufacturing interests are overshadowed by the resource sector, and fractured by disputes between large and small business and domestic and foreign-owned firms.

Perhaps even more important, however, has been the manner in which the character of economic development has profoundly affected the nature of regional conflict. Canada is geographically large, as well as socially and economically diverse. Since its creation, it has had an industrially developed centre which has been primarily reliant on the domestic market, and a series of resource- or staples-producing regions on the periphery, largely dependent on exports. As a result, different patterns of economic development and interests have evolved, with provincial governments becoming a natural focus for those interests. This has turned the issue of industrial strategy into one involving *territorial*-political conflict. The resource-producing provinces view industrial-policy issues as basically special pleading for favoured treatment by an already wealthy in-

dustrial centre represented by Ontario and Quebec. Just as important, this regionalization of economic interests has had an important
impact on the structure of industrial interest-group activity. Interest groups lack national coherence, partly because they are encouraged to express their grievances and aspirations on a regional
basis, often through provincial governments.

In a similar manner, the direction in which industrial policy is
evolving elsewhere, with its emphasis first on sectoral, and now on
firm-specific action, poses special problems for a country with ter-
ritorially diverse interests. The decision to support, or indeed, to rationalize a particular form of industrial activity, especially at the
firm level, inevitably has territorial implications when economic activity is so regionally specialized. Support for one industry or one
firm is seen as support for one region or province rather than
another. It is in this sense that it has become virtually impossible to
discuss industrial policy in Canada without immediately addressing
the problem of regional economic competition and its political mani-
festations - federal-provincial and interprovincial conflict.

These problems, combined with inexperience in the broad range
of industrial-policy instruments and coordinating mechanisms existing elsewhere, mean that we face particular difficulties in creating
and implementing a national industrial strategy. Now, however, international economic trends are forcing us to find a way to overcome
these difficulties. The question is: how?

Given that the problem of developing an industrial policy in
Canada is territorial in character and that in large measure the territorial conflict over industrial policy has found expression through
the 11 governments in Canada, it is through these governments that
at least a start to the solution of territorial conflict must be found.
Accordingly, this study focusses on three specific questions: 1) the
nature of the underlying regional economic conflict in Canada; 2) the
manner in which it has found expression at the governmental level
(in this case, the seeming weakness of the federal government and
the growing assertiveness of the provincial governments in the area
of industrial policy); and 3) the degree to which governments, either
jointly or separately, can find a way to harness their resources to effect necessary structural change.

Organization of the Study

The following chapter outlines some of the economic conflicts inherent in the Canadian federal system. Part Two reviews the emergence
of provincial industrial strategies as a response to those conflicts and
analyzes their significance for the development of national industrial policies. Part Three reviews the experience of federal-
provincial and interprovincial collaboration on industrial policy and

related matters. It also seeks some lessons from that experience for developing industrial policy in an intergovernmental context. Part Three is complemented by a discussion in Part Four of the role, both past and present, of the federal government in economic policy making, its relevance to the changing nature of industrial policy internationally and the shifting economic balance of power between the two levels of government. Finally, chapter XI offers some recommendations on how the provinces and the federal government can improve their collaboration and what role the federal government should play in a policy area that is becoming increasingly decentralized.

II. Canada's Centre - Periphery Economy

To hear it discussed today, one would think regional economic conflict is a relatively new phenomenon in Canada. The western resource boom in the 1970s and recent concerns about the impact of this new growth on the structure of the economy and the political balance of power has made people forget the West's long history of relative economic stagnation. On the surface today, the problem of regional conflict seems to be a dispute between an aggressive and selfish Alberta and victimized consumers in Ontario.

Historically, it was the reverse. Conflicts were between the wealthy and powerful industrialized centre, and a poorer and weaker group of commodity-producing regions. Even today, this broad and fundamental historical difference of interest is manifest in disputes over issues ranging from railway freight rates to the nature of trade policy. It is important to realize, therefore, that many of the conflicts we see today over the direction of economic policy are largely the result of a staples economy which encouraged regions to become highly specialized and highly unequal.

Canada has always depended upon the export of commodities.[1] Even today, commodities such as agricultural products and raw and semiprocessed materials (for example, smelted ores), comprise about two-thirds of the value of Canada's exports.[2] Not surprisingly, this continuing emphasis on raw materials and agricultural goods has prolonged past disputes.

After Confederation, the implementation of the National Policy, and the consequent expansion of both primary and industrial production, the full regional implications of a staples-based economy became a political issue. With the incorporation of Rupert's Land and British Columbia into Canada a few years after Confederation, a continent-wide staples economy was created. The planned and highly organized settlement of the Prairies, the construction of the

Canadian Pacific Railway and the introduction of tariffs to encourage manufacturing were all part of an attempt, through the National Policy, to structure an integrated national economy. However, it was to be a very particular integration, one which, ironically, institutionalized regional specialization and conflict. The West and, to a lesser extent, the Maritimes were to concentrate on the production of agricultural exports, and British Columbia, northern Ontario, Quebec, and the Maritimes were to provide mineral and forest exports. In return, these regions were to act as markets for the manufactured goods of southern Ontario and Quebec.

Whether any different geographical division of economic activity would have occurred and whether the regions would have been any better off without the National Policy is unclear. Indeed, good reason exists to believe that the problems faced by the regional economies were due more to their geographic location and staples base than the machinations of central Canada's economic policy makers.[3] It cannot be denied, however, that it was the regional economies of western Canada and the Maritimes which bore the principal costs of this staples-centred economy. They were the regions whose prosperity depended almost entirely on activities (such as agriculture) which traditionally generated lower incomes than those arising from manufacturing. Furthermore, such activities have generally offered less varied and secure job opportunities because they are dependent on the boom-and-bust cycles of world commodity markets. The legacy of this developmental pattern is an economy in which the regions have historically experienced very different costs and benefits from economic integration.

The Legacy of Inequality
The issue of regional economic inequality was undoubtedly one of the principal areas of conflict after Confederation. Since the Great Depression, the issue of regional disparities, and attempts to overcome them through a process of national income transfers, have been central to the Canadian federal system. Canada now has one of the most highly developed systems of regional transfers of any country and, indeed, one of the larger regional development budgets.[4] And well it should. Of the developed industrial countries, Canada has one of the greatest disparities in per capita income between its richest and poorest region. It is exceeded, depending upon the measure used, only by Italy, and equalled only by France (see Table II.1).

Historically, the nonindustrialized regions of Canada have suffered below average personal incomes and above average unemployment. For example, as shown in Figure II.1, personal income per capita has been below the national average for the Prairies, Quebec and the Atlantic provinces.[5] Only Ontario and British Columbia

Table II.1 – Regional Per Capita Product and Income Differences in Relation to National Average

Country	Year	Income or output measure[1]	Poorest region or state	Level average = 100	Richest region or state	Level average = 100	Mini /max ratio	Degree of inequality measured by Gini[2] coefficient
Australia	1973/74	Personal income	Tasmania	]87	New South Wales	]105	1.2	0.03
Canada	1973	Personal income	Newfoundland	54	Ontario	117	2.2	0.09
United States	1975	Personal income	Mississippi	60	Alaska	175	2.9	0.09 51 states
					Washington D.C.	125	(1.4	0.06 9 regions)
					Connecticut	120		
Switzerland	1972	GDP	Appenzell I.R.	69	Basel Stadt	151	2.2	0.07
Switzerland	1967	Personal income	Obwalden	72	Basel Stadt	143	2.0	0.07
Germany	1974	GDP	Schleswig-Holstein	84	Hamburg	149	1.8	0.05
					Bremen	118		
					Nordrhein-West	104		
Germany	1970	Personal income	Saar	81	Hamburg	133	1.6	0.05
					Bremen	113		
					Baden-Württemberg	108		
France	1970	GDP	Bretagne	81	Paris	139	1.7	0.09
France	1970	Personal income	Midi-Pyrénées	80	Paris	139	1.7	0.09
Italy	1973	GDP	Calabria	55	Liguria	137	2.5	0.15
Italy	1973	Personal income	Calabria	60	Liguria	134	2.2	0.14
United Kingdom	1974	GDP	N. Ireland	74	South-east	117	1.6	0.07
United Kingdom	1974	Personal income	N. Ireland	69	South-east	119	1.7	0.06

1. *GDP* at factor cost for Germany; market prices for other countries; regional GDP data do not exist for Australia, Canada and the United States. *Personal income* (as defined above) for all countries except Italy and Switzerland, for which net national product at factor cost is given, since official regional personal income data do not exist.

2. The Gini coefficient of inequality is a weighted average of per capita income differences between regions, where relative population shares are used as weights. A value of 0.0 means exact equality; a value of 1.0 denotes all income concentrated in one region; a value around 0.05 indicates relatively small interregional inequality, whereas a value of 0.15 indicates already substantial interregional inequality. This use of population share weights takes into account both the size of regions and also the distribution of regions falling between the richest and the poorest.

Source: *Report of the Study Group on the Role of Public Finance in European Integration*, vol. II, Commission of the European Communities, Brussels, 1977, p. 122.

Figure II.1 – Index of Personal Income per Capita by Region, 1930-1980

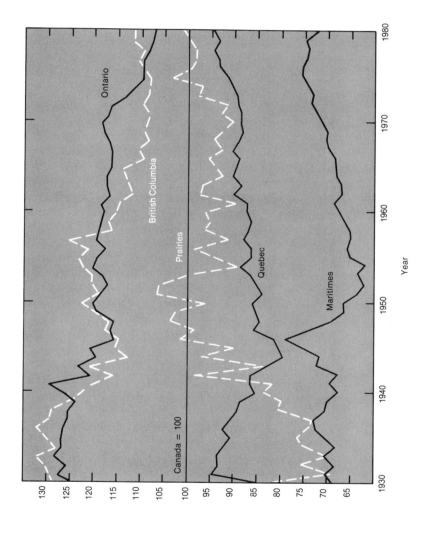

Source : Statistics Canada, 13-201, *National Income and Expenditure Accounts,* various issues.

31

have enjoyed above average income levels. More recent evidence indicates that provincial differences in per capita income are declining, largely due, in the case of the poorer provinces, to increased federal transfers. However, differences in provinces' gross domestic product per capita have increased. This indicates, according to Pestieau and Maxwell, that "disparities in the ability of provinces to generate their own income have widened considerably in the 1970s."[6]

Furthermore, unemployment data for the period 1946-80 (see Figure II.2) indicate that these disparities have also manifested themselves in lost job opportunities. Despite its high per capita income level, even British Columbia has had unemployment rates well above the national average, and only Ontario and the Prairies have remained significantly below the national average.[7] In the case of the Prairies, the level of employment maintenance was probably due, in part, to the high proportion of active farmers. Significantly, the only region which maintained *both* employment and income levels above the national average has been heavily industrialized Ontario.[8]

Average rates of unemployment or income do mask, however, equally significant qualitative differences in opportunity for residents of the various regions. The range of employment opportunities outside Ontario is less varied. And the facilities, both public and private, that residents have access to in Ontario are usually better than those elsewhere. There are also significant variations in such social indicators as accommodation, infant mortality and life expectancy.[9]

With increasing energy prices in the 1970s, western provinces broke this differential. In Alberta, for example, unemployment has recently been relatively low, and per capita income figures have been above the national average. Whether this situation will continue with the relative decline in oil prices is uncertain. Resource-based economies can, and do, experience boom-and-bust cycles as the staples they produce fluctuate in international markets. With proportionately fewer employment opportunities in other sectors, workers can find little in the way of alternative employment when the staple industry is in recession. In addition, seasonal unemployment, because of the staples nature of production (for example, in the forest industry and fishing), tends to be much higher in the peripheral regions than in Ontario. Finally, as these regions are fundamentally dependent on natural resources for their standard of living and employment, a decline in the economically exploitable reserves of a particular commodity can seriously cripple an entire provincial economy. The most dramatic example of this occurred on the Canadian prairies in the 1930s when a decline in international markets for wheat was compounded by a long period of drought. So severe was the impact on Saskatchewan, which was wholly depend-

Figure II.2 – Unemployment by Region, 1946-1980

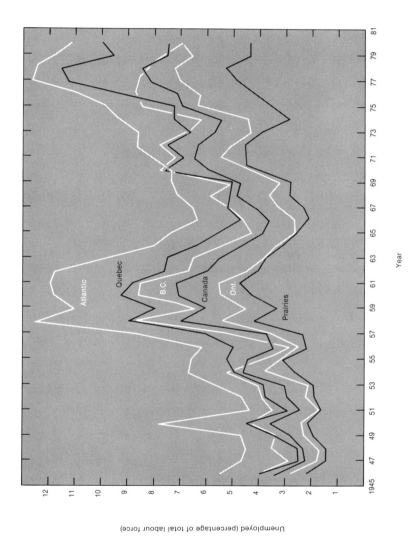

Source : Statistics Canada, 71-201, *Historical Labour Force Statistics Actual Data, Seasonal Factors, Seasonally Adjusted Data, various issues.*

ent on wheat, that by 1937 two-thirds of the rural population was on relief. Wheat yields fell from a predepression high of slightly more than 20.66 hectolitres per hectare in 1928 to about 2.42 hectolitres per hectare in 1937. By 1933 alone, it was estimated that per capita net income had fallen by 72 per cent.[10]

The collapse of the Saskatchewan wheat economy is the most dramatic example; but, it is by no means an isolated one. Changing international markets and depleting natural resources were responsible for the significant decline of Nova Scotia and New Brunswick as prosperous lumbering and commercial centres in the last century. And with the development of steam-powered, steel-hulled ships and the later emergence of railroads, the Maritime's merchant marine of wooden sailing ships, built from the region's forests, became obsolete. In addition, reduced demand for ship's lumber and overcutting of forest stands led to a decline in the squared-timber industry.[11]

All the country's resource-based regional economies have felt both the debilitating effects of collapse in international commodity markets for their products and the ever-present fear that their resource base will be destroyed or exhausted. In large measure, it is this legacy of inequality and uncertainty that explains the guarded attitude of many provincial governments towards the development of their own economies. For example, Alberta, which views its recently expanded oil industry as essentially transitory and short-lived,[12] seeks to obtain the maximum revenues possible from petroleum development and intends to use those revenues to establish a broader economic base. The province aims to build its economy based on technology related both to the extraction and management of the province's renewable and nonrenewable resource base.[13]

Our Divided Economy

Another consequence of the staples nature of the Canadian economy has been the high degree of regional economic specialization. A general picture of this can be obtained by examining the location quotient for a particular industry. Using a standardized base for comparison, location quotients indicate whether a particular region has a greater concentration in a type of industrial activity than would be expected if that activity were evenly distributed across the country. Table II.2 presents a series of location quotients for most of Canada's primary and secondary industries using population as the standardized base and employment levels in the industry as the measure. A location quotient of one in a particular industry indicates that the province has the amount of employment in an industry which would be expected if that industry were evenly distributed by population across the country. Numbers above one show a greater concentra-

Table II.2 – Location Quotients for Manufacturing Employment, 1979 (Population as Base)

	NFLD.	PEI	NS	NB	QUE.	ONT.	MAN.	SASK.	ALTA.	BC
Percentage of Canada's Population (1979)	2.42	0.52	3.58	2.96	26.55	35.92	4.36	4.05	8.50	10.86
Forestry	1.26	0	X	2.52	1.00	.57	0	0	X	2.96
Fishing and trapping	3.83	X	4.92	X	0	0	0	0	0	1.58
Mining	1.77	0	.98*	X	.63	.56	.91*	1.33	.37	.95*
Agriculture	0	2.89	1.46	.51	.64	1.02	2.64	6.11	2.44	.51
Mineral fuels	0	0	X	0	0	0	0	0	9.93	1.93
Metal minerals	3.48	0	0	X	.87	1.17	2.00	X	0	1.26
Nonmetal minerals	0	0	0	0	1.71	0	0	2.26	0	0
Food and beverage	2.03	1.66	1.37	1.45	.97*	1.03	1.05	.57	.78	.77
Tobacco products	X	0	X	X	1.75	1.00	X	X	X	X
Wood	.13	X	.48	1.19	.90*	.52	.38	.37	.67	3.85
Paper and allied	X	0	.69	1.63	1.31	1.00	X	X	.24	1.52
Primary metals	X	0	X	X	.89	1.65	.46	X	.37	.67
Printing, publishing and allied	.14	1.14	.42	.77	.95*	1.42	1.05	.53	.74	.74
Nonmetallic mineral products	.38	X	.38	.79	.92*	1.33	.67	.50	1.25	.67
Petroleum and coal products	X	0	.88	X	.75	1.63	X	X	1.25	.50
Leather	X	X	X	X	1.55	1.45	.45	0	X	.09
Textiles	X	X	.72	.14	1.83	1.28	.28	0	.14	.14
Knitting mills	0	X	X	0	2.11	.89	.56	0	X	X
Clothing	X	X	X	X	2.38	.69	1.57	.14	.24	.31
Furniture and fixtures	X	X	.18	.41	1.36	1.32	.95*	.05	.50	.32
Metal fabricating	.10	0	.25	.03	.91*	1.59	.14	.25	.67	.62
Machinery	X	X	X	.14	.79	1.65	1.02	.53	.63	.56
Transportation equipment	X	.12	.63	X	.76	1.81	.80	.10	.21	.48
Electrical products	X	.13	.27	X	.40	1.84	.43	.14	.20	.27
Chemical and chemical products	.12	X	.35	.14	1.14	1.59	.27	.05	.59	.30
Rubber and plastic products	X	X	X	X	.27	1.81	.27	X	2.96	X
Miscellaneous manufacturing	.11	.14	.14	.43	1.00	1.71	.46	.19	.39	.39

X = Confidential
0 = No significant change
* = Values above 0.9, but below unity
_ = Values above unity

Source: Statistics Canada, *Manufacturing Industries of Canada: National & Provincial Areas: 1979*, catalogue no. 31-203, and estimates based on unpublished Statistics Canada data.

tion of employment than would be expected if the distribution were even. A number less than one indicates a level of employment below that expected if there were an even distribution of employment. As Table II.2 illustrates, employment in industrial activity is concentrated in specific regions. Location quotients for resource production and the processing of raw materials are high in the peripheral economies of western Canada and the Atlantic region. Indeed, there is even a high degree of specialization in manufacturing between the two industrialized provinces. Quebec, for example, specializes in such industries as textiles, clothing and knitted goods – labour-intensive items, most susceptible to low-wage foreign competition.[14] Ontario, on the other hand, seems to concentrate more on such industrial sectors as transportation equipment, electrical and electronic equipment and machinery.

Although the data in Table II.2 give some indication of relative economic specialization, they do not provide any information on the economic linkages among the regions. Thus, while a region may specialize in a particular form of economic activity, the degree to which it is dependent on other regions of the country (or foreign countries) for markets cannot be measured by a location quotient. To form a better idea of this, the nature of interprovincial trade flows must be examined.

Tables II.3 to II.5 outline the relative distribution of interprovincial and foreign trade flows for each province on the basis of total merchandise trade, trade in raw materials and primary manufactured products, and trade in manufactured end products. The figures which follow are based on the results of a special Statistics Canada analysis of interprovincial trade flows using, in part, the 1974 analysis of the destination of shipments of manufactured goods. A similar survey, carried out by Statistics Canada in 1979 and released as this study was in press, indicates that for manufactured goods at least, the situation has remained relatively constant.[15] Unlike the 1979 survey of the destination of shipments of manufactured goods, the data presented here also cover raw material shipments and make some attempt to overcome the problems in the manufactured shipments data which, because they rely on the first and not the final destination of shipments from factories, can create problems when trying to accurately assign the actual shipments to each province. However, the statistics presented here do exclude interprovincial trade in services which are very large and could alter the overall distribution of trade.[16] Nevertheless, the figures do provide some basis for broad comparison.

The general trade distribution in Table II.3 demonstrates that, with the exception of British Columbia, Ontario and Quebec, no province manages to maintain more than half its trade within its own provincial boundaries. Furthermore, a large proportion of the

Table II.3 – Distribution of Interprovincial and Foreign Merchandise Trade, 1974 (percentages)

Province	(1) Within province	(2) Within region[1]	(3) Rest of Canada	(4) 2 + 3	(5) Exports abroad	(6) Total
Newfoundland	23.4	0.9	7.2	(8.1)	68.6	100.0
Prince Edward Island	45.4	18.9	27.0	(45.9)	8.7	100.0
Nova Scotia	44.8	11.6	19.4	(31.0)	24.2	100.0
New Brunswick	38.3	8.6	19.3	(27.9)	33.8	100.0
Quebec	53.6	—	28.3	—	18.2	100.0
Ontario	54.1	—	22.8	—	23.1	100.0
Manitoba	46.0	10.7	21.5	(32.2)	22.0	100.0
Saskatchewan	22.9	11.5	17.1	(28.6)	48.5	100.0
Alberta	38.5	13.7	16.5	(30.2)	31.2	100.0
British Columbia	52.7	6.3	4.4	(10.7)	36.5	100.0
Yukon/NWT	7.1	10.4	6.7	(17.1)	75.8	100.0

[1] Regional trade for Atlantic region includes the four Atlantic provinces; for the western region the four western provinces plus the Yukon and NWT.
Source: Unpublished data, Interprovincial Trade Project, Structural Analysis Division, Statistics Canada.

trade of most provinces in western Canada, and many in Atlantic Canada, is directed to destinations abroad. Many of these provinces also have a greater proportion of their domestic trade with the rest of the country rather than within their own region.

The pattern becomes even more pronounced when you distinguish between trade in raw and processed resource products and that in manufactured end products. Because all provinces other than Ontario and Quebec depend heavily for their industrial base on the production of raw materials, agricultural products and semiprocessed resource products, the pattern of trade for the periphery in these products (see Table II.4) becomes very revealing. Only Ontario and Quebec maintain over half the value of their shipments in raw and semiprocessed resource products within their own provincial boundaries, indicating their greater propensity to process resources into finished products. In contrast, virtually all the other provinces depend heavily on export markets and Canadian markets outside their own region. In fact, for most provinces, *export* markets are far more important than the Canadian market.

Turning to shipments of manufactured goods, an inverse picture emerges (see Table II.5). With the exception of Newfoundland and Nova Scotia (which together account for less than three per cent of national shipments), only Ontario ships more than half the value of its manufactured goods out of province. Manufacturing activity outside Ontario and Quebec is on a small scale (only about 17 per cent of shipments of manufactured goods originate outside those two provinces) and is mostly directed to local markets. Interestingly, only Nova Scotia, New Brunswick and Manitoba depend on regional and national markets for more than one-third of their market for manufactured goods. None of the provinces outside of Ontario or Newfoundland rely heavily on export markets for their manufactured goods.

We seem to have several distinctive economies. In manufactured goods, Ontario, with more than half of the country's trade in manufactures, dominates and is about equally oriented to national and export markets. Quebec, with more than one quarter of Canada's total trade in manufactures, is much more dependent on national markets. The rest of the provinces only account for a small proportion of manufacturing shipments and are much more oriented, especially in western Canada, to local markets.

On the other hand, in terms of primary products, Ontario and, to a lesser extent, Quebec are much more dependent on their local provincial markets, whereas the resource-producing provinces are heavily tied to export markets. In addition, trade in resources and resource products is much more important for the regions than for Ontario or Quebec; in many cases, it accounts for over two-thirds of shipments. Thus, unlike Ontario and Quebec, the other provinces,

Table II.4 – Distribution of Interprovincial and Foreign Trade in Unprocessed Materials and Primary Manufactured Goods, 1974 (percentages)

Province	(1) Within province	(2) Within region	(3) Rest of Canada	(4) 2 + 3	(5) Exports abroad	(6) Total	(7) Primary goods as percentage of province's total shipments	(8) Percentage of all Canadian primary goods shipments
Newfoundland	20.2	0.2	3.6	(3.8)	76.0	100	67.2	1.6
Prince Edward Island	43.5	18.2	28.9	(47.1)	9.3	100	89.1	0.3
Nova Scotia	42.5	8.2	16.7	(24.9)	32.6	100	50.3	2.0
New Brunswick	32.1	5.5	20.9	(26.4)	41.4	100	73.3	2.8
Quebec	54.7	—	20.0	—	25.3	100	44.7	22.0
Ontario	65.2	—	17.0	—	17.7	100	37.5	33.7
Manitoba	43.7	6.3	24.0	(30.3)	26.0	100	65.5	4.6
Saskatchewan	18.2	10.6	19.7	(30.3)	51.1	100	84.7	6.8
Alberta	30.1	12.7	20.0	(32.7)	37.3	100	69.0	11.0
British Columbia	42.7	5.4	4.7	(10.1)	47.2	100	75.3	14.8
Yukon/NWT	2.6	11.0	7.1	(18.1)	79.3	100	94.1	0.5
								100.0

Source: Unpublished data, Interprovincial Trade Project, Structural Analysis Division, Statistics Canada.

Table II.5 – Distribution of Interprovincial and Foreign Trade in Manufactured End Products, 1974 (percentages)

Province	(1) Within province	(2) Within region	(3) Rest of Canada	(4) 2 + 3	(5) Exports abroad	(6) Total	(7) End products as percentage of province's total shipments	(8) Per cent of all Canadian end products shipments
Newfoundland	31.6	2.6	14.5	(18.1)	51.2	100	32.8	.7
Prince Edward Island	74.6	20.4	4.6	(25.0)	.4	100	10.9	.0
Nova Scotia	48.5	14.8	21.6	(36.4)	15.2	100	49.7	1.9
New Brunswick	52.8	16.9	18.0	(34.9)	12.3	100	26.7	1.0
Quebec	52.9	—	34.8	—	12.3	100	55.3	27.4
Ontario	47.7	—	26.0	—	26.3	100	62.5	55.7
Manitoba	51.0	18.9	16.0	(34.9)	14.2	100	34.5	2.4
Saskatchewan	73.6	19.3	4.4	(23.7)	2.8	100	15.3	1.4
Alberta	64.3	17.0	6.0	(23.0)	12.7	100	31.0	4.9
British Columbia	76.6	10.0	4.2	(14.2)	9.3	100	24.7	4.8
Yukon/NWT	100.2	—	—	—	—	100	5.9	0.0
								100.00

Source: Unpublished data, Interprovincial Trade Project, Structural Analysis Division, Statistics Canada.

particularly those in western Canada, have a greater interest in markets *within* their own borders for manufactured goods and for markets *outside* Canada for their resources.

This pattern becomes even clearer if you examine the proxy provincial "balance of trade" which is derived from the shipments data. Figure II.3 presents these data broken down according to category of industry. Clearly, Ontario has by far the largest balance of trade surplus with the rest of Canada, a situation almost entirely due to trade in manufactured goods. Apart from Ontario, only Quebec and Alberta experience a substantial trade surplus with the rest of Canada, but for opposite reasons: Alberta, through resource shipments (principally oil and gas) to the rest of Canada, and Quebec, through interprovincial shipments of manufactured goods. It is significant to note, however, that while many of the resource-producing provinces have a domestic trade deficit, such is not the case with their export trade. British Columbia, Alberta, Saskatchewan and Newfoundland have positive balance of trade positions with countries abroad due to resource exports, while all other provinces, including Ontario and Quebec, run deficits.

Of course, these figures do not reflect total trade flows. As mentioned before, they ignore service industries (which can account for substantial earnings) and financial transfers through the taxation system or through regional development assistance. In addition, they may overestimate Ontario and Quebec's import deficit in manufactured goods, and may underestimate those of the resource provinces because Ontario and Quebec tend to be the ports of entry for many finished goods destined for other parts of Canada.

While the figures tend to indicate rather severe differences in the benefits provinces obtain from Canadian trade, the total picture may be far less stark. More important is the high degree of regional specialization revealed by such figures, and the consequent differences in economic interests.

The Political Protest

The great degree of economic specialization which has emerged in Canada has reinforced the traditional, and highly unequal, metropolis-hinterland relationship between the regions.[17] This does not mean that such a relationship has *necessarily* led to a lower standard of living in the hinterlands, although the evidence, until recently, suggests this has generally been the case. During periods of commodity power, when particular resources or staple products are in high demand, a regional economy can often have levels of economic activity, and, frequently, per capita incomes that may temporarily exceed those of the industrial centre. The boom-and-bust cycle, however, and the general uncertainty concerning employment

Figure II.3 – Provincial Trade Balances in Crude and Manufactured Goods, 1974 (in Millions of Dollars)

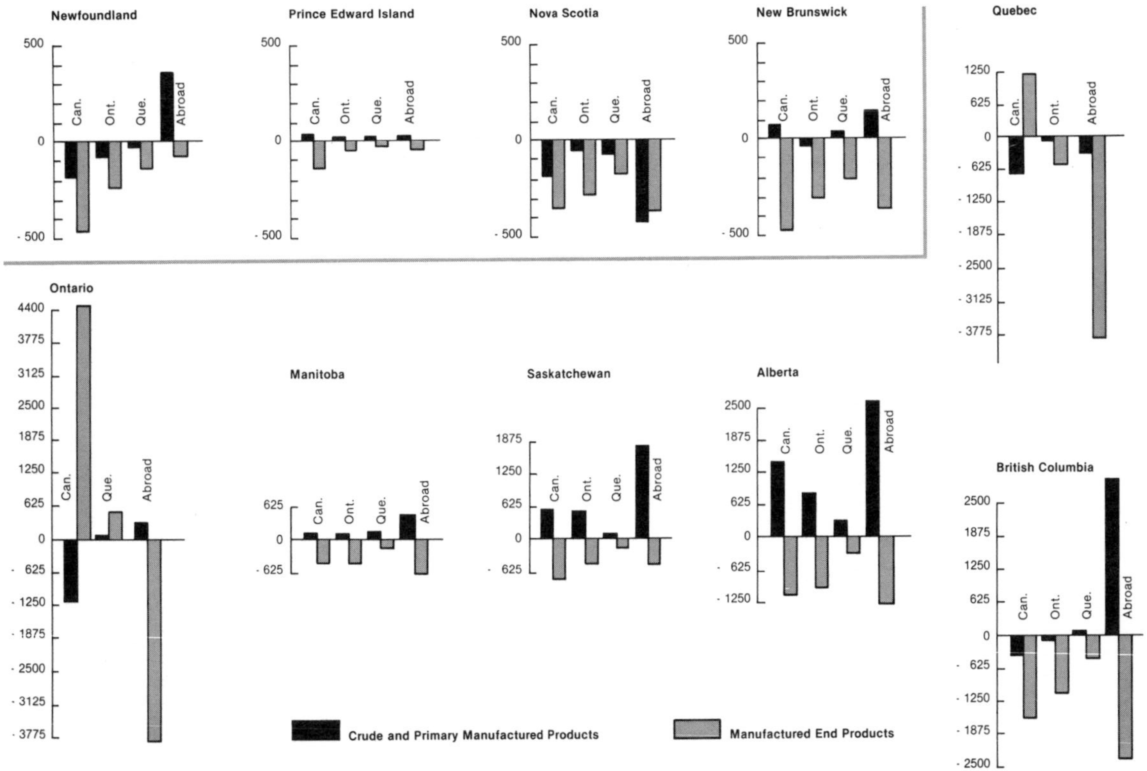

Source: Interprovincial Trade Project, Structural Analysis Division, Statistics Canada.

and income levels from year to year have generally resulted in less stable economic growth.

It is significant that the causes of the political protests which have emerged in Canada's regions since Confederation have not simply been due to the lower standards of living. They are also the result of the uncertainty that surrounds resource production and what is perceived as a discriminatory political and economic system, a sentiment most clearly articulated in the western protest movements of the 1920s.[18]

By 1930 the Progressive Party had failed in federal politics and regional protest was focussed at the provincial level with the emergence of the Social Credit party and the Cooperative Commonwealth Federation (CCF) in Alberta and Saskatchewan respectively. The political programs of these parties were originally directed at changing the pattern of economic management in Canada. However, as each party made little headway in federal politics, its focus shifted to the provincial level where it formed the government. The parties then attempted to promote economic change either by attacking the federal government's monetary powers by developing a provincial monetary system (Social Credit),[19] or by attempting to use provincial Crown corporations to diversify the industrial structure of the province (the CCF).[20]

Much of the rhetoric for change in western Canada during this period centred on the manner in which the federal government's economic policies (such as tariff protection for central Canadian manufactures) and the operation of the country's transportation and financial system discriminated against diversified economic development in western Canada. These themes have been a remarkably consistent aspect of western protest and can be seen even today in the communiqués issued by the Western Premiers' Conference (WPC) on national economic issues.[21]

Such protest has not been limited to western Canada. The Maritime provinces' opposition to the existing economic system led, in the last century, to the passing of secession resolutions in provincial legislatures.[22] In the early part of this century, discontent also produced the growth of the Maritime Rights movement which addressed itself to many of the concerns of the western protest parties.[23]

The Rise of the Provinces
Traditional regional grievances against the structure of the national economy seemed to be relatively mute after World War II. The dominance of the federal government during the economic expansion of the 1950s suggested that regional tensions might decline and that a greater level of national integration might ensue. By the early

1960s, however, a number of changes were occurring in the Canadian economy which would alter this trend. In the first place, the issues which had dominated the 1940s and 1950s – national defence, the rebuilding of the peacetime economy and Canada's role in assisting in the postwar international reconstruction process – no longer loomed as large. The central place these issues gave the federal government on the country's political agenda consequently declined. The 1960s also saw increased attention to those issues primarily concerned with providing social equity and infrastructure following postwar economic expansion, such as the establishment of medicare and the expansion of welfare and educational systems. This greater emphasis on distributional questions also brought to the fore a growing awareness of regional economic disparities.[24] While the federal role in regional development expanded significantly during the 1960s, concerns over regional disparities naturally shifted the focus of political attention from national issues to questions of regional balance.

At a more concrete level, the expansion of social welfare, health and educational services and the need to balance postwar growth with social infrastructure, led to an increase in the size and role of the provincial governments. This growth was truly remarkable. In 1950, provincial and municipal government expenditures accounted for about 45 per cent of all state expenditure, or about $4433 million. By 1978, this total had increased to $56 516 million, a 12-fold increase, and accounted for almost 60 per cent of all government expenditures in Canada.[25] The growth also resulted in the recruitment of a more professional provincial public service and a general increase in the administrative and policy-making capacity of provincial governments.

These alterations in public attitudes and provincial capabilities also occurred at a time of significant socioeconomic change in Canada's regions. By the early 1970s, Alberta, and later Saskatchewan, were experiencing renewed economic growth based on energy and other resources. Along with British Columbia, they began to achieve per capita income levels approaching those of Ontario and growth rates which were considerably greater. This growth was accompanied by the development of an indigenous business and commercial sector, most noticeably in Alberta, which created a political clientele anxious to see policies designed to encourage locally determined industrial development.[26]

In Quebec, as well, the early 1970s was a period of increasing self-awareness. The instruments for provincial economic development had been instituted during the Quiet Revolution (Hydro-Québec, the Caisse de dépôts, Sidbec, etc.) in response to a perceived need for Quebecers both to obtain greater control over their economic development and to expand francophone employment opportunities.[27] These initiatives were reinforced in the 1970s by two other trends. The first was a continuing concern with structural changes in the provincial economy which were widening the gap between Quebec's standard of living and that of Ontario, a gap most visible in a much higher unemployment rate.[28] The second was the rise, as in Alberta, of an indigenous business élite, which viewed the provincial government as the guardian of its interests.

An enlarged awareness of the very different economic situations of the regions, plus the enhanced capacity of the provinces to administer complex economic policies, has focussed attention on the role of provincial governments in satisfying growing regional aspirations. This phenomenon was more starkly revealed during the 1970s when the regionalization of the federal party system effectively isolated at least one major region of the country from the national governing process. Western Canada, in particular, has failed to attain significant representation in Ottawa for most of the decade, due to the Liberal party's diminished representation there. And the short-lived Conservative government of 1979-80 was unable to gain representation in Quebec.[29]

In light of these significant socioeconomic changes, it is hardly surprising that the 1970s turned out to be the decade during which the provinces assumed an economic as well as a social policy-making role. As the following chapter demonstrates, many of the creative and innovative aspects of industrial policy today in Canada are to be found, not at the national level, but within provincial jurisdictions.

Part Two

The Rise of Provincial Industrial Strategies

III. Policies on the Periphery: Industrial Strength Through Resources

The provinces on the periphery, particularly those in western Canada, have carried the concept of developing an indigenous provincial industrial capability the furthest. This is perhaps a comment on the historical sense of alienation and the present divergence of economic interest existing between this country's industrial centre and its resource-based periphery. But how far have attempts at creating more self-reliant provincial economies, or "province building" as it is more popularly known, really progressed? How different are the provinces' strategies from one another? As we will see, the form these attempts take, and even their objectives, are, in fact, somewhat different. However, the strategies share a common thread: the recognition that effective exploitation of resources is the key to prosperity.

The West

British Columbia

Any consideration of British Columbia's development strategy has to take into account its physical setting and the unique structure of the provincial economy. The data presented earlier (see p. 35, 37, 39, 40, Tables II.2 to II.5) clearly showed that the provincial economy is characterized by a high dependence on resource products, especially forest products and nonmetallic minerals. Prior to the 1970s, therefore, most of the provincial government's efforts were directed towards policies designed to assist these industries, rather than industrial diversification based on manufacturing. Because of the province's rugged terrain, and its reliance on offshore export markets, policies have been primarily directed towards the support of economic infrastructure, particularly transportation facilities. On a per capita basis, British Columbia has consistently spent more than most provinces on the development of such transportation facilities. This was particularly true during the 1950s when the province was heavily involved in road building.[1] But by the 1960s, the province also became significantly committed to other transportation services when it took over a major resources railway and an extensive coastal ferry network. Not surprisingly, therefore, government expenditure in support of trade and industry has traditionally been one of the lowest, on a per capita basis, of all the provinces, although its expenditure on the promotion of resource development is one of the highest.[2]

While the province has issued no formal industrial-strategy statement, some indication of its stand can be gained from a 1978 BC government position paper, "An Industrial Strategy for Canada."[3] The paper outlined the government's commitment to a free trade strategy, a strong domestic common market with few barriers to the movement of goods or people, a minimum of government intervention, the encouragement of regional labour mobility and a de-emphasis on regional development programs. Naturally, such a series of policies would significantly benefit a province that, as a large resource producer, needs to export widely, and prefers to import the least expensive manufactured goods from world markets. As a high-growth region, the province would also prefer a regional assistance scheme which encourages people and companies to migrate to growth centres rather than to provide financial assistance to expand industrial activity in the country's declining regions.

The province has been very forceful in promoting a more liberal national trade policy. It has, for example, established an International Economic Relations Branch within its Ministry of Industry and Small Business Development. This provided the analytical capacity for the government to become involved in federal-provincial consultations over the GATT negotiations and to make representations at the Federal Anti-Dumping Tribunal. In addition, the province assisted with the attempt by the 1978 WPC to present a common "western front" on trade negotiations, and has recently been active in examining other aspects of federal trade policy (for example, quotas) that provide protection for industries in eastern Canada at the expense of western consumers.[4]

Recently, a change has taken place in the priorities of the province's industrial and resources development policies. Due to the growth of concern in the past few years over the proper husbanding

50

of renewable resources, especially in forestry and fishing, greater emphasis is being placed on resource management and, in particular, on cooperative efforts with the federal government over such issues as reforestation. While the promotion of large resource export projects remains a central part of the government's development plans, increasing attention has been paid to diversification in order to help overcome the cyclical boom-and-bust nature of resource-based economic activity.[5]

This diversification policy has taken three forms. The first is an attempt to diversify activity outside the Lower Mainland to increase the stability of employment, and of economic activity in general, in the province's resource-producing regions. This has been attempted through the provision of a local industrial infrastructure, and loans and grants to businesses which are partly administered through a $110 million, shared-cost, Industrial Development Subsidiary Agreement with the federal government. A procurement policy for major resource projects has also been introduced to pressure resource companies to procure goods and services locally. The second initiative has been to develop programs to expand export markets. Again, the objective here is not only to expand economic activity, but also to soften the effects of highly cyclical resource markets by diversifying the geographical location of those markets. Third, the government is attempting to diversify the province's product mix by encouraging more resource processing and enhanced secondary manufacturing.

In this last case, the provincial government is placing an increased emphasis on technology-intensive industry. This has been given additional prominence with the establishment of a government ministry[6] to sponsor high-technology industry, the creation of a Science Council, and the funding of a Discovery Parks Foundation. The foundation will establish research parks housing facilities for high-technology industries at four institutes of higher education. In addition to supporting industrial research through a provincial research council, the government, through its Secretariat on Science, Research and Development, administers engineering and technology research awards and industrial postdoctoral fellowships to increase the availability of scientists to industry.

While these policies represent an important political initiative, they are not significant in terms of the resources they consume; the Discovery Parks Foundation has been budgeted at about $3 million, and the BC Secretariat on Science, Research and Development distributed only $1.25 million in research grants in 1979. What such policies do illustrate, however, is a growing awareness of the importance of directing R&D and research funds into appropriate industrial development projects. Towards this end, most of the research priorities outlined by British Columbia's new Science Council emphasize the development of research capabilities tied to local resource strengths, such as forests and forest products, ocean engineering, mineral extraction, and remote sensing technology.[7]

What is significant about British Columbia's industrial policy is the degree to which it is informed by an understanding of the particular needs of a resource-based economy. It advocates the maximum possible access to world markets for Canadian resource producers, and for government to limit its involvement in the economy to the provision of industrial infrastructure for a rapidly growing resource sector. This distinctiveness was perhaps most clearly recognized by Premier Bennett in his opening address to the First Ministers' Conference on the Economy in February 1978:

> "In listening to my fellow First Ministers here, I must say that what has come out clearly to me, is something British Columbia has advocated for some time, that we are not a single national economy; we are a country with distinct regions, with distinct economies unique to themselves, that need the attention and cooperation of the governments in meeting their own specific aspirations and needs."[8]

Alberta
Of all the western provinces, Alberta has pursued an industrial strategy the furthest. Ironically, the province has never published a document outlining its strategy, although the premier has issued several detailed industrial-policy statements.

The pressure to develop an industrial strategy comes primarily from two sources. First, from a widespread awareness in the province that its oil resources will be depleted in the medium term and will have to be replaced with other forms of economic activity. With about two-thirds of Alberta's industrial activity directly tied to hydrocarbons and minerals, it is hardly surprising that the government is concerned about this issue. Indeed, in a major speech in 1974 on Alberta's industrial strategy, Premier Peter Lougheed put the position more personally:

> "Since entering public life over nine years ago, my theme has been that this province's economy is too *vulnerable*, it is too dependent on the sale of depleting resources, particularly oil and gas for its continued prosperity.... . Frankly, I despair of the short-term thinking of a few Albertans who believe we can coast on the sale of our depleting resources for our continued prosperity."[9]

The second major driving force behind the provincial government's industrial policy is the emergence within Alberta of a confident, local business community which used the oil boom of the 1950s and 1960s to build up large provincially based corporations such as

Nova Corporation (formerly Alberta Gas Trunk Lines (AGTL)), ATCO, Loram and Dome Petroleum. As Richards and Pratt have pointed out, it was these companies, along with the rising middle class of professionals attached to the burgeoning oil and gas service industry, which formed the backbone of support for the diversification strategy founded on locally based enterprise.[10]

According to the premier, the province's diversification policies are guided by three main principles or foundations:

"The first one is to strengthen the control by Albertans over our own future and to reduce dependency for our continued quality of life on governments, institutions or corporations directed from outside the province. Secondly, to do this as much as possible through the private sector and to only move through the public sector if the private sector is not in a position or not prepared to move in essential new directions and then only in exceptional and very specific circumstances. And, thirdly, to strengthen competitive free enterprise by Albertans which to us means giving priority to our locally owned businesses. Our basic guide post was to maximize the number of our citizens controlling their own economic destiny. (This is not to say that we do not recognize and respect the contribution of large national corporations – we do – but our priority is to small and locally-owned business)."[11]

The diversification drive has resulted in an emphasis on several aspects of industrial activity including: nutritive food processing; further upgrading of natural resources (especially petrochemicals); tourism (now worth over $1 billion to the provincial economy); the growth of a financial industry (for which the Alberta Heritage Savings Trust Fund (AHSTF) has a special responsibility); the continued assurance of the province's role as an entrepôt for the northern territories; and finally, the promotion of high technology industry. In promoting these policies, the government has made a particular effort to stress the development of small business and to prevent concentrated development in Calgary and Edmonton.[12]

As one would expect in a province experiencing rapid growth, the level of direct government financing for industrial diversification has been modest. In 1981-82, the province's Economic Development Department spent $20.9 million, including the wages and salaries of departmental personnel.[13] In addition, the Alberta Opportunity Company (AOC) authorized about $41 million in loans to small business in 1982.[14] Indeed, the province has not developed any grant schemes which provide direct financial support to industry for industrial development outside of a single federal-provincial agreement designed to support the establishment of food processing plants.[15] Direct grants are provided, however, for technological development (see below).

The real thrust in the province's industrial policy has come from a series of unusual policy instruments which combine private- and public-sector capital. These include government-sponsored corporations, joint venture companies with the private sector and a judicious combination of administrative pressure and government ownership.

The earliest of these instruments was AGTL, established through special provincial legislation in 1954. The move was designed to ensure provincial jurisdiction over local pipeline companies; a move the government regarded as essential if Alberta was to maintain control over the depletion of its natural gas stocks. Although a private company, Nova's stock ownership has been arranged to ensure that effective control will always be divided among gas producers, distributors, exporters and the public at large. Some of the company's directors are considered "government representatives."

Nova, which originally had a monopoly on gas transmission within the province, has since diversified into a number of petroleum- and gas-related activities, often through joint ventures with Alberta companies. Nova is now involved in petrochemicals, pipelines, the manufacture of pipeline equipment and steel, and oil- and gas-producing properties (for example, Husky Oil). It is also involved, through Foothills Pipelines (Yukon) Ltd., in the Alaska Gas Pipeline project.

But importantly, Nova has been a crucial element in the province's attempt to increase local resource ownership and to encourage resource-related industrial activity. Its substantial size (1980 revenues of $2.1 billion and assets of $3.6 billion)[16] and rapid growth have assured its influence, and that influence has usually been exercised in close harmony with provincial interests. As the company candidly admitted in its 1978 annual report, it "has always remembered the importance of government policy in its formation."[17] Most revealing, however, was the rationale which the company provided for its dramatic expansion:

"In the 1970s when this was thought out, there were noticeably few companies in all of Canada which had the necessary combination of: autonomy for new investment choice; management and professional capability; and capacity to advance $5 million to $20 million of risk sponsorship funds to move on projects of sufficient scale to achieve national or international competitiveness. The noticeably few companies which did exist in Canada were almost all concentrated in Toronto and Montreal as to corporate headquarters and natural regional priorities. We thought it would be good for both Alberta and Canada if a few such organisations began to develop in the West and that Alberta Gas Trunk Line Company could be one."[18]

54

The provincial government has reciprocated Nova's provincial bias by maintaining the company's gas distribution monopoly and ensuring that its petrochemical developments obtain favourably priced, assured supplies of feedstocks.

More recently, the province established the Alberta Energy Company (AEC) which is 50 per cent owned by the government and 50 per cent by private shareholders. The company now holds Alberta's stake in the Syncrude project, a major oil and natural gas field at Suffield, an electronics firm and a lumber company. It has been involved in petrochemical and steel projects with Nova and in joint ventures in coal, electricity generation and pipelines with other companies. Though not as significant as Nova, AEC had more than $700 million in assets and generated about $232 million in revenues in 1980.[19] In keeping with the corporate objectives outlined in its 1977 annual report, the company is providing a vehicle to increase Canadian participation in Alberta's resource development (in 1977, 96 per cent of AEC's shareholders were from Alberta). It is also assisting with resource-related diversification through its investments in petrochemicals, electronic process control equipment and the manufacture of pipeline steel.

Perhaps the most remarkable instrument at the disposal of the government is AHSTF. It annually receives about 30 per cent of the province's oil and gas royalties. With $8.6 billion in assets in 1981, the fund is already a significant contributor to Canada's total investment capacity.[20] By the mid-1980s, however, some observers claim that the fund's assets will reach well over $30 billion, which, in the Alberta context at least, will make it a major investment pool.[21] To date, the government has refrained from extensive use of the fund to finance industrial diversification. The province's treasurer has claimed that such an objective is secondary compared to maintaining an investment reserve for the province's future generations.[22] The greater part of the fund's resources (about 53 per cent) have been invested through the Alberta investment division in projects designed both to make a return to the fund and to assist in strengthening or diversifying the provincial economy. To date, such investments have included the debentures of Crown corporations in housing, telecommunications, and industrial finance (AOC). Also in this category are investments in the Syncrude project and the government's equity stake in AEC.[23] The last three items are the closest the fund has come to fostering industrial diversification.

Considerable concern exists within the Alberta government about the future direction of investments of this kind as the opportunities for industrial diversification, which also promise a return to the fund, appear to be somewhat limited.[24] At present, there seems to be no great willingness to involve the fund in supporting large industrial diversification projects. Indeed, the recent decision to reduce the royalty paid into the fund from 30 per cent to 15 per cent, in order to finance a large incentive scheme for the oil and gas industry, and to use the interest on the fund's investments to finance a mortgage assistance program, would indicate that, for the time being, the fund will be used primarily for purposes other than industrial diversification. As the fund grows in the coming years, however, and as the province's resource-based industry expands, opportunities for such investments may increase. Significantly, in response to criticisms that the fund was too conservative, the AHSTF Act was amended in 1980 to allow investments designed to yield a commercial rate of return. And, to actively seek out profitable investments for the fund's resources, in 1983 the government announced in its budget the establishment of a Crown and venture capital firm, Ven Cap Equities Alberta Limited, to be funded by an initial investment of $200 million in Heritage Fund capital.

Finally, two areas of provincial policy towards industrial development deserve special attention. The first, concerns the promotion of technology within Alberta, and the second, the use of administrative arrangements to influence industrial location. Over the past five years, the province has been particularly mindful of the opportunities resource developments have provided for technology-intensive industries which can enhance natural resources exploitation. Early in the 1970s, the government established the Alberta Oil Sands Technology and Research Authority (AOSTRA) to develop *in situ* recovery technologies for bitumen oil sands. Apart from the significant expenditures on such research ($100 million from 1976-80), AOSTRA maintains an ownership stake in the results. It also insists on the use, when feasible, of Alberta and Canadian expertise in the research work it funds and reserves the right to ensure that Alberta or Canadian companies obtain the first opportunity to license any resulting commercial technology.[25]

The most comprehensive technology development initiative to date, however, has been the government's approval of a five-year R&D strategy by the Alberta Research Council.[26] The strategy is an attempt to harness public and private technological resources to develop key economic sectors. The program emphasizes increased efforts in energy resources, especially heavy oil and coal, a higher level of technical assistance to industry, (especially small business), and the development of capacity in emerging technologies especially applicable to Alberta. These include the use of biotechnology to develop crops suitable to the province's short growing season and the exploitation of existing technological strengths in the province (for example, telecommunications).

A number of steps have also recently been taken to strengthen the government's ability to deal with science and technology questions. A cabinet committee on research and science policy has been established (the membership of which includes a number of ministers from departments concerned with science and technology and the president of the Alberta Research Council) to assist in focussing cabinet discussions on science - and technology - related issues. In addition, a Research and Science Advisory Committee, composed of senior government scientists and officials, has been established to provide detailed advice on specific issues; this committee is assisted by a small office of science and technology which provides administrative and technical support.

A second aspect of Alberta's industrial diversification policy is the administrative pressure the government brings to bear on companies applying to develop Alberta's natural resources.[27] To obtain the maximum benefits for local companies involved in engineering, consulting and other services, the Department of Economic Development reviews in advance a company's plan for a resource development to make sure Alberta's capacity is being used. When the project is to be launched, the managing firm must apply for an industrial development permit which allows the government to review contracting arrangements. In addition, the firm is usually required to carry out its detailed design and engineering work and locate its procurement office for the project in the province. This helps to ensure that, when large projects are managed by foreign-owned firms, local firms have an opportunity to obtain some of the resulting subcontract work.

In summary, Alberta is pursuing an industrial policy designed to increase the level of local involvement in natural resources development, particularly in resource-related manufacturing and service activity. At the level of industrial policy, very little of this activity would seem to result in increased competition with, and duplication of, industrial policy efforts of other provinces, largely because most of the industrial diversification being sought is in highly specialized sectors unlikely to be important elsewhere in Canada. However, in one area of the province's diversification efforts, the prospect of severe competition does exist. That is in petrochemicals, where Ontario has a significant national capacity dependent on Alberta feedstocks.

Concern about the implications of the province's diversification drive should also be tempered by the relative effectiveness of the government's policies. Despite government efforts, there is now some concern within Alberta about the lack of an effective diversification of the structure of the provincial economy. Critics point out that during the 1970s the share of the provincial economy accounted for by manufacturing actually declined from about a fifth to about a tenth of all economic activity, due, in large measure, to the rapid growth in oil and gas activity. Thus, despite an absolute growth in the value of manufacturing production in the province, it still has a relatively low share of the provincial economy on a per capita basis (see p. 35, Table II.2) compared to many other provinces. Indeed, it would appear that the province is even more dependent on oil and gas production now than a decade ago.

The significant challenge which Alberta's initiatives pose to other provincial governments is not at the level of industrial policy, but rather at the level of fiscal and investment policy. Alberta's desire to obtain a larger share of the wealth from oil and gas production, and to store a portion of that money in the AHSTF, may create problems both for the country's equalization system and for Ontario and Quebec's industrial structure; higher prices will have an impact by increasing energy costs to both provinces' secondary manufacturing sectors. Second, while the present structure of the equalization system compensates the poorer Atlantic provinces for some of the increased transfers out of the region due to higher oil prices, it is placing a growing burden on the federal government and other provinces, most notably Ontario, to finance the system. One estimate put the increased burden on Ontario of oil-based equalization during 1979-80 at $345 million.[28]

Saskatchewan

Saskatchewan, like Alberta, has attempted to develop an economic strategy. Unlike Alberta, though, it has placed significantly less emphasis on industrial diversification, possibly as a result of the very disappointing experience with such schemes after World War II.[29] Traditionally, agriculture has dominated the provincial economy and in 1975 it accounted for over half of total primary and secondary activity compared to about 14 per cent in Alberta.[30] Recently, however, resource extraction has come into increasing prominence with the growth of potash mining and oil production. Consequently, the last NDP government emphasized ensuring provincial control over resource exploitation as well as a high rate of return to the provincial treasury from resource-based projects. These objectives have been met largely through public ownership. About half the province's potash capacity was purchased by the government in the mid-1970s and there was to be a significant level of direct government participation in new private sector oil and mineral developments (especially uranium). Government firms are also involved in processing resource products such as sodium sulphate and lumber.

Saskatchewan, though, has pursued a relatively active development policy which has sought to encourage manufacturing and resource processing. In 1976, the provincial Department of Industry and Commerce released a policy document, "An Industrial Development Strategy for Saskatchewan", which set out its priorities. These included the promotion of greater local manufacturing and resource processing and the encouragement of balanced regional growth. To achieve these objectives, the government would rely principally on public enterprise for major resource and infrastructure developments and joint ventures with the private sector in resource processing. With respect to secondary manufacturing, the government planned to depend much more on the private sector.

However, due to the province's small base of large local companies and a relative lack of interest in Saskatchewan's manufacturing prospects by foreign investors, industrial development efforts have had to be redirected to small local entrepreneurs. Saskatchewan has also had to be more activist than the Alberta government. Consequently, the Saskatchewan Economic Development Corporation (SEDCO) has a relatively important role. Its loan activities are broadly similar to its Alberta counterpart (the AOC), despite the fact that it operates in an economy less than half the size, a situation which may indicate the relative lack of private sector investment capital.[31]

Apart from SEDCO the province runs a series of small business aid programs ranging from counselling and promotional services to grants for trade shows. The province's largest direct program was for a major expansion of the prairies' principal steel maker, IPSCO.[32]

While the manufacturing sector is small relative to Saskatchewan's population (for example, in 1975, only 7 per cent of the province's work force was involved in secondary manufacturing compared to a national average of 21 per cent)[33], it is growing rapidly, particularly in specific sectors.[34] Apart from steel production, the province has a number of specialist manufacturers of farm machinery and a growing number of firms benefiting from the rapidly growing oil and potash resource base. Saskatchewan has also paid significant attention to technology. An expanding number of high-technology firms are being actively encouraged by the government, in part through the provision of financing and in part through the creation of a research park at the University of Saskatchewan.[35] For its 1983 budget, the government announced the establishment of a $50 million endowment from the Saskatchewan Heritage Fund, yielding about $5 million a year in funds to finance investments in research and new technologies.

In addition to a sizeable provincial research council which has a technology transfer role, and an advisory science council, the government also seems to be willing to use the purchasing capacity of its Crown corporations to develop new high-technology industrial capacity in the province. For example, the provincially owned telephone utility, Saskatchewan Telecommunications (SASK TEL), which is also responsible for cable TV distribution, is currently converting its trunk telecommunication lines to fibre optics cable. SASK TEL is one of the first telecommunications utilities to push the widespread

CAMROSE LUTHERAN COLLEGE
LIBRARY

use of fibre optics. And, on the basis of this large-scale contract, it was able to encourage Northern Telecom to establish a manufacturing and product development facility for fibre optics in the province.[36]

Presently, the province's development strategy seems to be at a crossroads. It is clear that, in future, resource developments, as distinct from agriculture, will be a significant growth factor. And with a high level of government participation in many resource developments, the question is: what forms of economic activity should be encouraged with resource revenues?[37] Or indeed, what role should the province be expected to play in light of the election of a Progressive Conservative government in the spring of 1982?

The new Conservative government has indicated its intention to emphasize private sector initiative in the development of the province's natural resource strengths, both through a more favourable tax environment and a restriction on the activities of the Crown corporation sector. A greater emphasis will also be placed on export promotion for both resource industries and secondary industry. However, to date, no detailed statement on industrial development policy has been forthcoming.[38]

In summary, over the past decade the thrust of the government's industrial development policies seems to be favouring backward linkages to resource production (for example, agricultural machinery, resource services) rather than significant resource processing. While manufacturing activity generally will likely receive less attention, some attempts have been made to stimulate specialized high-technology manufacturing in such areas as telecommunications and process control equipment for agriculture. But a move to broadly based industrial diversification does not, as yet, seem to be a priority.

Manitoba
Compared to its western neighbours, Manitoba is growing much less rapidly. With the exception of hydro power, and possibly potash, it has no large, new, resource developments. Unlike its western neighbours, Manitoba depends to a significant extent on secondary manufacturing for its wellbeing (over half its census value added in 1975 was in secondary manufacturing).

Although employment increased in secondary manufacturing during the 1970s, the sector's share of employment in goods production has declined slightly; in fact, the sector has generally had a rather mixed performance. Manufacturing's contribution to real provincial product grew during the 1970s and its growth rate of real output and employment was slightly higher than the national average. By other measures, however, the manufacturing sector's performance was less impressive. The rate of capital investment has been, until very recently, well below the national average, and the sector suffers from a number of structural weaknesses: many firms are small and tied to local markets while some are highly vulnerable to increased foreign competition (for example, the large clothing sector in Manitoba).[39] In addition, the growth of Edmonton, Calgary and, to a lesser extent, Vancouver, has outpaced the growth of Winnipeg; these cities are gradually replacing Winnipeg's role as an entrepôt to the West.

To a large extent, Manitoba's industrial policy over the past two decades has been directed at overcoming structural weakness in secondary manufacturing, although no industrial strategy as such has emerged from the government. During the 1960s, a number of attempts were made to address the problem of industrial decline, partly through a series of industry-government conferences and the establishment of provincial agencies such as the Manitoba Design Council, the Manitoba Development Corporation and the Manitoba Research Council. In the 1960s and 1970s, many industries received assistance, and several were eventually bought by the government.

Under the Conservative government of 1977, industrial policy shifted focus from individual projects to concentrate on selected industrial sectors. A new industrial support program (Enterprise Manitoba), jointly funded by both the province and the federal government, was established to increase the technological competence of local industry and provide industrial and financial assistance to small firms.* In addition, some attention was paid in the program to decentralizing the industrial base, now highly concentrated in the Winnipeg area. The industrial sectors which have been isolated for special attention are those in which there is existing commercial strength and those which have significant growth potential; they include food and beverages, health care products, light machinery, transport equipment, and the aerospace and electronics industries.[40]

Manitoba's future industrial development prospects will likely depend on its ability to maintain its position as a supplier of manufactured products to the rest of western Canada. In 1974, for example, western Canada took over half of Manitoba's domestic shipments of manufactured goods. Manitoba's industrial policies are unlikely to run into problems arising from the industrialization strategies of its neighbouring western provinces. Its chosen areas of concentration are based primarily on specialization within its relatively diversified manufacturing base. The other western provinces, in contrast, are diversifying principally on the basis of backward linkages to resource activities.

---

* A fuller description of Enterprise Manitoba is found in chapter VIII.

The East

Until recently, the Atlantic provinces had little in the way of newly found natural resources on which to base their economic development. They have long played the traditional role of peripheral regions. Economically depressed and suffering a population shift to the rest of Canada, they have served essentially as a market for central Canada's manufactured goods while their own industrial and resource bases atrophied. However, by the 1970s, circumstances in the Atlantic provinces began to change. With the declaration of the 200-mile fishing limit in the early 1970s, one of the region's principal resource industries faced prospects of a revival. At the end of the decade, oil and gas discoveries off the coasts of Newfoundland and Nova Scotia offered hope of a new resource base. Overall, though, the economic prospects of the Atlantic region are in a state of flux and the policies of the various provincial governments reflect this state. Although resource-based development offers hope for revived economic activity, there are still substantial problems. The population movement out of the Atlantic region ceased in the 1970s[41], and its share of Canada's real domestic product remained constant,[42] but unemployment rates are still the highest in the country. Further, evidence indicates that, despite the region's relative improvement in recent years, its dependence on outside sources of financial assistance is high and growing.[43]

New Brunswick

New Brunswick is heavily dependent on forest products and mining. But its industrial strategy has changed in the last decade; in the first half of the 1970s, extensive emphasis was placed on diversification of secondary manufacturing with the establishment of the New Brunswick Development Corporation and Multiplex, a joint federal-provincial Crown corporation which was to develop an integrated industrial complex in the Saint John area. By the mid-1970s, the strategy was largely abandoned due to a lack of success with either corporation and a number of other industrial development failures, most notably the Bricklin car assembly plant. The two corporations were disbanded and their development promotion activity was taken over by the province's Department of Commerce and Development.

More recently, greater emphasis has been placed on small business development and assistance, with less being placed on the "growth centre" approach to industrial diversification. In addition, attention has been focussed on forest products, mining and food processing - resource-based industries which were the economy's mainstays in the 1970s. Apart from the normal support assistance for industry supplied by virtually all provincial governments, and the maintenance of a research and productivity council to assist industrial research, the province kept a relatively low profile in the industrial development policy area in the latter half of the 1970s.

In the spring of 1982, the Department of Commerce and Development released a document outlining an industrial development strategy.[44] The document, essentially a review of past performance and the government's existing policy instruments for industrial development, did signal a greater concern for industrial diversification due to the prospect that low productivity and scarce resources would retard growth in the forest products industry and fishing in the 1980s. Indeed, concern for the future productivity of the forest products industry has been great enough to encourage the provincial government to enter into a major modernization agreement with the federal government. While mining activity is expected to do well, much of the government's efforts will be placed on encouraging the expansion of secondary manufacturing – especially in the metal-working sector (for example, through encouraging the introduction of Computer-Aided Design (CAD)/Computer-Aided Manufacturing (CAM)) – and promoting the development of small business. The document proposed no new industrial support programs or significant expansion of government funding; but it did state that greater emphasis would be placed on selectively tailored financial, infrastructure and technical assistance for major, new, nonresource industries.

Nova Scotia

Of all the Atlantic provinces, Nova Scotia has the most diversified economic base. It has significant fishery, mining, forest products and manufacturing sectors. But for a number of complex reasons, most of these sectors have been experiencing slow growth. Mining suffers from an unproductive coal industry, the forest products sector has wood stock and cost problems, and manufacturing is saddled with weak iron, steel, and shipbuilding firms.[45]

The province has a long experience with industrial development issues; in the 1950s, it established Industrial Estates Limited, a Crown corporation, to promote industrial diversification and development, and in the 1960s it rescued the province's major iron and steel mill (Sydney Steel) which is now publicly owned. In this period, the federal government also established the Cape Breton Development Corporation (DEVCO) to phase down the coal mining industry and encourage alternative industries. More recently, the provincial government, through joint agreements with the Department of Regional Economic Expansion (DREE) in the mid-1970s, has set up comprehensive development programs in the Strait of Canso and in the Halifax-Dartmouth harbour area.[46] Despite all of these efforts, however, only a limited amount of diversification has been achieved, with a number of costly failures (for example, Clairtone and Derterium).[47]

Recently, the provincial government published a green paper on what it sees as Nova Scotia's development issues and the potential role the government can play in economic development.[48] In its view, the province's development prospects are principally in manufacturing. It judges that the resource sector will be unable to supply sufficient expansion in future, either because of poor resource stocks (agriculture and forestry) or uncertain economic prospects (mining). Even the fishing industry, which has expanded significantly in recent years, promises only modest growth prospects and is currently in financial difficulty. Manufacturing, on the other hand, since 1972 has expanded at a rate above the Canadian average.[49]

As well, the provincial government is dissatisfied with its previous approach to industrial development which seemed to be a process of simply following federal precedents. It is proposing a series of industrial development initiatives based on a greater self-reliance for the Nova Scotia economy. This implies an increasing emphasis on technology-intensive and high-value added goods and services. Some of the initiatives include:

- a focus on improving labour resources and productivity as opposed to infrastructure and physical capital;
- greater stress on innovation, from product development to management and marketing;[50]
- more emphasis on industrial cooperation, especially among smaller enterprises;
- greater concentration on successful and innovative new industries and a shift away from existing weak industries.

Some of the mechanisms proposed to support these objectives include revised training and educational programs to assist small business. On the technology development front, the government proposes a provincial patent and licensing agency to assist in the procurement of technology for Nova Scotia firms. It also wants the Nova Scotia Research Foundation to assist more effectively in product and process design work and industry-government-academic exchanges of personnel. The government indicated that it would place greater emphasis on provincial assistance programs for export promotion and marketing, and encourage more business cooperation in such areas as bulk purchasing, marketing and research. Finally, the green paper proposed the establishment of a privately run export development corporation and an advisory service for business methods in small firms.

In terms of concentrating on existing strengths, the government advanced a "core enterprise program" to identify growth prospects for about 20 leading manufacturing firms and then tailor assistance to these firms' needs. The government has also proposed measures to improve public sector efficiency, an important element in a province where the public sector plays a relatively large role. Proposals included: budgetary reform; negotiation of federal transfers to emphasize investment rather than consumption; regulatory reform; more emphasis on income generation from provincially sponsored institutions; and a greater emphasis on subcontracting government work to the private sector.

Despite this emphasis on manufacturing, the Nova Scotia government still realizes that industrial development associated with resource exploitation is important. The natural gas discoveries off Sable Island will provide a needed replacement for expensive oil imports, while offering opportunities for local manufacturers and suppliers. And because its industrial base and infrastructure are generally more diversified than those of the other provinces in the region, Nova Scotia is also well placed to benefit from oil and gas activity elsewhere off the east coast. As a result, the government is aggressively pushing the province's capability in offshore work. In its recent agreement on offshore jurisdiction with the federal government, the province has not only managed to obtain all the significant government revenues which will flow from gas field development in the early years, but has obtained federal support for special development funds to assist with the provision of offshore industrial infrastructure, manpower training and R&D.

In short, Nova Scotia is pursuing a strategy which now emphasizes manufacturing over resource development, although it is cognizant of the opportunities posed by resource projects. And like New Brunswick, Nova Scotia has moved away from the pursuit of large industrial projects in favour of a more structural view of economic problems. This has meant a concentration on innovative small firms and targeted assistance to a few large "core" enterprises.

Prince Edward Island

Prince Edward Island has the smallest economy in the country and, in consequence, a somewhat limited industrial policy. In large measure, the province's strategy is a function of the Comprehensive Development Plan (CDP) which it signed with the federal government in 1969. The province suffers from slow growth, high energy costs and high unemployment. It heavily depends on agriculture, food processing and tourism, none of which is capable of generating significant increases in the standard of living (although all sectors have been improving their performance since the early 1970s).

The CDP has stressed improvements to the island's road network and assistance to increase productivity in agriculture, fishing and tourism. Some attempts have been made to reduce energy costs by experimenting with renewable energy sources, small-scale electricity-generation systems and the construction of a power cable to the mainland. Local industrial parks and malls have been created to attract secondary manufacturing, and low interest loans and grants are provided by the industrial development corporation, Industrial Enterprises Incorporated and the provincial department of Tourism, Industry and Energy.[51] However, with very limited fiscal resources, the province's activity has been relatively modest and has to be implemented principally within the context of the CDP.

Newfoundland

Newfoundland's standard of living has increased substantially in recent years, but it is still the poorest province in Canada with the highest level of unemployment. In 1979, for example, earned income per capita in Newfoundland was just over half the Canadian average, and the unemployment rate, at 15.4 per cent, was more than double the national average.[52] The economy depends heavily on exports of unprocessed or semiprocessed resource products such as minerals (principally iron ore), forest products and fish, and serious barriers exist to the further processing of these products due to the nature of the province's export markets.[53] As well, the economy has severe structural problems.[54]

Like other Atlantic provinces, Newfoundland has experimented with a number of industrial diversification policies. In the 1950s, attempts were made to establish provincially owned small-scale enterprises to shore up a declining manufacturing sector. The experiment failed and, in the 1960s, efforts were directed towards large-scale development projects such as oil refineries, liner board mills, shipyards and hydroelectric power projects. Many of these projects also ran into difficulties and suffered from unfavourable international market conditions. As they were poorly integrated into the narrow provincial economy, they provided few spillover effects.

In 1980, the government conducted a major reassessment of its economic development objectives and published a planning document, *Managing All Our Resources*. The statement set out in fairly explicit terms the government's current approach to industrial and economic policy. "The province," it stated, will "pursue a pattern of development based on the comparative advantages of the province's resource endowments. The primary objective is to retain as much as possible of the direct and indirect processing activity within the province."[55] The government aims not only to increase resource processing but also to seek forms of industrialization based on "backward" or "upstream" linkages to resource activities (for example, the manufacture of equipment for the fishing industry).

66

To pursue these objectives, the government is attempting to act in several areas. First, by assuming provincial ownership of resources, the government can obtain rents to finance further development and can control resource exploitation in order to increase local economic benefits. Second, the province intends to embark on a local procurement policy. And to assist with the provision of the necessary technical expertise, the government has committed itself to a provincial science policy.[56] It also plans to expand technical training and development facilities, particularly in the fishery sector. These efforts will build on initiatives taken during the 1970s to establish a technology base in marine operations for hostile northern waters. A Centre for Cold Oceans Resources Engineering (C-CORE) has been established at Memorial University with federal and provincial funding to conduct basic R&D work in marine engineering. On the operational side, the provincial government and DREE also established a Crown corporation, Newfoundland Oceans Research Development (NORDCO), to assist in the accumulation of data on operating requirements in the waters around Newfoundland and Labrador and in the commercial development of equipment and technology for marine operations. In addition, some attention is also being given to the improvement of local managerial and entrepreneurial capacity.

Much of the government's efforts will be directed to the province's newest resource sector, offshore oil and gas, although the fishing industry, with predicted heavy growth in catches until the middle of this decade, is also of considerable importance. Along with Saskatchewan, Quebec and Alberta, Newfoundland has been most direct in stating its desire to control its own resource base for industrial development. It has also taken strong stands on control of fishing rights and new jobs in resource developments for local residents. These positions, along with demands for ownership of offshore resources, have made the province seem the "bad boy" of Confederation. Yet, what is frequently not appreciated is that the government has little alternative. Its growing reliance on transfer payments and its lack of success with other strategies mean that it must pursue forthright policies which attempt to capture more of the value of resource developments. Such policies may offer the only way for the province to break out of its cycle of dependency.[57]

Conclusions

In the past decade the provinces of the eastern and western periphery have become aware of the importance of obtaining greater benefits from their resources. This draws in large measure from their historical experience and a growing appreciation that there are essential differences of economic interest between the centre and the periphery. They perceive that sustained economic development will only come from local efforts. In some provinces, such as Alberta, Saskatchewan and Newfoundland, this perception has resulted in a renewed commitment to obtain the maximum provincial share possible from resource revenues, and indeed, control over the future pace and direction of such developments. Their objective is to ensure that the revenues are used as much as possible for local, as distinct from national, development.

There is also a growing appreciation of the need to husband resources and to seek industrial diversification opportunities which build on existing strengths in resource industries. This is even noticeable in the Atlantic region where traditional industrial development approaches have largely been abandoned, partly in favour of more directed and focussed attempts at constructing backward and forward linkages to resource industries and to expand their existing manufacturing bases as a consequence. In their specialized diversification efforts, the western and eastern provinces are also placing a significant emphasis on the application of high technology. In effect, they are seeking a national, and international, market niche based on high-technology industry geared to their local resource endowments.

IV. A Troubled Heartland

If the provinces on Canada's periphery are finding a new role for themselves in industrial policy, those of Canada's heartland are discovering a new role in response to industrial decline. Both Ontario and Quebec are starting to experiment with policies more ambitious in their intended impact than those of the past – policies which bring government into a closer relationship with industry, and indeed, with individual firms. Ontario and Quebec are vitally concerned with the problem of restructuring existing uncompetitive industrial sectors. In some cases, they are seeking to strengthen ailing firms, and in others, to shift capital and labour to new industrial capability.

Despite their similarities, however, Ontario and Quebec are approaching industrial restructuring from rather different perspectives. In Ontario's case, restructuring is a response to an obvious, but still nascent, problem of industrial decline. The response, as befits a province used to being the economic leader of Confederation, has been somewhat restrained. In Quebec, the response has been to an immediate and manifest economic problem, one made more urgent by a growing sense of political dissatisfaction with the federal system. Along with the traditional alienation of the francophone majority from the economic mainstream, these factors have resulted in an approach to industrial policy which has tended to stress the role of government intervention to a far greater extent than in any other province.

Ontario

New Problems

To paraphrase a recent Ontario observer: "Other provinces have industrial strategies, Ontario has industry."[1] Ontario has tradition-

ally been the economically and some would argue, politically dominant member of Confederation. With more than 50 per cent of the
country's manufacturing sector, 35 per cent of its population, 41 per
cent of the national domestic product and 44 per cent of its export
trade, Ontario is clearly the single most important economic region.[2]
Serious problems, however, face the provincial economy. In general,
growth has been well below the national average; the province's annual rate of gross provincial product (GPP) growth between 1970-77
was exceeded by seven other provinces and its share of gross national product (GNP) over the same period dropped from 41.9 per cent
to 39.9 per cent. By many measures, income growth was the lowest in
the country. The value of manufactured shipments also declined,
making Ontario's growth rate the third lowest in the country.[3]
While these figures understate Ontario's still dominant position,
they are indicative of a province whose growth is unable to keep up
with the national average.

There are also concerns about the future role of Ontario within
Canada and the larger North American market. The province's competitive position is now being severely hurt by energy costs. It is
faced with a major adjustment well after most other countries have
incorporated high energy costs into their industrial structure.[4] Further, the province's most important economic sector, manufacturing, is undergoing considerable structural adjustment due to its
heavy reliance on branch plants. This form of industrial development is being made rapidly obsolete due to changes in both locational patterns of North American industry and the nature of international competition. On the first front, the steady movement of
America's manufacturing capacity away from the northeast to the
sun belt, and the desire of large American firms to rationalize production on a continental basis, have reduced the attractions of
Canadian branch plants particularly in light of the progressive reduction of tariffs through the Multilateral Trade Negotiations
(MTNs).[5] These trends are reducing Ontario's locational attractiveness as well as chipping away at the virtues of branch plants per se
as a way to serve the Canadian market.[6] Second, the types of products produced by Ontario's branch plants could become increasingly
uncompetitive with imported manufactured goods. This partly results from the traditional problem of productivity due to short production runs, but is also due to the changing nature of international
competition. Canada's industrial trading partners have increasingly
moved into technologically advanced production.[7] Unfortunately,
the US parents of many branch plants are falling behind technologically and, subsequently, are less able to supply subsidiaries with
competitive technology. There are also indications that Canadian
branch plants are getting what new technology is available from
their US parents less quickly than before.[8] Many of Ontario's tradi-

tional branch plants may have considerable difficulties adapting to a trading environment based on technology-intensive products and production.

Among domestically owned firms, there have been some successes in high technology, especially in telecommunications and aerospace products. However, the vast majority of the province's domestically owned firms are small and produce conventional manufactured goods. In addition, lower-cost producers in the NICs of Asia, the Mediterranean and South America are able to mass produce many conventional and established technology goods much more cheaply.[9] Ontario has an advantage over Quebec in that it has fewer of the labour intensive manufacturing industries (for example, textiles and footwear), which have been so adversely affected by competition from the NICs. However, many of Ontario's most important specializations in manufacturing, as, for example, automotive assembly and parts manufacture, are already under pressure from import competition and production rationalization due to the advent of new technology, new products and changing patterns of industrial location in North America.

Ontario has been uncertain about how to respond to this transforming climate. Traditionally, the province has benefited from sizeable foreign investment in manufacturing and has relied on an open Canadian domestic market to maintain its dominant position within the country's economy. Indeed, during the 1980 constitutional discussions, Ontario was virtually the only province backing federal proposals which would ensure the maintenance of a strong national common market.[10] However, as the changes in the province's economic circumstances indicate, Ontario has also realized that its traditional, relatively free-market approach to industrial development will have to change if the challenges facing its manufacturing sector are to be met.[11] As well, Ontario seems to be unsure about the future location of its markets. Much emphasis has been placed on seeking new opportunities for Ontario in the United States, particularly in the industrial northeast. However, difficulties with the auto pact, and an increasingly protectionist attitude in the United States, have tempered this enthusiasm. Recently, the province's former industry minister, Larry Grossman, claimed that moves to closer trade ties with the United States should be pursued on a case-by-case basis and should not be undertaken if they weaken Canadian economic integration.[12] Finally, as its experience in energy pricing disputes indicates, Ontario can no longer rely entirely on the federal government to protect its interests, or to pursue policies which will automatically benefit the province. With western Canada emerging and Quebec still restive, Ontario's interests are not as central as they once were in Ottawa. Not surprisingly, therefore, a former industry minister recently stated that: "it makes sense to me that Ontario should speak for manufacturing, just as the prairie provinces have traditionally spoken for grain farming and the Atlantic provinces for fishing."[13]

The Response
In broad terms, the province's industrial development policy consists of the following elements:

1. An attempt to improve the business environment through taxation, deregulation and reduced government expenditure on noneconomic development items.[14]

2. An emphasis on both export promotion and import replacement. Ontario has an extensive network of trade missions abroad and is expanding its export promotion and financing activities. In addition, the province is pressuring the federal government to pursue vigorously violations of the GATT agreement on nontariff barriers which limit access to foreign markets for Ontario goods. The province has also launched an import replacement program designed to encourage consumers to buy Canadian-made goods and to inform Ontario manufacturers of import replacement opportunities. This program has been reinforced with a provincial government purchasing policy allowing up to a 10 per cent premium on Canadian goods purchases. This policy has recently been expanded to cover Crown corporations and the procurement of private firms whose expansion or investments are funded by government grants.[15] The government is also attempting to encourage other provinces to cooperate in the collective procurement of goods and services which have import replacement or industrial development potential.[16]

3. A focus upon shifting North American industrial patterns. The first initiative in this area was the establishment of the Employment Development Fund (EDF). It was designed to meet the industrial incentives being offered by other jurisdictions in the United States. Its $200 million 1979-80 budget was intended to "top up" existing provincial investment incentives. The EDF has been used for two major projects: a $28 million grant for the Ford Motor Company to establish an engine plant in Windsor; and grants totalling approximately $100 million to Ontario pulp and paper companies to help purchase pollution abatement devices and modernize production equipment.[17] With respect to the EDF, the government indicated that it formed a new direction in funding policy for industry, a policy which, in the words of a former industry minister, "must be based on... tough, shrewd, selectivity." This selectivity is to be based not only on the

government's assessment of a firm's viability, but also on the degree to which a firm fits the province's development strategy.[18]

In November 1980, the Ontario government announced that EDF was to be superseded by the new cabinet Board of Industrial Leadership and Development (BILD) as part of a more intensive approach to industrial development. The board now coordinates all the government's development spending on industrial, resource, transportation and regional development, human resources and community infrastructure. These items were budgeted at just over $2 billion in 1980-81. In addition, BILD will manage a new series of economic and regional development incentives which will amount to $750 million over the five years from 1980. In a move designed to increase the coherence of Ontario's relationship with the federal government on economic development issues, the board will also be responsible for reviewing all federal-provincial consultation and cooperation.[19]

4. A rationalization of its industrial strategy. Although the provincial government has never issued an industrial strategy as such, nor has it isolated a group of industrial sectors for specific attention, it has published an outline of its economic development policies for the 1980s under the aegis of BILD. This isolates five aspects of the provincial economy for specific policy attention: increased emphasis on nuclear generation capacity and rail and transit electrification to reduce Ontario's dependence on imported oil; special attention to transportation, particularly in the manufacture of advanced transit systems; and resources development, principally centring on agricultural and forest resource management techniques and mining machinery. In addition, the province intends to assist technology-intensive industry through a new Crown agency, the Innovation Development for Employment Advancement Corporation (IDEA Corporation). The corporation will fund R&D projects with the private sector or public institutions and may also take an equity stake in private technology development ventures. It will also manage the government's share of a joint venture with a private firm to establish a major biotechnology company. Along with IDEA Corporation, the government established a number of technology development centres in microelectronics, auto parts, CAD/CAM, resource machinery, robotics and farm equipment and food processing machinery. In total, the centres will receive $128 million for their first five years of operation. Finally, the province intends to increase the quality and level of on-the-job training, youth employment counselling and

additional assistance for postsecondary institutions to expand high skill-training in such fields as, for example, microelectronics.[20]

5. Cautious moves in the direction of establishing private-sector advisory committees on certain key industrial sectors, or issues, in order to develop consensus on industrial policies. To date, joint labour-industry committees have been established in the electrical goods and microelectronics sectors, and a committee made up of senior executives of some Ontario multinationals was formed to advise the government on world product mandating.[21]

Summary

The Ontario government realizes that significant structural changes are occurring in the province and that new measures are required; this is particularly noticeable in the major efforts being made to encourage high-technology innovation and the institution of EDF and BILD. However, as the "catch all" nature of the new R&D program indicates, the government has so far refrained from advancing any overall industrial strategy. Indeed, the government has come under considerable attack; both the opposition and the press claim that the BILD program is merely a repackaging of existing support programs. Although some of the money spent for high-technology projects is new, a significant element in BILD's five-year, $750 million budget consists of infrastructure programs such as employment training, road construction and tourist facilities.[22]

Many of the government's objectives, such as trade promotion, greater access to the US market and fostering a better business climate, are based on the assumption that Ontario manufacturing is basically strong and that by removing certain market imperfections it will continue to prosper. The truth of this depends on the degree to which Ontario industry makes significant structural changes. However, the indicators are not overly promising. The continued economic viability and importance of foreign-owned manufacturing subsidiaries and even the province's central role as a supplier of manufactured goods to all of Canada are by no means certain.[23] The automobile industry, the backbone of the province's manufacturing sector, is also facing rather bleak long-term prospects. But at least the gradual move to address underlying structural weaknesses – as seen in BILD's emphasis on skills training and technology development, and in the government's attempts to encourage branch plants to adopt world product mandates – indicates that the province is seriously re-evaluating some aspects of its traditional industrial policy. How sharp and radical a departure this re-evaluation is, remains to be seen. What cannot be denied is that a new and more aggressive pursuit of the province's industrial interests is certain to be a hallmark of Ontario's future policies.

Quebec

Of all the provinces, Quebec has attempted to establish the most comprehensive industrial strategy. It also has the most clearly developed official analysis of its problems and prospects. Neither of these facts should be surprising given the socioeconomic circumstances of the past two decades. Since the late 1950s, Quebec's relative economic position within the country has declined. Population growth has been slow, its share of Canada's total population has dropped, and it has the country's second highest regional unemployment rate. Personal income and investment growth has been significant, especially in the 1970s, but much of it has been due to transfer payments and public-sector investment. In manufacturing, growth in shipments, employment and capital expenditures were all below the Ontario and Canadian averages. The primary sector has experienced a net decline in its contribution to GDP and employment. Agriculture, mining and forestry are experiencing significant problems.[24]

The province is faced with a number of notable structural problems as well. Compared to Ontario, Quebec suffers from a disproportionate share of uncompetitive industries in its manufacturing sector producing nondurable goods. For example, traditional industries based on forest products, clothing, textiles and food processing provide about 41 per cent of total manufacturing employment.[25] These industries are under significant international competitive pressure, either because of a poor capital plant and dwindling resource base, as in the case of the forest products industry, or a high-cost labour content when competing against Third World producers, as in the case of textiles. In addition, manufacturing firms tend to be smaller than their Ontario counterparts, and less able to engage in marketing, risk taking and R&D.[26] Like the rest of Canada, Quebec suffers from low R&D expenditures; only about 275 firms are engaged in industrial research.[27]

Finally, Quebec suffers from a poor integration of some industrial sectors with the rest of the provincial economy. This is particularly true of producer goods and consumer durables. In the primary sector, the processing of mineral products suffers from similar problems; in some areas (for example, copper refining) processing facilities are isolated from their source of raw material. In others, resources are refined within the province but shipped out for final manufacturing (for example, asbestos).[28]

All these factors are more striking when viewed in the context of the profound social changes over the past two decades. During this period, the province's francophone majority began to move up the social and professional ladder. Francophones have increasingly entered technical and commercial professions, the historical preserve of the anglophone minority. Many have interpreted the expansion of the state sector in Quebec and, in particular, the nationalization of the power companies and the establishment of numerous commercial Crown corporations, as an attempt to meet the aspirations of this rising francophone middle class.[29] However, this is only a partial explanation of a much more complex socioeconomic process.[30]

The need to generate more francophone white collar and professional jobs in industry coincided with a significant growth in the size of the labour force during the 1970s and with rising unemployment which hit francophones more severely than anglophones. Clearly, a continued expansion of government would not generate the needed jobs. In addition, employment in the private sector was scarce, partly because of the structural problems of the economy, and partly because anglophone or foreign-owned firms were not providing sufficient French-speaking employment opportunities, particularly in the skilled and managerial categories.[31] And most francophone firms were too small to provide the needed French-speaking jobs.

By the late 1970s the government faced a dual crisis: it had a declining industrial base; yet it needed to substantially increase employment opportunities. To meet this challenge, it has been forced to seek far more comprehensive and radical policies than other provincial governments. One example has been "francization" of the work place under Bill 101.[32] More important has been the industrial strategy announced in the government's white paper, *Bâtir Le Québec*.[33] The strategy outlined in the document has basically five goals: i) to increase linkages between the resource and manufacturing sectors by tying resource development to industrial development policy; ii) to expand the level of government assistance available to the small and medium-sized business sector; iii) to protect declining industries; iv) to use the public sector and Crown corporations to achieve major development goals; v) and to increase the level and quality of private sector R&D.

Resource Linkages
In the case of resource industries, the government is proposing to play a greater role in the management of resource development to ensure further processing in the province. A principal instrument will be its control over hydroelectric capacity. Electricity is important for industries such as smelting (for example, aluminum, zinc, magnesium), newsprint manufacture and the production of industrial chemicals. At present, only 38 per cent of the production of such primary products is incorporated into other manufactured goods in

the province – the rest is exported. This compares to 90 per cent of such production being incorporated into manufactured products in the United States.[34] To change this, *new* electricity supply contracts over 5MW will be subject to review, and applicants will be required to demonstrate some of the following: increased backward or forward linkages to the economy; integration with other planned major capital investments; employment of local residents; and the location in Quebec of head offices, management and other service functions.

The government is also pursuing special efforts with respect to forest products. Because of its important role in the provincial economy, the forest products industry will receive financial assistance broadly similar to Ontario's. Grants to improve forestry roads and reforestation projects, plus tax incentives and grants to encourage plant modernization, make up the principal elements.

Finally, the government is seeking selective, direct participation in the resource sector. Since the mid-1960s, Quebec has tried to influence the pace of resource development and the use of its resources through government-owned mineral and petroleum exploration corporations (for example, Soquem and Soquip). However, these firms have remained relatively small and have had a modest impact on resource development. Hydroelectric resources are, however, effectively controlled by Hydro-Québec and the James Bay Development Corporation, and these companies have tried to ensure that electrical energy projects promote provincial industrial development. So far, this has involved Quebec firms supplying goods and services to these corporations for ongoing operations and for massive hydro construction projects.

Perhaps the most controversial use of public enterprise by the government in the resource sector, however, has been the attempt to nationalize the asbestos industry. Traditionally, the industry has been under total foreign control and most of the asbestos mined in Quebec has been shipped out or semiprocessed in the province. By establishing a national asbestos corporation (SNA), the government hopes to capture the economic rent and to expand processing, including the incorporation of asbestos into a wider range of manufactured products. To this end, the SNA has already purchased a significant proportion of the province's asbestos mines[35] and has established a research facility to develop new products. In addition, the corporation is investing in a plant to extract magnesium from asbestos residuals and in firms concerned with secondary products (for example, manufacture of brake shoes and linoleum backing).

Small and Medium-Sized Firms
Government support for small and medium-sized firms is designed primarily to help overcome the limitations of size, and to promote

growth through private-sector collective action in such areas as marketing, exports and R&D. As well, government resources and financial assistance are used for expansion. Table IV.1 lists some of the government's proposed actions. Particular attention is being paid to increasing linkages between small and large firms.

Table IV.1 – Proposed Quebec Government Actions Primarily in Support of Small and Medium-Sized Business

- support in a variety of ways the amalgamation of firms for research, exporting, and transportation purposes;
- eventually set up a subcontracting exchange in the Montreal region to facilitate contracts between major multinational corporations and small local suppliers;
- provide technical and financial assistance to large firms for organizing exhibitions of products which could be manufactured by subcontractors;
- strengthen the government's purchasing policy by emphasizing the following: pooling of purchases, closer supervision of construction estimates, maximizing technological impact;
- expand existing programs aimed at bringing interest groups together: all types of mergers of interest groups would be eligible as long as they brought about savings and accelerated development of the enterprises involved;
- set up one-stop-shopping for government assistance by establishing multidisciplinary teams in regional centres which could analyze the needs of people in business and inform them of the full range of government assistance available;
- set up the Office québécois du commerce extérieur (OQCE) to collect foreign market data, organize export promotions, and promote the organization of private-sector export consortiums;
- set up the Société d'exportation du Québec (SEQ): this government corporation would be a minority partner in the organization of temporary or permanent export amalgamations, corporations or consortiums.

Source: Ministry of State for Economic Development, *Challenges for Quebec: A Statement for Economic Policy*, Éditeur officiel, Quebec, 1979, pp. 168-172.

Declining Industries

For industries in severe decline (for example, textiles), Quebec's response has basically been to pressure the federal government for effective tariff and quota protection. However, the Quebec government has also made it known that it will provide financial support to individual firms which exhibit above average growth potential.[36]

Use of the Public Sector and Crown Corporations

Much of the use of the state sector in the developmental process involves a greater coordination of the already existing, and extensive, provincial participation in the private sector. In addition to the Crown corporations' involvement in resource development, the government has a significant presence in iron and steel. However, the most interesting aspect of the government's Crown corporations is the size and variety of the financial institutions involved. The government currently controls three financial corporations: the Société générale de financement (SGF), an investment and holding corporation; the Société de développement industriel (SDI), a vehicle for the delivery of industrial development loans and grants; and La Caisse de dépôt et de placement (CDP), an investment agency for the assets of the Quebec Pension Plan. In the 1970s, the first two were particularly active in industrial restructuring.

The SGF frequently pursues investments on a joint venture basis with other firms. It has significant interests in pulp and paper, and is increasing local participation in this crucial industry. In addition, SGF is taking part in a major Montreal petrochemical project with foreign interests, has a significant stake in MLW-Worthington and has assisted in the merger of three furniture manufacturers. With assets of more than $800 million and interests in shipbuilding and machinery, SGF has become a major holding company and a vehicle for increasing local ownership.[37]

SDI, on the other hand, has functioned as a traditional development corporation, providing loan capital at concessionary rates. While many of SDI's loans are to small firms, it also lends significant amounts to larger firms. About 40 per cent of its loans are disbursed to firms owned by nonresidents.[38] While it does act as an instrument of provincial policy, SDI's loan pattern reflects more the existing structure of industry than that of the SGF. There are indications, however, that SDI will become a more direct instrument for industrial restructuring. The legislation which established SDI has been redrafted to allow the corporation to administer government assistance programs to firms and to provide a wider range of financing, including equity capital. SDI has also been given a special mandate to seek firms for assistance in microelectronics, biotechnology and high-technology service industries.[39]

Finally, is the CDP, better known simply as "The Caisse." It is one of the largest sources of capital in the province, but is also the least involved in industrial restructuring. Because of its pension fund role, it has traditionally avoided risky investments. In 1978, only 19 per cent of its capital was invested in corporate securities, when its allowable limit was 30 per cent,[40] and, unlike the SGF, it has not taken an active management role in the firms it has invested in. It has, however, had a role in supporting the brokerage community in Montreal and 60 per cent of its industrial assets are invested in Quebec-based companies such as Provigo, Bombardier and Marine Industries Ltd.[41] Recently, the Quebec government has indicated that it would like The Caisse to take a more active industrial investment role in the province. But whether the government will be able to harness the CDP for a more active role is uncertain, as such a role has become an issue of some political controversy in the province.[42]

R&D

R&D is the final area of significant government interest. Quebec for some time has had a number of government agencies responsible for assisting in the development of science and technology policy, including an advisory science policy council, and an office for science and technology in the Ministry of Education. In the industrial field, the province, like many others, has a provincial research council, the Centre de recherche industrielle du Québec (CRIQ), although it is a relative newcomer compared to those in the other provinces.[43] In addition, the government manages a mineral research centre and Hydro-Québec operates a world-class electrical technology research centre, the Institute de recherche d'Hydro-Québec (IREQ).

The following year the government released another white paper, *A Collective Approach: Statement of Policy Objectives and Plan for the Implementation of a Research Policy for Quebec*, which seeks to recast and improve government policies and institutions in support of scientific (including industrial) research.[44] In the white paper, the government outlined general measures on scientific research, mainly concerned with improving the research infrastructure, the provision and use of research manpower, and increasing the coherence of government policy mechanisms for research policy, including the naming of a minister of state for science and technology with a small support staff (known as the Ministre délégue à la science et à la technologie). In the white paper, the government also announced a number of initiatives to increase Quebec's industrial technological capacity. These proposals include expanding the budget and activities of CRIQ and IREQ, particularly to provide consulting, testing and technological diffusion services to industry. Among the other diverse measures proposed by the government were: a series of awards to stimulate interest in industrial innovation; possible research subsidy programs to encourage industrial research, especially in electronics and textiles; and support of cooperative research programs carried out by industry associations.

A New Departure

Three years after its first major statement on industrial policy, the Parti québécois government released a new policy review in the spring of 1982. *Le Virage technologique*,[45] basically reaffirmed the directions laid out in the earlier *Bâtir Le Québec*. But it also elaborated the government's intentions in high technology. The review addressed three main issues – new industrial development opportunities, the adjustment problems of existing manufacturers and natural resources issues. In the latter two, it re-emphasized the pressing need to improve the management, technology, marketing and export capabilities of many of Quebec's conventional manufacturers and the need to improve the efficiency of resource industries.

More importantly, the review outlined a significant policy for new industries. Attention would be devoted to three principal areas: industrial spinoffs from megaprojects; financial and technical assistance for high technology service industries; and specific assistance programs for electronics and biotechnology. To implement these objectives, the government has established the Office of Major Projects to assist firms in identifying commercial opportunities and to help them in marketing products and services to major project sponsors. In the promotion of new technology services, SDI has been assigned responsibility, along with the Quebec office of external commerce, to assist in the promotion of engineering and other export-oriented services to federal agencies such as the Export Development Corporation (EDC) and the Canadian International Development Agency (CIDA). SDI may also assist in the provision of finances to help establish export consortia.

In the area of new industries, the government is committed to: providing financial assistance through SDI (including equity stakes) to electronics firms; establishing a development plan for specific electronics specializations; establishing a state corporation, Société de Développement des industries de la culture et des communications (SODICC) to promote the application of new electronics technologies in communications; and using CRIQ to provide assistance on product development in data processing, office automation, data communications and telecommunications. In biotechnology, increased support will be given to research laboratories and institutes, and there will be a new emphasis on technology transfer from academic research establishments to industry. In addition, SGF and several Crown corporations are to make major investments in bio-technology along with private sector partners. The government has indicated that biotechnology specializations in the following four fields will have priority: health, agriculture and food, forestry and the environment.

Summary

Quebec probably has the most diversified instruments to implement an industrial strategy. It also has the most pressing political imperative in light of its industrial weakness and its need to involve the francophone majority in the economy. Given the pattern of socioeconomic development, the Quebec government has long felt it necessary to play an active and interventionist role. But attempting a structural transformation of Quebec's manufacturing and resource sector will be a great challenge.

Whether Quebec will be up to the challenge is an open question. It is one thing to propose a policy, another, to implement it. With a marked budgetary crisis and an economy which has been particularly hard hit by the recent recession, the government's room for manoeuvre is somewhat limited. Its industrial development expenditures are already the highest of any provincial government (see Figure IV.1), and managing the short-term social problems created by the recession and expenditure restraints may sap a good deal of the current government's energy to promote change. In any event, it is still too early to tell whether the announced measures will all be implemented, or indeed, if implemented, whether they will be successful.[46]

There are some indications as well that the Quebec government has avoided, or at least toned down, its significant commitment to the more difficult structural problems facing the provincial economy. In textiles, footwear and clothing, the sectors likely to cause the most significant problems in the coming years and in which there is a heavy proportion of the Quebec labour force, the proposed measures have been limited. Apart from some assistance with the promotion of innovation and exports, the provincial government has stated that it will be forced to rely on federal government initiatives to prevent further import competition in this sector. Thus a very difficult structural problem in the Quebec economy is left squarely on the federal government's doorstep.

Certainly, Quebec's objectives pose little threat to the rest of Canada. Most of its present manufactured exports do not directly compete with those of the other provinces, and a strategy encouraging new manufacturing specializations that would compete with those in other provinces is unlikely for several reasons. The costs would be prohibitive and the social and economic uncertainty would be politically undesirable. Economic uncertainties and social dislocations are likely to be minimal if the government attempts to restructure industry within the framework of the existing industrial base. In fact, in its most recent pronouncement on industrial policy, the government has explicitly stated that, in the area of new technology support, it will ensure that its policies complement those of other provinces.[47]

In the resource sector, government policy is also unlikely to cause conflicts. With the exception of Ontario, only a small proportion of the province's resource wealth, which is shipped out in an unprocessed or semiprocessed form, goes to other provinces for further processing. It is also evident from government statements that the principal target for further processing is export markets or markets within Canada which are met by imports. The most significant example of this is the attempt to ensure further processing of asbestos within the province. Problems can arise in areas where Quebec shares a similar resource-based industry with other parts of Canada

Figure IV.1 – Provincial Government Spending on Trade and Industry, 1976-1980

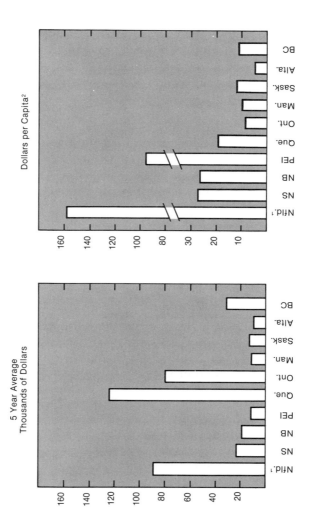

5 Year Average
Thousands of Dollars

Dollars per Capita[2]

[1] Newfoundland's expenditure figures reflect the writing off of a very substantial industrial investment in 1978.

[2] Based on 1978 population estimates.

Source: Statistics Canada, *Provincial Government Finance, Revenue and Expenditure*, 68-207, various years.

and pursues policies which essentially create surplus capacity. This is most likely in an industry such as forestry. However, as we shall see in chapter VIII, this particular problem has resulted in some very interesting forms of cooperation with Ontario and the federal government.

The real potential for conflict may relate more to the manner in which government policy is implemented than to its objectives. For example, the extensive tariff and nontariff protection for the high proportion of Quebec manufacturing activity which is vulnerable to international competition will require the provincial government to pressure federal authorities for more protection and financial assistance. This will bring Quebec into conflict with western provinces pressing for trade liberalization, particularly in manufactured goods,[48] and even the federal government, which is committed to liberalization under GATT. Also, a good deal of the province's current economic performance has been maintained through transfer payments and public investment. A sizeable element of this aid has been in the form of federal income support payments, financial assistance and incentives to investment.[49] In future, though, Quebec may no longer be the pre-eminent claimant. For example, the current structural problems facing the Ontario economy may cause that provincial government in future to seek increased federal assistance. Thus, although Ontario and Quebec are unlikely to engage in disputes over trade or industrial policy, significant differences could arise between the two provinces over the allocation of federal largesse for industrial restructuring.

Another possible cause of tension is the degree to which Quebec's desire for local control works against the interests of other Canadian firms in the province. This may lead to clashes that could even reach ideological proportions if, for example, provincial Crown corporations in Quebec expropriate private Ontario-owned assets. Significantly, differences between Ontario and Quebec over the CDP's plans to acquire companies through the Toronto Stock Exchange have already surfaced.[50] Despite its commitment to greater local control though, the Quebec government has often chosen to assist and promote the expansion of foreign-owned firms when growth and employment prospects have been better than those available from locally owned firms.[51] As a result, conflicts with other provinces over the promotion of locally owned firms would, at most, be limited. The fighting will more likely develop over Quebec's procurement policy where discrimination against out-of-province firms is significant.

V. Provincial Industrial Policies: Ten or One?

In the last decade, the scope and range of provincial industrial policies have expanded significantly. The provinces' functions are starting to mirror in extent, if not in form, those of the federal government. This is occurring at a time of rapid change in the various provincial economies, particularly in the role they play within the national economic system. In western Canada, economic expansion has created a renewed awareness of the importance of industrial diversification linked to resources. The economies of Quebec and Ontario, meanwhile, occupy a less certain place at the centre of the national economy; both provincial governments have to restructure an economic base which is now under increasing competitive pressure.

There is clearly considerable variety and sophistication in provincial industrial policies. But are they incompatible because of the new vigour with which they are practised?

The Character of Provincial Policies
The provinces have traditionally lacked the ability to practise the fiscal and monetary stabilization policies on the effective scale available to Ottawa. Consequently, they have been forced to rely on direct policy instruments such as the selective provision of grants and other financial incentives to firms. Further, because of their concern with the primarily local effects of industry, provincial governments have had a more direct political interest in the detailed consequences of business behaviour and have developed very specific, often interventionist policies to deal with them. For example, in the promotion of industrial R&D activity, provincial governments have been much more prone to take a direct role in technology development and diffusion through the use of provincial research councils

and organizations such as AOSTRA and NORDCO than to use the provincial tax system to promote R&D activity in industry.

Interestingly, provincial industrial-policy instruments resemble those of other advanced industrialized countries more than they do federal policy instruments, mainly because of their emphasis on directly influencing individual firms. Like western European countries, Ontario, Quebec and the western provinces have a similar need to restructure their economies. Hence, provincial governments have seen the need to create government corporations to guide resource and industrial development and to take an equity stake in important private sector resource and manufacturing companies. It may be, therefore, that the experience of provincial governments with these more direct forms of intervention enables them to practise the type of firm-specific policies which are becoming more common with many of our industrialized trading partners. This is not to say that the federal government has not been involved in similar activities, such as the operation of Crown corporations in industrial sectors, or direct types of intervention in the form of the regulation of specific corporate activities. However, these aspects of federal policy have usually taken a secondary place to demand management policies.

This situation could well change with the growing limitations on federal fiscal and monetary policy resulting from accumulated deficits and monetarist anti-inflationary efforts. Such factors may shift attention to more selective vehicles for the provision of public funds to industry and the creative use of regulatory and administrative powers. Provinces, on the other hand, have more recently attempted to use those parts of the taxation system under their control (for example, sales taxes) to establish provincially specific stabilization policies.[1]

A larger question, however, is the compatability of the various provincial strategies. In terms of their intent, they seem to fall into two categories. The first is the strategy of diversification based on existing resource strengths. This, in essence, is the strategy of most, but not all, of the peripheral provinces, including British Columbia, Alberta, Saskatchewan and Newfoundland. The object is to increase further processing of resource products within the province where feasible, and to obtain the maximum employment opportunities from resource development. Where this is not feasible, the provinces usually attempt to ensure the maximum extraction of rents from resources to finance alternative activity. This surplus is then spent to improve the existing renewable resource base (as in Alberta's investments in crop research and irrigation) or invested in industrialization opportunities which service the principal resource industry (for example, oil extraction equipment and technology in Alberta or fishing equipment and technology in Newfoundland).[2] In large measure, these policies seem to be encouraged by a growing provincial recognition of the very finite nature of nonrenewable resources, and their present limited capacity to fully regenerate many renewable resources, particularly forests. Because of their emphasis on diversification based on one or two principal resource strengths, these provinces' industrial policies tend to be more focussed and coherent than those of other provinces. This is particularly clear with respect to R&D strategy. Alberta, British Columbia and Newfoundland have placed a special emphasis on technology related to resource development and on mechanisms to implement effective research strategies (for example, AOSTRA, C-CORE and NORDCO).

The second strategy is directed at restructuring manufacturing in light of significant changes in the capacity of each province's industries to adapt to changing international, continental and regional trade patterns. This is characteristic of the industrial policies of Nova Scotia, Quebec, Ontario and Manitoba. Their approach emphasizes the improvement of the technological, marketing and management capacity of manufacturing firms and seeks to increase the sector's ability to maintain regional, national and international markets.

Conflicting Strategies?
Provincial strategies seem to be compatible, *at least in intent.* The attempt by many peripheral provinces to increase the processing of local resources does not appreciably affect central Canadian manufacturing. This is because most resource production is destined for foreign markets in the first place and it is foreign, rather than domestic firms which are denied the added possibilities in further processing the resource. Indeed, with the exception of Prince Edward Island, no province relies on the rest of the Canadian market for more than a third of its shipments of resource and primary products (see p. 40, Table II.5), and in many cases it is substantially less. In addition, further processing of raw materials benefits the entire country because it creates new markets for central Canadian suppliers of capital equipment and services.

Further processing of resources has been seen as a problem almost entirely because of a dispute between Ontario and Alberta over the supply of feedstocks for petrochemical refineries.[3] While this is a serious dispute, it is also one over a strategic commodity central to the economic prosperity of an industrial region. There would be a dispute whether the Alberta government wished to keep the resource for further processing, or export it in crude form for higher royalties or taxes. It is unlikely this dispute would be repeated with any other resource commodity, given the pattern of Canadian interprovincial resource shipments.

The restructuring strategy of the more industrialized provinces also raises few interregional problems. The attempt by Ontario and Quebec to shift away from uncompetitive industries can only strengthen the national economy, decrease protectionism and help provide cheaper and more technologically competitive goods. Difficulties might arise if new industries were developed in an industrialized province which were also being developed elsewhere. Fortunately, this does not seem likely; the provincial economies are already highly specialized and the directions for future specialization outlined by the various governments do not appear directly competitive. For example, even though a number of provinces have announced plans to expand microelectronics research and there seems to be some duplication of effort, any duplication will be mitigated if the commercial applications for such research differ in each province. There are indications that this is already happening. In Saskatchewan, for example, microelectronics research is directed at agricultural implement control and fibre optic telecommunications equipment, but in Manitoba it is linked with mechanical engineering.[4]

The real conflicts are more likely to be felt in two principal areas. First, arguments could arise over the modification of federal industrial and trade policies required by the restructuring of Quebec and Ontario industry. Second, provinces may attempt to insulate their economies from the effects of economic forces at the national level.

The first issue has already been partly discussed at the end of chapter IV and seems to divide into two parts. First, problems may emerge if both Ontario and Quebec require significant restructuring assistance from the federal government at the same time. Second, and perhaps more important, are the potential interregional conflicts over the content of federal industrial policy.

Conflicts between Ontario and Quebec over the allocation of federal funds may create a significant dispute in the future, particularly because, as recent developments in the automotive industry indicate, Ontario's economy is likely to become more vulnerable over the next decade. A demand by Ontario for more federal industrial assistance could cause serious problems for Quebec because, until recently, it has received by far the most significant levels of federal, industrial-development assistance.[5]

A broader concern, however, is the reaction of the whole country to the needs of the two central provinces. Not only will such central restructuring require federal funds, but it will also require significant federal trade-policy support, particularly to control imports in industrial sectors under pressure from such goods. Given the growing militancy of the western provinces over protectionism and the traditional contention of both the western and Atlantic provinces that Ottawa's industrial support policy unduly favours central Canada, trade policy could easily become an issue of considerable controversy.[6]

From Strategies to Barriers: Conflict Between Centre and Periphery

There is a more significant cause of interregional conflict however, relating to the *manner* in which provinces apply economic policies, as distinct from longer-term strategic *objectives*. In the attempt to implement their economic policies, provincial governments increasingly try to insulate their economies from negative national developments, while seeking to capture all the benefits of a particular opportunity. All provinces seem to be doing this, regardless of their stated strategic objectives. It has even prompted a growing body of literature about provincial infringements on the Canadian economic union.[7] The issue is complex, covering questions of constitutional authority, trade in goods and services, mobility rights of workers, fiscal policy, and discretionary actions on the part of provincial governments or provincial agencies in such areas as procurement and investment. The attempt to insulate provincial economies derives its force from a perception in much of western and Atlantic Canada that the Canadian common market works against regional interests. This perception manifests itself in policies which treat much economic activity as a zero-sum game in which the benefits of one region are the liabilities of another. These policies break down into two categories: restrictions and barriers, principally applied to goods and labour; and incentives, principally applied to capital investment.

Barriers
Barriers are by far the most plentiful of these policies and affect the free movement of both people and goods. In the area of labour, elaborate provincial systems to regulate and set standards for professions and trades can pose significant barriers to movement.[8] While there are systems of reciprocal recognition of trade and professional qualifications, their application is uneven and inconsistent, as the recent dispute between Ontario and Quebec over construction workers illustrates.[9] Recent moves by both Newfoundland and Nova Scotia to limit employment opportunities from resource developments to local residents indicate that the scope for provincial action may be considerable. However, a province's ability to apply such controls in a highly restrictive manner to a wide variety of employment categories may be limited in practice. Areas of high growth to which people usually wish to migrate tend to be short on skills; so it is usually not in the interests of a provincial government to be unduly restrictive.

Many hiring restrictions, such as those of Newfoundland, Saskatchewan (for northern development projects), and even federal industrial development projects funded by DREE, exist simply to ensure that developments absorb as much of the locally unemployed as possible before new workers come in from outside. It is hard to see how such restrictions harm other Canadians.[10] Indeed, inefficiences could only result by insisting that local untrained labour be used in place of skilled external labour, and these can be overcome by phasing in local labour requirements in conjunction with training programs.

It is important to remember as well that other unintended barriers to interprovincial labour mobility are also present in our federal system. They include: provincial differences in educational systems;[11] differences in the level of social services; and, of course, language barriers. All of these in some way limit the mobility of labour. Further, it is not at all certain what real impact provincially imposed barriers have on a person's ability to relocate in Canada compared to more fundamental limitations such as income level or job skills. In short, the issue is complex and concern with explicit provincial mobility restrictions may be misplaced as these may be only a small part of the overall problem of labour mobility in Canada.

Barriers to the movement of goods are, however, more numerous and varied. Perhaps the most controversial are provincial marketing boards. There are well over 100 in Canada[12] under both federal and provincial jurisdiction. Many, though not all, are concerned with supply management within a province of various agricultural commodities through the allocation of production quotas to farmers. In the early 1970s, there was significant conflict over interprovincial agricultural shipments (the "chicken and egg" war),[13] and subsequent court rulings have limited the ability of provinces to control imports from other Canadian provinces.[14] However, the net result has been the establishment of national marketing boards in commodities where interprovincial shipments can cause disruptions (poultry, turkeys, eggs and potatoes).

This re-emergence of national marketing boards, with significant provincial participation, indicates the strength of the "orderly marketing" concept in agricultural products. It also means that free movement of agricultural goods is restrained not only because the provinces want barriers to trade, but also because of the serious disadvantages posed by a common market on a large scale to many small commodity producers.[15]

Another area where provincial barriers have been an issue is in the regulation of business and commercial activity. Provincial regulations relating to employment standards, industrial safety, product standards, consumer protection, contract law, and transportation often mean additional expenses and complications for companies selling nationally.[16] However, two factors must be balanced against these costs: first, there is a great tendency for provincial regulations to be broadly similar; indeed, in some areas institutional devices encourage a certain commonality (for example, interprovincial regulations on truck transport). Second, in a country of considerable social, geographic, cultural and economic diversity different regulatory environments may be essential to ensure a good match between standards and local conditions. At present, therefore, despite the publicity they have attracted, the barriers outlined above do not seem to significantly damage the relatively coherent nature of the national market.

The most important provincial barriers to economic integration, however, relate to three areas: control over resource depletion, procurement policy and the regulation of capital flows. As owners of natural resources, provinces can set conservation regulations on resource exploitation and insist that further processing be done within the province. A province cannot set the price of a resource entering interprovincial trade, nor restrain it from such trade, except for conservation purposes.[17] However, the ability to withhold a resource from trade, for whatever reason, or to be able to insist on a specific level of processing, is a significant power. It may also inhibit interprovincial trade and cause interregional disagreements. The conservation power, for example, is the basis upon which Alberta withheld a certain proportion of the province's normally available oil reserves from production during its 1981 oil pricing dispute with the federal government.

Another significant barrier to economic integration is provincial government procurement policy which discriminates against out-of-province producers. All provinces practise favouritism in one form or another. Some of these policies are outlined in Table V.1. In addition to these general government preferences, provincial Crown corporations, particularly hydro and telephone corporations, also practise some form of discriminatory purchasing. Such practices obviously split the Canadian market and create barriers to large-scale capacity. And when combined with lowest-cost bid approaches, such preferences result in the purchase of many finished goods from abroad, particularly in provinces with a small manufacturing base. Yet attempts by Ontario to encourage "buy Canadian" procurement policies are viewed with some suspicion by other provinces as simply a device to encourage them to buy more expensive Ontario goods.[18]

Table V.1 – Provincial Government Procurement Policies, 1981

Newfoundland[a]
- 15 per cent price premium for local suppliers, plus benefit/cost analysis (local preferred when benefit is 1.5 times added cost)
- four-tier preference policy on consulting contracts, (for example, by location of office in province)
- overall Canadian preference

Prince Edward Island[b]
- no stated local preference policy
- some informal preferences on local supplies

Nova Scotia
- up to 10 per cent price premium, applied selectively to specific local industries[c]
- general local preference applied to smaller contracts[d]
- restricted to local suppliers, if three or more are available, or in other selected circumstances[c]

New Brunswick
- since October 1977, evaluates tenders by both cost and local benefit
- includes subcontracting sources
- restricted to local suppliers, if three or more are available
- some development of local source through "cost plus" contracting and product development assistance

Maritime Provinces[e]
- Council of Maritime Premiers, 12 March 1980 announced changes in purchasing policy of New Brunswick, Nova Scotia and Prince Edward Island to include "regional" value - added in criteria for awarding contracts and purchase of materials
- informally, five to ten per cent premium accepted before contracts granted to out-of-region firms

Quebec
- ten per cent price premium on contracts exceeding $50 000[c]
- in some circumstances (related to amount of competition within Quebec) restricted to local bids[d]
- restrictions also used for provincial industrial development objectives
- local and Canadian content must be specified; this includes subcontracts

Ontario
- ten per cent price premium to *Canadian* suppliers, also applied to all provincially funded agencies and industries receiving provincial assistance as of November 1980
- preference to Ontario firms only when bids competitive[df]

Manitoba
- preference only if price, delivery, quality equal[d]

Alberta
- no local preference in purchasing of supplies, some large contracts (for example, tourism programs) let only to Alberta firms
- on natural resource exploration and extraction permits and leases, firms allowed to tender restricted to those licensed to do business in Alberta
- bidders on certain major projects (tar sands, pipelines) must specify local employment, purchasing[g]

British Columbia
- ten per cent price premium
- "committed" to provincial preference
- may use regional or sectoral unemployment, general health of industry as procurement criteria[c][d]

Sources : [a] Government of Newfoundland, Department of Industrial Development;
[b] Interview with Prince Edward Island official;
[c] Government of Canada, *Powers Over the Economy: Securing the Canadian Economic Union in the Constitution*, CCMC, Doc: 830-81/036, July 1980, pp. 29-31;
[d] J. Maxwell and C. Pestieau, *Economic Realities of Contemporary Confederation*, HRI, Montreal, 1980, p. 87;
[e] Council of Maritime Premiers, "Regional Preference in Provincial Purchasing and Tendering Policies," press release, March 1980;
[f] F.S. Miller, *Supplementary Measures to Stimulate the Ontario Economy*, Government of Ontario, November 1980;
[g] Interview with officials, government of Alberta.

It is very difficult to measure the market-splintering impact of provincial procurement policies because these policies are frequently hard to identify even when they are operating. For example, preference policies can take the form of a price premium to local firms or an outright limitation of contract awards, or bidding, to local firms. All of these practices are usually invisible, unless they are stated public policy. However, one area where provincial procurement policy does seem to have had a particularly negative, and visible, effect is in public utility supply contracts. The major manufacturers of equipment and supplies for public utilities such as provincial hydro and telecommunications corporations often find that, to obtain access to a provincial market, they must establish a local production facility. As is often the case, a suboptimal facility manufacturing an existing product line is established. This makes it difficult for the industry to make full use of the economies of scale of the entire domestic market. It also makes Canadian industry internationally uncompetitive by restricting export opportunities and promoting import penetration. There may be some link between this situation and the fact that Canada is the only major producer of electrical equipment which also has a sizeable trade deficit in this sector.[19]

The final category of provincial economic barriers is capital flows. This barrier is relatively new, reflecting in part, a growing desire by provincial governments to exercise some control over capital movements. Interestingly, although the federal government has control over banking and credit, there are no constitutional prohibitions against the provinces limiting capital movements.[20] Much of this potential control derives from the provinces' ability to regulate provincially incorporated companies. The most significant provincial powers to this end are regulations governing financial institutions such as trust companies, caisses populaires, credit unions and insurance companies. Quebec, Manitoba and British Columbia have legislation requiring insurance companies to have a certain portion of their assets in the province of incorporation. Quebec also has a law requiring that loan and mortgage companies' transfer of shares be approved by the government. As well, British Columbia and Quebec (in different degrees) require that their pension funds be invested in their province, and under an agreement with the federal government, Canada Pension Plan funds are reinvested in all provinces (except Quebec, which administers its own fund) in proportion to their contributions.[21]

Apart from restrictions concerning the investment of pension and insurance funds, provinces have not actively used their powers to block the movement of capital. However, in exceptional circumstances, they are willing to use both their normal financial regulatory powers and other areas of jurisdiction which impinge on business (for example, control over natural resources) to control capital movements. This has happened when there were regional concerns about the loss of local control over important financial or industrial companies. The most celebrated was the Quebec government's use of its legislative powers to prevent the sale of Crédit Foncier to non-Quebec interests, and its threat to use its regulations over the location of investment to prevent Sun Life from moving its head office out of the province. Most surprising, however, was British Columbia's move to prevent the sale of MacMillan-Bloedel to Canadian Pacific Investments, particularly in light of the province's often-stated opposition to foreign investment controls and its desire to have unimpeded access to foreign investment. Clearly, if these actions were repeated in a number of cases, they could seriously affect ownership patterns throughout the country.

Despite these exceptions, the barriers issue seems of limited importance. And the degree to which it has attracted the attention of policy makers over the past few years is probably the result of the few isolated and spectacular cases which have arisen. Barriers are still the exception rather than the rule, and their real impact on the efficiency of the Canadian market is as yet very much a hypothesis. What they do demonstrate, however, is the *potential* for disruptive action if many of the larger provinces were to decide that their interests lay in thoroughly challenging the existing economic structure of the country.

Incentives

More important than barriers to the movement of goods, labour and capital in Canada are the inducements that provinces can use to influence industrial location and development. These relate primarily to expenditure and taxation powers.

Traditionally, the provinces have not competed among themselves in taxation rates and methods. In 1981, the lowest provincial personal income-tax rate was in Alberta (at 38.5 per cent of the federal tax) and the highest in Newfoundland (at 58 per cent). But the corporate income tax has been much more standard, ranging no more than about six percentage points. However, Ontario, Quebec and Alberta have implemented separate corporate tax systems which allow them greater flexibility in tailoring fiscal policy to local requirements, and in the case of the wealthier provinces, allow lower tax rates. Some provinces have also established special taxation provisions to encourage investment in companies carrying on all, or a substantial part, of their activities within the province.[22]

These new forms of fiscal inducement have sometimes taken quite bizarre turns. In 1975, when the Ontario government temporarily suspended the retail sales tax on motor vehicle sales to boost automobile production, it declared the reduction applicable only to cars assembled under the Canada-United States Automotive Agreement, 1965. Volvo cars assembled in Nova Scotia from imported Swedish parts were excluded. Ironically, the result of the program was a tax stimulation encouraging the sale in Ontario of cars assembled under the agreement in the United States – while discriminating against cars assembled in another Canadian province.

In addition to fiscal incentives, the provinces provide a significant level of direct financial support for firms. Provisional estimates for 1979-80 indicate that the provinces spent a total of about $330 million in direct support of trade and industry. Of this amount, about a quarter probably consisted of direct cash transfers to businesses.[23] In addition, provincial governments, often through development corporations, lend significant sums of money to businesses to assist with new plants or expansions. At the end of 1977, for example, loans outstanding to business and industry from provincial governments came to $779 million.[24] Obviously, these significant inducements are open to abuse in the form of competitive bidding among provinces. Although in principle such activities *can* be kept to a minimum by ensuring that provincial industrial policies are complimentary rather than competitive, evidence exists that this is not, in fact, what usually happens.

Several provinces have attempted to compete by encouraging the establishment of industries, or maintaining declining industries, despite the fact that similar, and successful, industries already exist in other provinces (for example, steel in Saskatchewan, Quebec and Nova Scotia and automobile production in Nova Scotia, New Brunswick and Quebec).[25] In most of these cases – steel in Quebec and Nova Scotia and automobiles in New Brunswick – such competitive facilities have not been successful. Further, it is difficult to know the extent to which additional industrial capacity in automobiles and steel – which *is* commercially viable – has harmed Ontario producers of similar products. At least in those two sectors it would seem less likely that market fragmentation has occurred owing to the special-ist products of the steel facility in Saskatchewan and the car assembly plant in Nova Scotia.

On the other hand, as Allan Tupper has pointed out, competition among provinces also allows businesses to play one jurisdiction off against another to obtain the best subsidy. In regions which may not be able to offer the locational advantages of central Canada, or the resource endowments of the west, such bidding tends to have a negative impact on other areas of government policy. Provincial governments such as Nova Scotia, for example, have felt it necessary to enact restrictive labour legislation to prevent the organization of workers at specific factories in order to ensure a sizeable foreign investment.[26]

In the past, the poorer provinces have attempted to influence the location of new industries, or the expansion of existing ones, with various forms of industrial incentives. Now, however, even the more wealthy provinces are willing to dangle carrots. In the case of Ontario and Quebec, industrial incentives are used largely to restructure their industrial bases. For the western provinces, particularly Alberta, the temptation will be great to use accumulated resource rents to bankroll new industrial development - which may pre-empt developing industries in central Canada.

In such a competitive environment, the weaker provinces will suffer dearly. As Figure IV.1 (p. 83) illustrates, the resources provincial governments have to devote to industrial development are clearly uneven. The burden placed on the poorer provinces to support industry, as seen in the per capita expenditures on trade and industry, is already significantly greater than it is for wealthier provinces. In a highly competitive environment, these inequities can only increase.

Conclusions

Provincial barriers to trade and competitive economic incentives are more embryonic threats than immediate crises. Certainly, as the previous discussion indicates, the capacity for "barrier and bidding wars" is great; yet, despite the potential for harm, the provinces have, until now, been *relatively* restrained. The existing barriers and incentives are, with some exceptions, either symbolic or have been implemented to offset the negative effects of the Canadian common market in particular provinces. Further, the provinces do not seem to have set out to actively compete with one another in setting industrial priorities – which is hardly surprising, given the highly special-ized structure of the Canadian economy and its rather weak internal linkages. What the various divergent provincial industrial strategies do indicate is a *drifting apart* of economic interest, a desire to

96

seek provincial, rather than national or regional solutions to industrial problems.

However, the significant changes occurring in the country's economic structure and the growing sense of differing regional interest suggest that embryonic conflicts over industrial policy could grow. The problem is how to overcome these difficulties and, at the same time, lay the institutional framework and policy objectives that will encourage provincial policy makers to work in harmony and contribute to a national industrial policy. The next section reviews some of the recent attempts to accomplish this at the intergovernmental level.

Part Three

Intergovernmental Coordination and Industrial Policy

VI. A Nation of Governments

More than any other federation, Canada relies on intergovernmental negotiation to help resolve political differences. This is partly because many of our political differences are expressed in regional rather than class, ethnic or religious terms. The fact that both levels of government are responsible for a wide range of functions also makes contact between them essential and unavoidable. This applies particularly to industrial policy inasmuch as the question has often been not simply *what* industry to promote, but *where* the benefits are to be located.

The geographic distribution of industrial activity in Canada tends to overshadow questions of efficiency (which type of activity to encourage), or even those concerning the social distribution of industrial benefits. But how effective are our intergovernmental mechanisms for settling regional industrial policy disputes? Are they capable of generating consensus and coherence in the design and implementation of industrial policy? The following chapters seek to answer these questions by examining some of the attempts at intergovernmental cooperation over the past decade. The case studies that follow have been broken down into two major categories – interprovincial collaboration and federal-provincial collaboration. The former includes both attempts at regional cooperation (for example, the Council of Maritime Premiers (CMP)) and more broadly based intergovernmental collaboration (for example, interprovincial industry ministers' meetings). The latter comprises attempts at multilateral collaboration (that is, the federal government and several, or all ten, provinces) and on a bilateral basis (the federal government and one province).

The Extent of Intergovernmental Relations

It is not possible within the confines of this study to review the extent of interprovincial and federal-provincial collaboration and consultation in any depth.[1] In general, however, it would be fair to say that intergovernmental activity has increased substantially in recent years. A vast network of federal-provincial and interprovincial organizations now exists, ranging from large formal organizations with their own permanent staffs (for example, the Council of Ministers of Education and the CMP) to informal working groups concerned with a specific technical issue or problem. Between these two extremes there is virtually every combination and permutation imaginable.

It is perhaps a comment on the fluidity of intergovernmental relations that *no* authoritative statistics exist on the actual number of intergovernmental organizations or the frequency of their meetings. In 1972, the Privy Council Office (PCO) prepared a list of 482 federal-provincial organizations, but estimates since then have grown considerably.[2] Gérard Veilleux, a senior federal official, has undertaken a survey on the number of federal-provincial consultations and some of his results are presented in Table VI.1. As he readily admits, the list greatly understates the potential activity.[3] Nevertheless, it does indicate that intergovernmental activity increased dramatically between 1957 and 1977.

Table VI.1 – Number of Federal-Provincial Organizations* and Frequency of Their Meetings

Category	1957	1967	1973	1977
Ministerial				
Organizations	5	14	20	31
No. of Meetings	—	17	30	39
Officials				
Organizations	59	105	62	127
No. of Meetings	—	142	121	296
Total				
Organizations	64	119	82	158
No. of Meetings	—	159	151	335

*Organizations defined either as a continuing conference, committee or working group.
Source: Gérard Veilleux, "L'évolution des mécanismes de liaison intergouvernementale," in *Confrontation and Collaboration: Intergovernmental Relations in Canada Today*, R. Simeon ed., Institute of Public Administration of Canada, Toronto, 1979, p. 37.

The activity is not limited to meetings of civil servants and ministers, however. In 1982, there were several hundred formal agreements between the federal government, the provinces and municipalities involving over $9 billion of annual federal expenditure, exclusive of equalization payments.[4] These figures do not include provincial expenditures under those agreements, nor the large number of interprovincial agreements in existence.

The system has become so vast and complex that most provincial governments, and Ottawa, have created special organizations simply to handle intergovernmental relations. The organizations vary in size and significance (see Table VI.2), but it is noteworthy that five of the largest provinces and the federal government have felt that intergovernmental relations are sufficiently important to require the establishment of separate ministries.[5] In Quebec and Alberta, these ministries exercise significant control over the manner in which negotiations are conducted by provincial line departments with other provinces or the federal government, and their consent must be obtained before any intergovernmental agreements can be signed. Further, all the intergovernmental affairs' agencies attempt to ensure that their province adopts a consistent "line" or position in dealings with other governments. As well, they try to keep their own government informed of policies being pursued by other federal and provincial governments.

Table VI.2 – **Intergovernmental Affairs Agencies Within Canadian Governments, 1981**

Government	Agency	Date Created	Type
Canada	Federal-Provincial Relations Office	1974	A
Newfoundland	Intergovernmental Affairs Secretariat		B
PEI	Executive Council Committee[1]		
Nova Scotia	Department of Intergovernmental Affairs	1980	C
New Brunswick	Office of the Premier		B
Quebec	Ministère des Affaires intergouvernementales	1968	C
Ontario	Ministry of Intergovernmental Affairs	1978	C
Manitoba	Cabinet Committee on Dominion-Provincial Relations[1]		B
Saskatchewan	Department of Intergovernmental Affairs	1979	C
Alberta	Department of Federal and Intergovernmental Affairs	1972	C
British Columbia	Ministry of Intergovernmental Affairs	1980	C

Types: A. Independent department, headed by prime minister
B. Part of executive council
C. Full department with minister in cabinet
[1] Financial issues usually dealt with by provincial Treasury Department, constitutional affairs by the attorney general's department, other issues by line departments.

The Quality of Intergovernmental Relations

Despite the new ministries, the intergovernmental process is unevenly developed. In policy areas such as taxation and equalization, there have been fairly structured arrangements for collaboration since the mid-1950s. Intergovernmental consultation also seems highly developed in health and welfare, transport and natural resources (including agriculture and the environment).[6] In other areas, and most notably in industrial policy, this is not the case (see Table VI.3).

Table VI.3 – Number of Federal-Provincial Liaison Organizations by Sector of Government Activity, 1977

Sector	No. of Organizations	Meetings
1. General government services	40	105
2. Justice, protection of persons and property	12	16
3. Transport and communications	25	44
4. Health	11	27
5. Welfare	2	3
6. Culture and recreation	8	12
7. Education	6	16
8. Natural resources and primary industry	49	100
9. Industrial and commercial development	5	12
Total	158	335

Source: Veilleux, op. cit., p. 50.

One should be very careful, however, about confusing institutional arrangements and *effective* action. As the Council of Ministers of Education illustrates, even an elaborate secretariat and regular meetings of officials and ministers has done little to produce a coherent and integrated educational system across the country. The best the council can do is provide a useful arena for information exchange and technical cooperation.[7]

This spotty record raises the question: what intergovernmental processes are the most useful for industrial policy issues? Unfortunately, most of the research on federal-provincial collaboration has been concerned with issues which do not bear on industrial policy questions as such. The areas of policy most heavily studied include fiscal and equalization issues, constitutional questions and topics relating to pensions, health and social security, manpower, and regional development policy.[8] The conclusions from these studies have been rather mixed in that they relate to both the *process* of federal-provincial relations and the *substance* of the issues involved.

On the process side, the elements which seem to have encouraged harmonious federal-provincial relations include, first, shared professional norms and commitments which allow policy issues to be reduced to technical questions, and second, formal or informal networks connecting officials and ministers from different jurisdictions. In addition, institutional arrangements promoting continuous liaison have helped governments sort out problems and promoted collaboration early in the development of policies. Successful intergovernmental negotiations also depend in particular on the degree to which the governments involved are flexible about achieving objectives and the degree to which they are willing to involve the other level of government at an early stage.[9]

Federal-provincial relations have succeeded largely because both levels have recognized the need for a common solution, or at the very least, an acquiescence by one level of government to the objectives of the other (for example, collaboration over medicare and pensions). This acquiescence is usually due to the superior resources one government can bring to bear on an issue – a situation common during the 1940s and 1950s when Ottawa dominated the federal system due to both its superior financial resources, and its greater access to bureaucratic expertise in proposing and implementing policies.

Intergovernmental Collaboration and Industrial Policy

If we apply the above experience to the industrial policy arena, intergovernmental cooperation should be based on well-organized, highly specific, technical subject areas. Further, the process would be best conducted on an incremental basis, using agreements on specific subjects to build an even wider consensus on broader issues.

Such a scenario is not fully applicable. First is the problem of developing policies in an environment characterized by agreements on isolated issues. This is by no means unacceptable, especially in areas requiring technical collaboration, but it cannot be the sole basis on which industrial-policy collaboration proceeds. If a government has a coherent industrial policy, positions on specific industrial development opportunities are linked to the overall industrial strategy. Changes weaken the strategy, making bargaining over specific industrial-policy issues difficult. *Indeed, the process of trying to develop an industrial strategy highlights the existing regional differences in the country's economy. It can make manifest conflicts which in a disorganized and ad hoc policy environment were largely dormant. This is not to say that some progress cannot be made, as some of the following case studies will illustrate, but simply that very special difficulties must be faced.*

There is also disturbing evidence that the direction of federal-provincial relations will make intergovernmental bargaining over industrial policy more difficult. There is a growing tendency for governments to attempt to rationalize the policy-making process through methodologies such as planning by objectives, and through institutions such as central policy coordination agencies.[10] In the intergovernmental arena this has manifested itself in the creation of intergovernmental affairs' departments. In the words of one prominent observer:

> "These central agencies restrict the capacities of program officials and departments to effect federal-provincial agreement based on professional and/or technical norms. . . the thrust of federal-provincial relations agencies is to link narrower purposes with broader and more political ones, and in respect to these latter it is less likely that federal and provincial governments will agree. This implicit and single-minded purpose of intergovernmental affairs managers at the provincial level is to safeguard and if possible to extend the range of jurisdictional autonomy, including of course the revenues that provincial governments have under their unshared control."[11]

This general politicization of intergovernmental bargaining has been compounded by a growing tendency for each level of government to take a keen interest in affairs under the exclusive jurisdiction of the other level, be it federal interest in civil rights or provincial interest in international trade policy.[12] The result has been that the scope of subject matter under consideration at federal-provincial meetings has increased markedly. Most notably, questions of economic policy have loomed large on the agendas, either as subjects themselves as, for example, at the First Minister's Conferences on the Economy in 1978, or as aspects of other negotiations, as in the debate during the 1980 constitutional discussions over the maintenance of the Canadian common market.

Despite what seems to be substantial inherent limitations, seeking an intergovernmental route to harmonize industrial policy in Canada and harness the country's collective efforts in industrial policy has a number of attractions. It does provide a channel to reconcile and harmonize regional political and economic differences. Because intergovernmental relations are inherently regional in their structure they address this fundamental problem directly. The real question, however, is what type, or form, of intergovernmental relations are best suited to solve the problem? The next two chapters address this question in some detail.

VII. Interprovincial Collaboration in Action

Extensive cooperation among provinces has become a permanent feature of the Canadian federal system. Much of it is related to technical issues, such as the harmonizing of transport regulations, where the actions of one government can seriously affect another. Such collaboration is not limited to geographically linked provinces nor even to widely separated provinces as the large number of cooperative agreements with American states indicates.[1] A good deal of this activity is informal and difficult to investigate.

In the area of industrial policy there have been a number of interprovincial cooperative initiatives, but the most notable is the conference of provincial ministers of industry. It has been held for a number of years, usually on an annual basis, to discuss issues of mutual interest. (Provincial deputy ministers of industry also meet to prepare agendas for the ministers' meetings and to exchange information.)

It is less than clear exactly what is accomplished in these meetings as they are held on a confidential basis and communiqués are rarely issued. In fact, apart from keeping their colleagues up to date on their respective industrial policies and activities, the meetings seem geared to federal-provincial conferences inasmuch as they provide provinces with an opportunity to review their reaction to federal industrial policy initiatives. Indeed, this latter role seems to be a common one for many interprovincial meetings. For example, in November 1977, the Council of Provincial Energy Ministers was established. Its official role is to provide a forum to "develop policies, priorities and programs, including guidelines and strategies for research and development."[2] However, its principal achievement in its first year of operation was, in the words of the Alberta Department of Federal and Intergovernmental Affairs, "the development of a unified provincial position on the [federal government's] Canadian Home Insulation Program for the federal-provincial energy ministers' conference."[3]

There is also some reason to suspect that the exchange of information and positions at these meetings may not be as full and frank as possible when it comes to industrial policy. Provincial industrial policy can involve the attraction of new industrial investment either from existing firms in the province or from outside companies. Naturally, provinces compete to a certain extent when it comes to such issues as public assistance to firms, procurement policy and so forth. Thus, the extent to which such interprovincial meetings are capable of producing effective initiatives in industrial collaboration is, to say the least, open to question.

The most developed forms of interprovincial cooperation do not take place nationally, but regionally, as can be seen in the work of the CMP and the WPC. These organizations have moved the farthest in terms of interprovincial cooperation and reveal the limits of such action, given a degree of common regional interest in, and need for, collective action, and an established institutional mechanism for carrying out such activity. In addition, because both these organizations have taken public action, it is possible to evaluate the results in a way that is not possible with the normally highly secretive interprovincial conferences.

The Council of Maritime Premiers

Established in May 1971 by the three Maritime provinces, the CMP was a response to the recommendations of the Maritime Union Study commissioned by Maritime governments several years before.[4] This study had recommended a more elaborate structure which, in addition to a premiers' council, would have established a maritime provinces' commission and a joint legislative assembly. In effect, it sought a structure somewhat like that of the European Economic Community (EEC) and intended to create an administrative and political structure which would encourage unification. By opting for a premiers' council, the heads of the three provinces decided to institutionalize cooperation rather than work towards political union.[5] The legislation which established the CMP requires that the premiers meet four times a year and that council decisions be unanimous. A secretariat of about 20 employees provides basic administrative and policy coordination.

In 10 years, the CMP has encouraged a significant level of regional cooperation. In addition to the secretariat, the CMP has established a number of regional agencies which provide services to all three provinces in such areas as higher education, municipal training and land registration (see Table VII.1). The council was also instrumental in founding the Atlantic Policy Academy to train municipal police officers. Of the council agencies, the most significant in terms of political cooperation is the Maritime Provinces Higher Education Commission. This commission is now responsible for making recommendations to the three provincial governments on higher education funding and administering transfer payments to universities for out-of-province students as well as the universities' operating and capital grants. It also encourages regional planning for higher

Table VII.1 – Agencies of the Council of Maritime Premiers, 1982

Agency	Created	Staff (Person years)	Budget 1981-82 ($ 000)	Function
Land Registration Information Service	1973	211	8 802	A common, comprehensive land registration system (including mapping) for the Maritime provinces.
Secretariat	1972	22	1 111	Administrative coordination.
Maritime Resources Management Service	1972	70	2 898[1]	Provides specialist technical services for government and private sector developments, including engineering services, air photo and mapping and planning services.
Maritime Municipal Training and Development Board	1974	4	200	Funds development implementation of training programs for municipal officials.
Maritime Provinces Higher Education Commission	1974	11	571[2]	University funding.
Total		318	13 582	

[1] Operates on a fee-for-service basis.
[2] This commission is budgeted to distribute in 1981-82 capital and operating assistance grants to the universities of about $215 million.
Source: Council of Maritime Premiers, "Estimates of Revenue and Expenditure for the Fiscal Year 1982-83," Halifax, 1982.

education facilities and courses. The commission has played an important role in rectifying problems arising from interprovincial movements of university students and in helping to prevent the costly duplication of specialized training facilities.

The CMP has also encouraged the development of a large number of interprovincial committees on a variety of technical issues. A recent estimate by the CMP secretariat claimed that, of 41 Maritime and Atlantic regional bodies, the council has influenced the creation of 24.[6] Progress has been most marked in standardizing government regulations in such areas as securities and the environment. The most developed of the technical committees is the Maritime Provinces Transportation Commission which comprises the senior transport policy official from each province. It has made significant progress in standardizing regulations on trucking and highway transport, traffic safety, and the transferability of licences and vehicle registrations within the region. The commission has also helped develop a regional position on federal transportation policies, and, in particular, the attempt by the federal government to incorporate a "user-pay" principle into the National Transportation Act.

However, while the provinces have cooperated on specific technical questions or issues relating to federal policies, the level of cooperation on broader economic policy issues has been less impressive. This lack of progress is doubly discouraging in light of the significant initiatives, particularly in recent years, taken both by the premiers and by officials of the council to encourage cooperation.

The basic problem seems to be that economic cooperation can often clarify the trade-offs essential for joint action and make the process appear to be a zero-sum game (that is, one party is the winner, the other, a loser). In some cases, of course, collaboration can be either inexpensive (such as when there is agreement on a regional position on a federal policy), or involve cooperative projects in which the benefits are easily divisible (such as when a service is established that brings equal savings or benefits for all).[7] In these cases, cooperation can be fairly easy to promote and maintain. However, if cooperation takes on the character of a zero-sum game, (for example, a facility can be located in only one province), problems can develop. It has taken more than five years, for example, to settle the location for a regional veterinary college, due to the inability of the Maritime governments to agree on which province was the most suited to house the facility. In the end, agreement was reached only when two of the provinces finally threatened to go ahead and build the $27 million college if the third, Nova Scotia, refused to join.[8]

Early in its history, the CMP did attempt to formulate a regional economic development policy through the ministerial Committee on Economic Development and Transportation. Unfortunately, the

110

initiative met with little success, and a more recent effort has also been deferred. But in the area of government procurement, some progress has been made. An effective regional purchasing policy directing more government procurement to firms in the region is of some relevance to the Maritimes due to the losses they incur as a result of substantial purchases of manufactured goods from central Canada.[9] Regional purchasing policy has been discussed off and on by the council since it was first established. A concerted effort has been made since 1977 to work out a procurement policy and the premiers approved it in principle in 1978. The chief roadblock to agreement on this policy had been an inability to find an effective mechanism to ensure regional preferences when procurement decisions were made by each government. The result, after three years of negotiations, was a policy statement in March 1980 which committed each province to give preference to regional suppliers if no local (that is, provincial) supplier exists. In addition, each province is pledged to standardizing purchasing practices and exchanging information on local suppliers. The three provinces have also agreed that, where no regional supplier is available, they will support the establishment of such a supplier in the Maritimes.[10]

Although this effort is clearly superior to three separate procurement policies, it does suffer from a number of weaknesses. It only provides a regional governmental market in those sectors where there is a *single* regional supplier. This is a problem because there are suboptimal producers in each province in many industrial sectors. Regional procurement could provide perhaps one or two suppliers in such sectors with large enough contracts to allow them to produce as efficiently as out-of-region suppliers, but the new policy does not require this. It is also less than clear how the three provinces are to decide where to locate the new industrial capacity they are to encourage through purchasing. Efficiency may dictate a single location, but the structure of political accountability within the region is unlikely to allow this to happen if it appears that one particular province will benefit more than the others.

Perhaps even more indicative of the limits of regional cooperation, however, is the saga of the Maritime Energy Corporation (MEC). All the Maritime provinces suffer from unusually high electricity costs and Nova Scotia and Prince Edward Island are particularly dependent on imported oil to generate electricity.[11] Regional energy policy began to be discussed in 1976 after the federal government refused to provide additional oil import subsidies for electricity generation. In early 1977, the CMP decided that a regional energy agency would benefit the Maritimes by allowing the development of large-scale energy projects such as Fundy tidal power. The three provinces and the federal government agreed in February 1977 to establish

MEC to study regional power projects, and if approved, develop them. MEC was also to manage the region's power grid.

By January 1978, agreement had been reached on funding, with the Maritime provinces and Ottawa each contributing $5 million to MEC's initial capitalization.[12] In the following months, progress was slow, partly because the federal government was reluctant to commit its funds until the provinces had agreed on the corporation's first major power project.[13] By February 1979, a new agreement had been reached between the three provinces and Ottawa on the projects to be undertaken by MEC.[14] Under the new agreement, the Point Lepreau nuclear project in New Brunswick, which had been experiencing serious cost overruns and delays, would be taken over by MEC. The federal government, in turn, would take an equity stake in the corporation and guarantee its loan obligations, thus reducing its borrowing costs.[15] What followed this agreement, however, is a classic case study in the problems of negotiating intergovernmental cooperation.

In the spring of 1979, when the Liberals were defeated by the Conservatives, their energy policy was put under review. Ottawa began to raise questions about its original promise to guarantee MEC borrowing. Some officials speculated that the federal government had too little control over the corporation and that it was reluctant to finance regional energy projects not a part of an overall national policy.[16]

Growing federal reluctance, however, was only part of the problem. In the face of Ottawa's lukewarm commitment, the Maritime provinces began to reassess their positions. New Brunswick's principal interest was to find a vehicle to fund the mounting costs of its nuclear power station at Point Lepreau; if federal participation did not lower its financing costs, there was no particular attraction to joining MEC.[17] Nova Scotia, on the other hand, was concerned that MEC would be principally a device to fund New Brunswick's power developments and that no benefits, aside from less expensive nuclear power for a part of its energy requirements, would accrue. The new Conservative administration in Nova Scotia, like its Liberal predecessor, also wanted to see greater emphasis placed on indigenous power generation based on coal-fired generating stations using Cape Breton coal. In fact, a provincial energy review had indicated that the development of coal resources and potentially, tidal power, should be its top priority. Finally, a new Conservative government elected in Prince Edward Island was totally opposed to nuclear power. It hardly wished to participate in a corporation whose first project was to be a nuclear power station.

By the early summer of 1979, it looked as if the project was doomed to failure. However, that fall, the CMP made one last attempt to revive it. After some hard bargaining, it was agreed that the corporation's second project would be to increase the capacity of a new coal-fired generating station at Lingan, Nova Scotia, a station that was to use Cape Breton coal. The new arrangement would also allow Prince Edward Island to participate on a selective basis, so that it would not have to contribute to the Point Lepreau project, but would contribute to the coal-fired station in Nova Scotia. The form of the federal government's financial participation, however, was still uncertain.[18]

Despite the agreement, the provincial commitment to MEC waned in 1980 as each province concluded that its own objectives could be accomplished outside MEC. Even the study of Fundy tidal power, a project originally envisaged as one of MEC's principal responsibilities, was arranged in this period on a bilateral basis between the federal government and Nova Scotia. Consequently, at its September 1980 meeting, the CMP decided not to proceed with MEC.[19] In its place, the CMP and the federal government agreed to establish an informal organization to provide studies and advice on future energy developments. This has since been modified into a coordinating committee of the three Maritime utility companies whose function is to assist in planning new exchanges in power generation capacity and provide a regional focus for future projects and R&D activities.[20]

Thus, even when it was possible to arrange MEC operations to enable each province to eventually experience some direct investment, the desire to seek individual solutions still prevailed. This situation also greatly diminished the ability of the provinces to argue for the type of financial assistance they required from the federal government. But it must also be remembered that MEC was a unique departure in the region. Upon its creation, the corporation would have immediately possessed assets of about $1.7 billion and been responsible for the region's future major power projects. It would have been a unique intergovernmental undertaking without precedent in North America.[21] It is hardly surprising that such an ambitious project met with difficulties.

Despite these less than impressive results, the CMP still has a firm commitment to continue to take initiatives in economic development, partly because of a realization that a firm base of economic cooperation is essential for the region's future prosperity. In the last half of the 1970s, the Maritime governments became increasingly aware of their economic vulnerability. The election of a separatist government in Quebec raised the possibility that the region could be geographically cut off from the rest of Canada. There was also a growing realization that the region was becoming too dependent on federal transfer payments, a dependence indicating that self-sustaining growth was not developing in the region.

To help meet the need for more cooperation in the area of industrial development strategies, and to help construct a political consensus in the business community for a regional strategy, the council established the Voluntary Advisory Committee on Regional Economic Development (VACRED) in 1978.[22] This committee, made up entirely of businesspeople appointed by each premier, has met several times with the council on regional development issues and acted as a catalyst for establishing the regional purchasing policy. VACRED has also been instrumental in encouraging the council to commission a study on fisheries and development opportunities available to marine and offshore industries, and to establish a committee on regional R&D.[23]

Despite these more recent initiatives, however, the council has been able to encourage only modest economic cooperation. This limitation can be attributed to the structure of the council itself. It can only proceed on a project when it has the full agreement of all three heads of government who are, in turn, responsible to three different political constituencies. When the council was created, it was decided that no attempt would be made in the foreseeable future to create an institution with a political life or constituency of its own. Instead, the premiers decided to establish a body directly under their own control. The lack of success the council has had in the economic arena is fundamentally linked to this lack of a regional political constituency, a situation against which the original Maritime Union Study cautioned the three governments. The study's authors thought that establishing a body such as a premiers' council was inadvisable, for:

"While many useful things could be accomplished in this way [that is, by creating a Council of Maritime Premiers] in regard to professional, technical and specialized matters, not much of substantial significance could be expected in the realm of basic policy decisions. The political representatives who must make these decisions will continue to be responsible to provincial legislatures and their political lives will continue to be dependent on local political support. . . . In these circumstances it is very difficult to cope effectively with the interests of the region as a whole especially when compromises and accomodations inside the region are involved, as they almost always are."[24]

Certainly, the council has dealt effectively with technical collaboration, and it is doubtful that the cooperation achieved to date on more substantial matters would have occurred without the council's presence. But the political mechanisms necessary to promote a regional consensus on economic issues, independent of the provincial constituencies represented by each premier, are clearly absent. In the words of one former premier:

"... I rather think that, although the Council of Premiers is an absolute necessity at the present time, it will have to be augmented by other structures to bring about alterations to the manner in which government has functioned traditionally."[25] The need for an extraprovincial political entity which could provide greater impetus for regional development and act as a regional lobby (for example, a Maritime commission or a joint legislative assembly) has been advocated by Premier Hatfield and will be essential if progress is to be made on economic policy issues.[26]

While all three provinces need to seek cooperative action, their economic difficulties sometimes work against it. The great need for outside investment, for example, can cause governments to compete more vigorously. And a modest level of prosperity means governments are more reluctant to sacrifice any existing benefit or opportunity no matter how much sense it makes in terms of increasing regional economic efficiency. Cooperation usually occurs only when the returns to *all* parties are immediate, equal and obvious.[27]

In addition, there are often sufficient differences in the structure of the various provincial economies to thwart collective action, even in a region as seemingly homogeneous as the Maritimes. Indeed, even when there is a perceived common need or problem, the solutions required for each province are often quite different. This was readily seen in the attempt to establish MEC. The project involved a complex, and ultimately unmanageable, series of compromises to ensure the participation of each province. Clearly, even in a highly structured example of interprovincial cooperation, such as the CMP, the opportunities for significant collaboration on economic or industrial development policy appear to be limited.

Western Premiers' Conference

The WPC began as the Prairie Economic Council (PEC) in October 1965. It was founded by the three prairie provinces to encourage economic cooperation within the region.[28] The council met annually and was composed of the premier, plus an additional minister, from each government. An informal secretariat was provided by the host province and the provinces agreed to share the costs of collective studies. The council mainly emphasized seeking solutions to the periodic conflicts which emerge among the prairie provinces. As such, the issues which came before the PEC tended to be discussed in an isolated context. Issues covered at these meetings included provincial preferences in procurement policies, interprovincial highway transportation and the use of the port of Churchill.[29]

In 1968, however, attention shifted to broader regional positions on national issues. PEC developed a western position on transportation policy for the December 1969 constitutional conference.[30] This

115

resulted from the growing dissatisfaction in western Canada with what was regarded as federal insensitivity to western Canada's interests. The council's move to stress regional perceptions of national issues was reinforced in 1973 when the federal government decided to hold a Western Economic Opportunities Conference (WEOC) to restore its profile in western Canada.[31] The federal government intended the conference to be a platform from which it could demonstrate how federal policies could be tailored to suit the needs of western Canadians. However, the prairie provinces saw the conference as an excellent opportunity to present a unified western position on a number of national issues. Consequently, they invited British Columbia to join them in the preparation of several detailed position papers consolidating their views on transportation policy and industrial development assistance for WEOC.[32] In addition, the four provinces agreed to monitor the progress achieved on the submissions after WEOC was over. This new group, the Western Economic Council, held its first meeting in March 1973. The following year, its name was changed to WPC in keeping with the broader role of the organization and its emphasis on executive action.

Since 1974, WPC has held annual meetings in all four western provinces and has been responsible for a number of intergovernmental initiatives. Most of these have occurred in transportation and economic development policy, and constitutional or jurisdictional questions. Cooperation has grown at the practical level as well. A Prairie Agricultural Machinery Institute was established to assist in the development of agricultural equipment and a joint Veterinary Infectious Diseases Organization was created to help overcome communicable diseases in livestock. In addition, various exchange arrangements have been implemented which allow regionalization of specialized postsecondary training programs. The provinces have also cooperated in grain handling, the investigation of fertilizer prices and feasibility studies of a western Canadian power grid.[33] Some idea of the extent of this cooperation can be seen in a recent survey for the WPC; it revealed more than 300 cooperative agreements among the four western provinces on technical or administrative matters.[34]

But while much of this cooperation has been practical and useful, cooperation on broad policy matters has been directed much more at taking regional stands on national issues. This is clear from the very successful initiatives taken to develop a common western position for the MTNs[35] and the lobbying of Ottawa to ensure that western interests were represented in Canada's negotiating position. WPC has also issued a series of "constitutional intrusions" reports.[36] These reports in particular have resulted in joint action by the two levels of government to reduce outstanding constitutional disagreements over federal actions in what the western provinces feel are areas of provincial jurisdiction or interest.[37]

In both constitutional issues and trade negotiations, a common regional perception of the inappropriateness of national policy made joint action possible. In fact, a perusal of the communiqués issued after each premiers' conference indicates that most of the items discussed relate to difficulties with aspects of federal policy rather than with interprovincial cooperation.[38] This is confirmed when one looks at the indifferent results from attempts at cooperation on interprovincial economic policy issues.

In 1974, the Committee of Western Industry Ministers was formed to increase industrial cooperation, and it met with modest success.[39] It was responsible, for example, for drafting a western position on tariff and trade policy for the federal government prior to the MTNs in Geneva. In addition, it also initiated a western Canadian trade mission to Latin America.[40] However, despite attempts to work out coordinated regional approaches to industrial development (for example, attempting to establish a common western procurement policy) this committee has made little progress – indeed, in recent years it has met infrequently.

In 1979, the premiers established the Western Economic Policy Liaison Committee to identify common aspects of federal-provincial financial and fiscal relations. The idea was to develop a coherent western position in such areas as transportation, trade policy, and R&D.[41] This committee, composed of the deputy minister of finance and the deputy minister of intergovernmental affairs from each province, met on a regular basis. It was hoped that this group would build on the initial success of the Committee of Western Industry Ministers in developing a common trade position, and attack other, broader policy areas. To date, though, the group seems to have had very little success in developing common positions, even on federal financial policies.

The problems facing WPC in generating significant levels of policy cooperation relate to the underlying structure of the four western economies. As resource-based, export-oriented economies, all four provinces share certain common economic objectives, particularly in national transport and trade policy. In addition, due to geographic proximity and some shared problems, a great deal of practical cooperation has developed, particularly in the agricultural area. These factors have encouraged two types of collaboration: 1) limited technical cooperation on specific issues; and 2) broader policy cooperation on common concerns about national policies. What is missing is a significant level of interprovincial cooperation on exclusively regional issues.

The reasons for this lack of cooperation are complex, but they are partly the result of the rather different economic structure of each province (see p. 37, Table II.3). As well, provincial governments have, at times, been of considerably different ideological persuasions. The former factor has prevented cooperative economic development projects because, with very different resource-based, exporting economies, the provinces have had very little need to collaborate on specific areas of resource or industrial development. Cooperation comes only where there are issues which affect resource or staples production in general (such as a federal transport policy) or the provinces' access to the international trading system (such as a federal trade policy). The different political persuasions of the governments has also meant that appropriate policy instruments are difficult to achieve. This is due in large measure to their very wide differences of opinion about the proper role of government in society – a situation that prevents agreement on the form that policy instruments should take, or indeed, even on the necessity for public sector action.

VIII. Federal-Provincial Collaboration Over Industrial Policy

Federal-provincial collaboration is probably the most widespread and highly developed mode of intergovernmental cooperation in Canada. In general, it takes two forms: *multilateral* cooperation involving the federal government and some or all provinces; and *bilateral* cooperation, involving the federal government and only one province. From the point of view of developing an industrial policy, each form has its own drawbacks and advantages.

Multilateral Relations

This form of collaboration is the one familiar to most Canadians when they think of federal-provincial relations. It is, in short, some variation of the traditional meeting of the representatives of Canada's 11 governments. Unfortunately, as indicated in chapter VI, despite the highly developed nature of this type of intergovernmental collaboration in Canada, federal-provincial relations in industry, science and technology are poorly developed.

A conference of federal-provincial industry ministers usually meets annually and is preceded by a federal-provincial meeting of deputy ministers of industry. However, in recent years such meetings have tended to be sporadic. The deputies' meeting is usually concerned with preparing the agenda and exchanging information. As is the case with interprovincial meetings on industrial issues issues, these meetings and their agendas and minutes, are confidential. But from interviews with the participants, it would seem that they exist mainly to exchange information and to discuss issues of common concern, or as is frequently the case, disputes over federal, industrial-policy initiatives. Interestingly, apart from meetings convened by nongovernmental groups such as the Association of Provincial Research Organizations, there are no regular meetings of provincial and federal ministers responsible for industrial R&D policy, despite the growing importance of such policy at both the federal and provincial level.

To get a better appreciation of the nature of federal-provincial collaboration, three case studies are examined. These studies provide at least some indication of the nature of the process and its limitations, especially because they vary from a highly institutionalized process embracing many issues over the long term (the Canadian Council of Resource and Environment Ministers (CCREM)) to an essentially *ad hoc* process limited to a single issue (the modernization of the forest products industry).

*The Canadian Council of Resource and Environment Ministers**
While not directly concerned with industrial policy issues, CCREM is the closest example of intergovernmental economic cooperation that has involved the establishment of a permanent organization or secretariat. It provides us with an excellent case study of what intergovernmental cooperation can achieve when it has two important advantages: a relatively uncontroversial policy area of common concern to all 11 governments; and a permanent secretariat which is capable of providing continuous and fairly intensive bureaucratic support. This latter feature is very important. On the list of a public servant's priorities, intergovernmental relations rank very low, unless, of course, he or she is an intergovernmental relations official. Thus, the presence of a permanent secretariat to structure relations, maintain dialogue and keep attention focussed on common issues prevents individual provincial and federal officials from concentrating exclusively on issues within their own jurisdictions.

CCREM grew out of concern expressed in the late 1950s over Canada's renewable resource base, particularly in forestry. This resulted in the Resources for Tommorrow conference, held in Montreal in 1961 at the initiative of the federal government. Demonstrating to the federal and provincial governments the need for a more coherent national approach to resource management, the conference was a success; many of the participants realized that a continuing forum on renewable resource issues would be useful. In early 1964, the two levels of government decided to establish a Canadian Council of Resource Ministers with a secretariat in Montreal[1] to foster better management of renewable resources – later this mandate

---

* Much of the material for this section was drawn from a paper on CCREM prepared for the Science Council by Professor M.S. Whittington of Carleton University.

was extended to include environmental protection. The council's membership consists of the federal and provincial ministers responsible for renewable resources or the environment,[2] although many officials from both levels of government participate in CCREM's work through various coordinating committees and working groups. Unlike a number of federal-provincial organizations, CCREM decided to establish a permanent secretariat, independent of any government, which would provide professional and administrative support. In the nine years to 1973, the council grew in size and scope. By 1973, it had a permanent staff of about 16, half of whom were professionals, assisted periodically by consultants and part-time employees. Apart from holding an annual ministerial meeting, the council became involved in activities ranging from workshops on resource and environment issues to the publication of periodicals, newsletters and conference proceedings.[3] A sophisticated network of ministers and officials concerned with environmental and resource issues was constructed through CCREM's working groups and the secretariat staff. This network acted as a catalyst for new collective projects and as a clearing house for information. In a policy area in which technical issues assume some importance, and where, in the late 1960s, there was a favourable public attitude towards conservation, conditions encouraged close intergovernmental collaboration. CCREM, in fact, provided an excellent institutional base from which to consolidate and increase intergovernmental collaboration.

The result was not only considerable informal cooperation in the environmental field, but a growing similarity across the country in environmental and renewable resource policies and legislation. Michael Whittington has noted that a good deal of this similarity can be attributed to the council's ability to act as a bridge builder:

> "Many resource administrators interviewed mentioned. . . that the jargon, the vocabulary of the environmental policy area, had become similar in all parts of the country, largely as a result of the information distributed by CCREM. This was. . . borne out in practice by the fact that the same "buzz words" kept coming up in interviews with these people. Moreover, what was objectively apparent in these interviews, was that the same basic priorities were articulated by resource administrators from St. John's to Victoria. When asked to comment on major trends in the future of the field and major new policy concerns for the provinces to tackle, it was remarkable how close the responses were to the current concerns expressed by the members of the [CCREM] Secretariat."[4]

The council still exists with many of its earlier functions intact, but there was a decline in its role after 1973; the reasons for this are significant. In 1973 CCREM held its largest gathering, the Man and Resources conference, to herald a new phase in its work. Involving more than two years of organizational work and a lot of CCREM's resources, the conference was intended to include the general public, as well as academics and civil servants, in a wide-ranging discussion of Canada's renewable resource and environmental policies. In a sense this inclusion of the public was the culmination of a gradual change in the CCREM secretariat's view of its role; rather than serving the information and liaison needs of the provincial and federal governments, CCREM now felt its job, at least in part, was to encourage public discussion of resource and environmental policy issues. This new role caused concern in government circles because public reviews of existing policies, and public input on the direction of future programs seemed to question the legitimacy of the policy-making process within the member governments.

This concern over CCREM's changing role was parallelled by a growing uneasiness in smaller provinces because of the time-demands CCREM's activities made on their limited staff resources. Their financial contribution was never great, but the smaller provinces had always had difficulty contributing fully to CCREM's ongoing staff work. Indeed, there was some resentment that CCREM's professional staff was often as large as those of some smaller provincial governments in such policy areas as natural resources or environment. These resentments came to a head in the early 1970s when the workload of the Man and Resources conference began to eat into the council's resources and make increasing demands on provincial officials.

There were other problems as well. After 1973, rising oil prices and a general perception of resource shortages diminished public concern over environmental issues. And by the early 1970s, several provincial governments were establishing, on their own, substantial capabilities in intergovernmental affairs. That made them less dependent on CCREM as a provider of information – a role which comprised an important part of the council's total functions. To these governments, CCREM's usefulness seemed to decline at the very time when the secretariat was trying to generate public awareness – a task which seemed more likely to create problems than benefits.

CCREM also faced more mundane organizational problems. After the Man and Resources conference, CCREM's secretary general left the organization. He has been the director of the organization since its inception and in many ways the person to be credited for CCREM's sense of purpose and direction. Some of CCREM's identity and purpose went with him, a loss compounded by a wholesale change in official and ministerial representation on CCREM. The council lost many of its original supporters, particularly on the bureaucratic side.

The result of these changes was a significant scaling down of the organization and its activities. Today, the council consists of a small staff of five with offices in Toronto. The annual ministerial meetings are still held, and the structure of a coordinating committee of senior officials and various working groups of more junior officials has been maintained. CCREM also holds workshops and seminars for ministers and officials on policy issues of common concern and assists in drafting reports for ministers. Most of the council's current work, however, is intergovernmental consultation – attempting to provide a framework in which government policies and potential opportunities for shared action can be discussed. Recently, it was involved in a major review of provincial forestry policies resulting in publication of a compendium study of management policies.[5] The study contributed to the launching of a major federal-provincial effort to improve forest management techniques and the operating capacity of the forest products industry. It also appears that, in contrast to earlier years, the council is putting greater emphasis on substantive ministerial consultations on policy issues, rather than relying on more extensive meetings of officials.[6]

The expansion and contraction of CCREM tell us a little about the dynamics of a federal-provincial organization. In the first place, such organizations do play a useful role in helping to structure a network of officials and ministers. They can create an environment conducive to the development of common policies or practices in a specific area. In the environmental and renewable resource area, this role was reinforced by the fact that the issues themselves were, relatively speaking, not controversial. There were no fundamental underlying differences between governments over broad objectives, and the mechanisms which could achieve those objectives were technical enough to depoliticize any latent conflicts. CCREM probably had the most favourable circumstances for cooperative intergovernmental activity, and indeed, it met with some success.

A permanent organization such as CCREM has its costs, however. Continuous consultation bonds officials and ministers from several governments; but it makes demands on the staff resources of smaller governments. In addition, once a separate intergovernmental bureaucracy has been created, there is a risk that the organization can develop its own internal objectives and work towards goals which may not be shared by the member governments.

It is far from clear if the permanent and highly organized form of intergovernmental collaboration that was reasonably successful in the case of CCREM can be applied in a policy context where the issues are more contentious (for example, industrial policy). Indeed, CCREM's success may have been due to both a unique combination of organizational structure, which encourages governments to meet, *and* an uncontentious policy area.

The following example shows just how limited collaboration can be when there is no such institutionalized process and when the policy area under discussion is more likely to be contentious.

The 1978 First Ministers' Meetings on the Economy
Of all the examples of intergovernmental bargaining over industrial and economic issues, the first ministers' meetings on the economy in 1978 were the most significant federal-provincial attempt to deal with intergovernmental economic policy making. Two separate first ministers' conferences took place that year, one, in February and the other, in November. Each conference was preceded by a series of meetings of senior officials and ministers from the "economic" departments (for example, industry, agriculture, energy, and natural resources). The whole process was a gargantuan effort, involving hundreds of individuals in a complex series of meetings and the drafting of literally dozens of position papers, reports and communiqués.

It is not possible in the space available to provide a detailed review of the events surrounding the conferences, and in any case, they have been fully described elsewhere.[7] What will be attempted here is a brief overview of some of the conferences' strengths and weaknesses, and what had been achieved by the time the conferences were over. Before doing so, however, it is necessary to outline some of the special factors which both provided the political commitment to hold the conferences and prevented the participants from making effective decisions.

The most obvious pressures encouraging the governments to participate were the twin problems of low economic growth and high inflation that characterized the economy at that time. Considerable uncertainty also arose over how the economy would perform after the removal of wage and price controls, which in the 1976-77 period had moderated the rate of inflation. Finally, there was also a concern that business needed to be given a firm signal that government policies would assist, rather than hinder, economic expansion, particularly after the extensive period of government intervention during the controls period.

Despite these real incentives for all governments, and particularly the federal government, to take joint constructive action on the economy, a number of constraints were operating as well. The conferences were scheduled in the midst of another massive set of intergovernmental negotiations, the constitutional conferences which divided the attention of the politicians and bureaucrats, and also complicated the economic conferences by injecting jurisdictional and other constitutional issues into them. It was also known at the end of 1977 that the federal government would be facing a general election within a year to eighteen months – raising suspicions that the conferences were partly a political exercise for Ottawa. To compound these problems, the lead time to the first conference was so short that thorough preparation was impossible. The prime minister raised the possibility of an economic summit with the premiers in the autumn of 1977, confirmed the conferences in mid-December and held the first session within two months. That it would be possible in such a very short period to provide the analytical basis for the 11 heads of government to discuss what the prime minister hoped would be a medium-term economic strategy for the country seemed, at the very least, optimistic.

In any event, the prevailing political mood was not very conducive to a major governmental initiative to establish an industrial strategy. If there was any political consensus among the 11 governments, it was that the role of government should be curtailed rather than expanded and that deficits and expenditures should be reduced. Indeed, the medium-term strategy which was to be the focus of the conference had much more to do with monetary and fiscal restraint than industrial policy. Nevertheless, the conferences remain the best example of a concerted attempt to develop joint economic policies.

Because of their complexity, an assessment of the conferences is best made at two levels: first, the problems raised by their organizational form; and second, the substance, or content, of the conference discussions and of the resulting policy initiatives.

Perhaps the most serious organizational problem facing the conference officials was that of focussing an agenda that was an economic "grab-bag." It was intended that the conferences address broad macroeconomic questions (for example, the labour market, economic outlook, regional development, energy and trade policy) as well as much more specific issues such as the prospects and policies for particular industrial sectors. Some attempt was made to rationalize the issues by having senior officials, and then ministers, meet before each first ministers' conference – it was hoped that this would assist in structuring the discussions at the first ministers' meetings by obtaining prior agreement on less controversial issues and setting out the alternatives open to the first ministers on the more difficult questions. But the strategy did not work as planned. The ministers' conferences lacked a sense of direction and the ministers were reluctant to make decisions.[8] Despite the large number of papers prepared, and the fact that seven of the nine ministerial meetings produced reports for the first minister's conference,[9] most issues remained unfocussed and unresolved. Consequently, the first ministers faced a barrage of diverse and controversial issues which had to be settled in a few days of discussion. Progress was slow and the areas of final agreement were few in number and general in content.

These problems were not helped by the uncertain role played by the federal government in the conference discussions. In some cases, particularly at the ministerial level, there were complaints that federal departmental consultation with the provinces had been weak or ineffective. Some provinces also found that a federal leadership role was lacking. Federal preparations for the conference were basically a "bottom-up" exercise: policy papers developed by separate departments were reviewed, first by the Committee of Deputy Ministers on Economic Issues and then by the Cabinet. The federal position papers were thus largely an amalgam of departmental views, rather than a coherent federal economic development strategy – probably a reflection of fundamental uncertainty within the federal government itself about the content and direction of an industrial strategy for the country.[10] One participant, a provincial official, commented that the lack of focus and clarity was due, at least in part, to the fact that the federal role was too diffuse. In other words, the federal government had no clear idea of what it wanted from the process. As the provincial official put it:

"[Consultation] has to be part of any effective policy, but the problem is that consultation can so easily be an alternative for policy. I think that the frame of mind of the federal government in 1978 was such that, in practice, the consultative process was a substitute for policy, not a means for getting policy."[11]

The final difficulty with the conferences was their highly public nature. Preliminary meetings were held in private, but the two main first ministers' conferences were open to the press and televised nationally by the Canadian Broadcasting Corporation (CBC). This led to two rather different types of problems. In the first place, the presentation created unrealistic expectations in the public mind about what could be achieved. Second, it encouraged the premiers to speak to their home audiences, making them reluctant to become involved in any real bargaining because their constituents would see them making concessions over regionally sensitive issues. The result was little opportunity for the "horse trading" essential to good bargaining. The only opportunities for private bargaining came during luncheon and dinner breaks – hardly enough time for indepth discussion.

However, more fundamental than the organizational and operational difficulties were the deep divisions over the *content* of economic and industrial policy. The consensus on the broad outlines of economic policy barely survived the level of pious hope. Each provincial delegation came with its own particular view of the issues. On commercial and industrial policy, for example, delegates agreed that the private sector should be encouraged to adapt to changing international circumstances and that government intervention should be rolled back (significantly, Quebec and Saskatchewan were silent on this issue). But how these objectives should be carried out was open to considerable disagreement, partly because the manner in which they would be implemented could have very different implications in different parts of the country. For some provinces, less intervention meant a relaxation of regulations and a reduction in direct subsidies to individual firms. For others, it simply meant a more positive attitude to the private sector's needs, such as the provision of more effective financial and fiscal benefits. For British Columbia, effective commercial policy consisted of infrastructure support for industry (transport, power, etc.) and seeking a more open environment for international trade.[12] For Ontario, on the other hand, effective commercial policy was understood more as assistance to specific firms and sectors facing severe international competition.[13] The two provinces thus had very different views on the substance of commercial policy and the manner in which it should be implemented, despite what initially seemed to be a consensus on the appropriate role of government in the economy. Similar differences in interpretation surfaced in other policy areas, especially regional development and energy.

The final conclusions to the February first ministers' conference (which turned out to be the high point of intergovernmental agreement) demonstrate the general and rather diffuse nature of federal-provincial cooperation in economic policy matters. With respect to medium-term economic objectives, a good deal of the agreement was, in the view of one observer, platitudinous.[14] It stressed the importance of private-sector employment expansion and a desire on the part of the governments to restore price stability. Unfortunately, it was not made clear how this would be achieved.

Some progress was made in the area of expenditure restraint. Governments agreed to limit total spending to less than the growth rate of Canada's GNP, to accept the Bank of Canada's strict monetary targets and to be commited to preventing public sector compensation from leading private-sector wage settlements. Governments agreed that the Economic Council of Canada (ECC) would establish a wage and price monitoring agency and launch a study on government regulation of industry. An agreement was also reached to review petroleum and mining taxation, and a promise extended from Ottawa to continue to involve provinces in GATT negotiations and to press for greater access to world markets for Canada's processed raw materials. Finally, it was decided to proceed with two energy projects (a hydro development in Newfoundland and a heavy oil plant in Saskatchewan), and a list of 12 priority projects for federal-provincial attention was drawn up. Typically, the 12 projects provided something for each province, from a grain-handling terminal for British Columbia, to a joint effort to increase investment in the auto industry for Ontario. The first conference was not without its achievements; but most of the agreements were general and lacked coherence.

At the second conference in November 1978, very few new initiatives were taken. The federal government expanded its GATT commitment to include efforts to seek freer international markets for Ontario and Quebec's high-technology industries. In addition, the first ministers agreed that, as a principle, the Canadian market should not be fragmented "unnecessarily" by government purchasing policies – although no mechanisms were established to prevent this from happening.[15] An Alberta and federal task force was set up to study expansion of natural gas pipelines to eastern Canada, and a consensus was reached on the taxation of resource industries.

The two other principal areas of agreement, transportation and regional development, provide a classic example of the bargaining so typical of federal-provincial conferences. On regional development it was agreed that assistance should only be provided to "viable economic opportunities resulting from natural strengths,"[16] a position reflecting British Columbia and Ontario's concerns that some regional development assistance was affecting harmfully existing industry (by subsidizing regional competition or preventing productive capacity from moving to high-growth regions). On the other hand, it was agreed that the federal government's proposed National Transportation Act should explicitly state that transportation policy is a tool for regional development, a position which pleased the Atlantic provinces and western Canada, but which rejected Ontario's support for a "user pay" principle.

In short, the achievements of the two conferences were limited by the need to reach a consensus in a group whose participants had very different economic interests. On balance, the conferences were capable of galvanizing the various governments to act on issues where there was an emerging consensus (for example, limiting government expenditure). However, in practical terms, the specific policies that emerged were those not seriously affecting the interests of *any* of the participants. The results of the conferences tended to be either agreements on general principles that later turned out to hide very real differences, or agreements on isolated issues which did not, in themselves, add up to a coherent program of political action (for example, the trade-offs over regional development and transport policy).

The major achievement of the conferences may have been the development of a more sophisticated process for intergovernmental consultation. Indeed, many of the participants saw this, rather than policy making, as their role.[17] The conferences provided a valuable experience for the participants in learning to coordinate a broad and complex economic-policy agenda. As well, the first ministers tended to delegate complex issues to specialist working groups. Both these developments could increase the capacity for such intergovernmental meetings to deal more effectively with economic-policy issues.

However, underlying these assumptions is a belief that a more sophisticated approach to the *process* of intergovernmental negotiation will assist in overcoming significant differences of economic interest over the *content* of policy. This proposition is by no means proven. Indeed, there was a growing gulf evident at the conferences between those officials concerned with intergovernmental relations who saw the conferences primarily as a process, and those officials from the various "line" departments who tended to see the conferences mainly in terms of the substantive policy initiatives which were taken. The former group was, relatively speaking, rather pleased with the outcome (particularly that of the February conference). The latter group was disappointed at what they saw as a disjointed and minor achievement in policy terms.[18] An emphasis on intergovernmental negotiations tends to heighten the importance attached to the process of intergovernmental meetings. It may be that if we came to rely on such meetings to develop industrial policy, that is how our success will be judged.

Unfortunately, therefore, given their present state of development and their emphasis on process rather than substance, intergovernmental meetings of the first ministers' variety seem unlikely to produce the type of coherent and forceful policy on industrial issues that are essential for an effective national industrial strategy.

The Federal-Provincial Forest Products Strategy
When we consider an example of successful federal-provincial cooperation involving a specific industry, we find the process much more focussed and the outcome much more positive. Understanding the reasons for this requires some background on the industry itself and on the pattern of federal-provincial interaction.

The forest products industry is one of Canada's largest industrial sectors, accounting directly and indirectly for about 900 000 jobs[19] and approximately 40 per cent of Canada's exports of fabricated products.[20] In addition, the industry represents a vital component of some provincial economies; in the case of New Brunswick and British Columbia, it amounts to almost half the value of all provincial manufacturing activity.[21] The political importance of the industry is further heightened by the fact that it is frequently located in communities which are almost entirely dependent on it for employment.

By the 1970s, a number of structural weaknesses in the industry became manifest. New producers of pulp and paper, particularly in the southern United States, began to compete effectively in traditional Canadian export markets. Their access to lower labour, production and resource costs, plus a wood supply that regenerates itself more quickly meant that these producers had a considerable price advantage. Also during the 1970s, studies suggested that Canada's economically exploitable forest resources were much less plentiful than expected.[22] A lack of long-term planning had resulted in insufficient forest protection and poor use of some timber species. In addition, poor harvesting techniques and rudimentary silviculture practices meant that much potential usable timber was wasted and that reforestation did not keep pace with harvesting.[23]

In eastern Canada, these problems were compounded by outdated capital equipment in the pulp and paper sector that wasted energy, caused pollution and required labour-intensive production techniques. Also, low profit margins and low energy and wood supply costs gave little incentive to producers to re-equip. Thus, by the mid-1970s, a significant investment backlog had developed. Producers faced rising energy costs, more stringent pollution control regulations and machinery that was rapidly reaching the end of its productive life.[24] The need for forceful public action was obvious, and the particular structure within which forestry issues were discussed gave the forest products initiative both its unique character and successful outcome.

Traditionally, there has been considerable informal cooperation between the two levels of government on forestry issues. Ottawa does not have formal responsibility for forests under the Constitution Act, but it has taken an interest in the industry because of its responsibilities for commerce and international trade and concern with industrial development. In addition, the federal government has traditionally provided technical services such as resource mapping, and research on silviculture techniques, pest and disease control, forest protection and the manufacture of forest products.[25] The provinces, as the principal owners of forest reserves, have been responsible for setting and collecting royalties for the timber harvested by private companies. They also have the ultimate responsibility for ensuring effective reforestation and for providing the protection necessary to maintain the forests' productivity (for example, pest and disease control programs and fire-fighting services).

There has, in consequence, been a good deal of informal cooperation between the two levels of government, with each having a more or less complementary set of responsibilities. This pragmatic cooperation has been reinforced by other characteristics of forestry policy making. In the first place, a number of mechanisms promote federal-provincial dialogue. Since the mid-1960s, CCREM has acted as a major forum for forest resource management issues. As mentioned earlier, the council sponsored a major cooperative review of forest management practices in the mid-1970s which provided a stimulus for the provinces to reform their forest management practices. There have also been a number of federal-provincial working groups in the forestry area, the most notable being the Forest Industry Development Committee (FIDC). Second, the policy area has been dominated in large measure by technical and professional considerations. Effective forest management is highly specialized, and matters for policy consideration tend to be very technical or scientific. As a result, conclusions about appropriate policy tend to vary between governments only to the extent that the physical conditions of their forests differ.

There are, however, significant differences between the structure of the forest *products* industry in eastern Canada and in British Columbia. In British Columbia the emphasis is more on the production of lumber and plywood; in eastern Canada it tends to be on pulp and paper.[26] Eastern companies have older equipment, a greater need for pollution control and, accordingly, greater capital investment needs. West-coast firms generally possess newer equipment, but depend on export markets (for example, the construction industry in the United States) that tend to be more cyclical.

Even so, similar problems and well-developed mechanisms to reach a consensus have produced a fairly coherent national approach to forest management policy. In the mid-1970s, a number of provinces changed their forest management programs, placing greater emphasis on reforestation and restructuring royalty payments to encourage better conservation practices and a more efficient use of various tree species.[27] In order to assist the provinces, DREE has signed forest management agreements with all five eastern provinces and with two western provinces (Saskatchewan and British Columbia). The programs, representing a total expenditure by all governments of about $677 million, of which about $451 million comes from the federal government,[28] are designed to improve silviculture techniques, pest control and road access to timber reserves.

The most interesting example of federal-provincial cooperation in the forest products industry was, however, the attempt to improve and modernize pulp and paper mills in eastern Canada.[29] This program in a sense dates from 1970-71 when senior officials from Ontario, Quebec and the federal government formed a committee with private-sector executives to review the structural problems of the pulp and paper industry. By 1973, the federal Department of Industry, Trade and Commerce (IT&C) recommended to cabinet that a modernization program be implemented and administered by DREE. The recommendation was never taken up. The following year a Forest Industry Development Committee (FIDC) was established. Composed of the representatives of seven federal departments and two representatives from each province, it was intended to encourage cooperation on forestry development.[30] By 1976, from FIDC deliberations and various studies by both levels of government, it was clear that action on pulp and paper plant modernization was needed. Both the FIDC and a number of federal interdepartmental committees began to examine the potential policy alternatives. In addition, both Ontario and Quebec approached DREE about subagreements for the pulp and paper industry.

By 1978 Ontario and Quebec had become impatient with the process and started to push the federal government to take action. With the depreciation of the Canadian dollar and resulting increases in pulp and paper exports, the provinces felt that the industry's financial position was sufficiently strong enough for investment incentives to produce an industry commitment to new capital equipment. Ontario and Quebec were both anxious that the incentive program be composed largely of grants; but federal departments were divided over what form assistance should take. In order to increase the pressure, both provinces announced their own incentive schemes (Quebec in June 1978 and Ontario in January 1979).

Even though a consensus had been reached on the need for modernization, in the summer and autumn of 1978 federal officials became concerned that uncoordinated provincial programs would create unnecessary competition over the location of new capital investments and that announced and contemplated provincial policies could stimulate surplus production capacity. A positive federal response to provincial action was delayed, however, until February 1979, in part because of reorganization of the federal government's economic policy-making machinery. The new Board of Economic Development Ministers (BEDM) reviewed the various federal policy proposals that had been worked on by four departments and coordinated the assembly of a final package announced by BEDM President Robert Andras on the first of February 1979.

The federal assistance offer consisted of a $235 million grant program for the modernization of plant equipment and the purchase of pollution abatement equipment. To be administered by DREE on a cost-sharing basis with the provinces for five years, the program would apply to all provinces willing to establish their own programs meeting federal criteria.[31]

Over the following months, negotiations were pursued with Ontario and Quebec, the two provinces which had announced modernization programs. While the federal government had gone some way to meet provincial objectives (for example, a grant-based, as opposed to a tax-based incentive scheme), several outstanding differences remained. While Quebec wanted the joint program to include expansion of production facilities, Ontario favoured a fairly broad program to improve production facilities. By mid-May 1979, however, there was sufficient agreement to allow two programs to be established, one for Ontario and the other for Quebec. Broadly, they followed the federal proposals; no production expansion was to be allowed and funds could only be used for modernization of plant or pollution abatement equipment. However, there were some differences between the two programs. The application procedures for assistance varied, as did the relative provincial contributions. In Quebec, the program amounts to $150 million of assistance with the provincial share 40 per cent of the total. In Ontario, the provincial share is 60 per cent of an identical budget.[32] In addition, Quebec operates a separate, modest incentive program designed to encourage the expansion of pulp and paper production facilities.

Approximately a year later, in August 1980, a third modernization program was established with New Brunswick. In recognition of New Brunswick's less significant revenue base, the federal government agreed to contribute 80 per cent of the funds.[33]

Like most DREE agreements, each program has a joint federal-provincial management committee to review applications for assistance and oversee its operation. So far, the programs seem successful. Ontario moved the most rapidly and, by the end of March 1980, had six modernization agreements in place, representing more than $880 million in investment,[34] and, Quebec had implemented three, representing slightly more than $100 million.[35] In Ontario's case, more than seven dollars of private-sector investment has been attracted for every dollar of public incentive – considerably more than expected. Further, in both the Quebec and Ontario cases, Canadian procurement has been favoured in the agreements; in Ontario, a 10 per cent Canadian procurement premium is required for all private-sector investment covered under the agreement. Provincial officials estimate that, of the total planned procurement covered by the program in the province, more than 80 per cent will be sourced in Canada.

The modernization program can be criticized with respect to the advisability of granting large subsidies to firms which are usually part of corporate conglomerates with significant capital resources of their own.[36] However, a number of important industrial policy objectives have been achieved through the program. First, progress has been made towards improving the productive efficiency of a Canadian industry which is a major employer and exporter. Second, despite the fact that responsibility for the industry's development is effectively split between two levels of government, it was possible to develop a coherent, noncompetitive approach to industrial assistance that provided for a consistent policy, but also one flexible enough to allow adaptation to specific provincial circumstances. This success was in large measure due to the relatively well-developed federal-provincial consultation on forestry issues which helped to promote a consensus; and the proven DREE mechanism of subagreements which provided a model on which to structure modernization agreements. Indeed, the consensus and the subagreement mechanism allowed a rapid federal-provincial decision on the issue of plant modernization once a federal commitment had been made. For example, the two agreements between Ontario and Quebec and the federal government were negotiated, ratified and implemented within about four and a half months of the federal government's policy announcement. Perhaps even more important, however, the provinces managed to avoid being competitive as they rebuilt a major industry. Without federal participation, there is every indication that Ontario and Quebec would have engaged in competitive bidding since both were anxious not only to modernize, but also to expand pulp and paper production.

One final advantage to this form of federal-provincial policy making needs to be mentioned. Plant modernization in the pulp and paper industry was a problem unique to eastern Canada. Although money was made available for all provinces, in fact none was taken up in western Canada because of the different structure of the industry. In consequence, the federal government proposed a separate program for the special needs of the western industry.[37] The federal government, then, specifically tailored its forest products industry assistance for two very different regions of the country. This flexibility in program design and implementation, essential if the federal government is to maintain its leadership in industrial restructuring, suggests that mechanisms allowing specific bilateral compromises within broader multilateral programs are also imperative if such programs are to be successful. We now turn to this essential bilateral element.

Bilateral Relations

When a number of provinces are involved, generating sufficient consensus to allow cohesive action is often difficult, if not impossible. One solution is to narrow the range of the subject matter to a specific set of shared problems in the anticipation that this will focus attention on a mutually acceptable solution. This strategy has been followed in the case of CCREM and the forest products industry.

Another solution is to work bilaterally so that a number of issues can be discussed between two governments who share a desire to come to an agreement. This working strategy has a number of advantages, not the least of which is the ability to seek agreement over a wide range of issues. With respect to an industrial strategy, this advantage is particularly important, as the coordination of policy in a wide variety of areas is required if the strategy is to be truly effective.

The General Development Agreements

Bilateral agreements between Ottawa and individual provinces over industrial policy issues have not been numerous.[38] One exception, however, to this otherwise rather underdeveloped area of federal-provincial relations is the General Development Agreement (GDA) system created by DREE. The GDA system is significant on two counts. First, is the sheer scale of financial commitment to these agreements by both levels of government – commitments amounting to over $4.3 billion in 1979-80.[39] Second, these agreements have provided a framework making it possible to use bilateral relations to attack the general question of economic development, rather than some specific issue relating to a province's economic structure.

The GDA system is quite complex, but basically works as follows. The federal government, through DREE, and a particular province negotiate an agreement (known as a GDA) outlining objectives both governments are willing to support with respect to the development of the provincial economy. The objectives are usually phrased in general terms that indicate the particular economic problems the two governments wish to overcome and the aspects of the provincial economy they wish to see developed. Under this umbrella agreement, usually based on some form of agreed analysis of the provincial economy's problems, there are a series of subagreements on specific development opportunities or problems; they are the GDA's policy instruments. Subagreements are usually implemented by a provincial government department and supervized by a management committee of federal and provincial officials. Usually a province suggests the subject matter for a particular subagreement and submits it to the local DREE office for analysis and negotiation.

Subagreements range widely in subject matter from the provision of infrastructure (for example, funding the building of provincial highways) to assistance programs for specific sectors (for example, tourism, mining, forestry, agriculture, etc.). In some cases, more general social development issues such as community infrastructure and job-training problems are tackled in these agreements as well. The instruments used can vary from traditional grant and loan programs to the establishment of provincial Crown corporations. Such corporations have been set up under subagreements to encourage the establishment of an integrated manufacturing complex in St. John, New Brunswick (Multiplex Corporation) and in Newfoundland to assist with the development of marine technology (NORDCO).

Enterprise Manitoba
Perhaps the most interesting subagreement signed to date is the Industrial Development Sub-Agreement (Enterprise Manitoba) between the federal government and Manitoba.[40] The Manitoba example is especially significant because it attempts to establish an overall sectoral approach to the development of the provincial economy. Most of the industrial subagreements signed with other provinces have either been concerned with a single industry or with general forms of financial or industrial infrastructure assistance (for example, constructing industrial parks).

Enterprise Manitoba is a five-year program which has been in operation since April 1978. It involves total financial commitments on the part of the two governments of $44 million, of which Manitoba's contribution is $17.6 million.[41] Enterprise Manitoba's major objective is to assist in expanding Manitoba's manufacturing base which encountered serious difficulties in the 1970s. The program is the latest in a long series of attempts, starting in 1961 with the Roblin government's Committee on Manitoba's Economic Future, to improve Manitoba's manufacturing sector.[42] These attempts have included the creation of several industrial development agencies - the best known being the Manitoba Development Corporation (MDC).

The subagreement itself is broken down into seven program components, the most interesting of which are concerned with the creation of Industrial Sector Advisory Boards (ISABs), the provision of technology development centres, and a program to support new manufacturing firms through Enterprise Centres. The ISABs, consisting of private sector executives assisted by civil service committees, essentially perform two functions: the integration of private sector advice into the policy development process and the identification of new industrial opportunities. A total of six ISABs has been established for key industrial sectors including health care products, light machinery, electronics, aerospace, transportation equipment and food products. It is hoped that private sector involvement and the focus on a few key sectors of the economy will give Enterprise Manitoba's other support programs a sense of coherence and direction.

This emphasis on specific sectors has been reinforced by the establishment of two technology development centres, one for food products at Portage la Prairie and a second for general industrial technology in Winnipeg which has specialized, at least initially, in health care products and electronics. The centres are designed to assist in the dissemination of technological information to firms, test products and assist with product development. They are advised by a board which is drawn, in part, from ISABs' membership. Complementing the technology development centres are two enterprise centres, one in Brandon and one in Winnipeg. These enterprise centres offer consulting and management services to small business and provide factory space and on-site services for firms starting operations. New firms located in the centres' factory spaces will have daily access to business advisory services (and technical services in Winnipeg) for up to two years. Although the enterprise centres are open to all types of firms, it is clear from the linkage in Winnipeg to the technology centres that they are intended to encourage technology-intensive projects in the six sectors identified as priorities in the Enterprise Manitoba agreement.

One final point concerning Enterprise Manitoba: integrated into the agreement is a coordination and assessment function involving both officials from the DREE Manitoba office and senior officials from the Manitoba Department of Economic Development, the provincial department responsible for the subagreement's implementation. The objective of this assessment function is to provide a constant review of the programs in the subagreement and to provide joint analysis by the two governments on changing economic conditions which could affect the program elements.

It is too early yet to assess the extent to which Enterprise Manitoba will make a positive contribution to the provincial economy. But some judgements can already be made on the viability of the agreement from an intergovernmental perspective. In the first place, it is important to emphasize that both governments have gained something substantial. In Manitoba's case,[43] it is obvious that the subagreement has brought in a significant level of federal funding. Equally important, however, has been the implicit federal commitment to recognize Manitoba's special industrial development problems. This more political objective was viewed as important by provincial officials because of what they saw as the federal tendency to identify the problems of Canada's manufacturing industry with those of Ontario and Quebec alone. This recognition is particularly relevant for Manitoba, for of all the western provinces, Manitoba's economy is the most dependent on manufacturing.

From the federal viewpoint, the subagreement also has a number of important advantages.[44] Like their provincial counterparts, DREE officials saw the subagreement as an opportunity to introduce a regional element into federal industrial policy. The subagreement helps DREE fulfill its mandate and also helps to involve IT&C in regional concerns – officers from IT&C's Manitoba regional office sit on many of the committees which are responsible for overseeing the agreement's operation. The federal department also signed the subagreement and will contribute to the costs of the technology development centres.

Equally important, the subagreement allows Ottawa to influence provincial priorities and directions in an area, industrial policy, in which it has a vital interest. Further, because the negotiation of an industrial development subagreement requires both governments to reach some consensus on the nature of the province's economic problems and the types of policy instruments required, it provides a mechanism for ensuring that some harmony and coordination exists between the two governments' industrial policies. In this sense, the industrial development subagreement can ensure some coherence in the development of industrial policy for a specific province.

However, difficulties exist with such subagreements as well. In the first place, negotiations for, and operations of, subagreements are highly bureaucratic. An average subagreement takes about a year to approve and sign following its first proposal, usually by the provincial government.[45] The potential agreement must not only pass through the DREE provincial office but must also be approved at the regional office and national headquarters in Ottawa, all of which requires consultations with other departments in Ottawa. This makes it difficult for the various governments to react quickly to specific proposals and can cause difficulties if a subagreement program is intended for a specific industrial project. More generally, there tends to be difficulties in the negotiation process between DREE and provincial officials because of differences in political outlook and function. Part of the problem is due to the natural suspicions which emerge as a result of two rather different bureaucracies having to work together. However, it also reflects the different political commitments of the governments concerned, particularly over such a contentious issue as industrial policy.

Such "political" problems are also compounded by the rather different functions which provincial and federal officials carry out. For example, senior federal officials in DREE provincial offices are in some ways more autonomous than their provincial counterparts. They usually have greater authority to make expenditure commitments under a GDA. On the other hand, provincial officials are much more closely integrated into their own political process. The small size of a provincial bureaucracy also provides its officials with a wider view of policy issues, especially with respect to the relationship with federal departments and the federal government in general.

The distance from Ottawa, and the general mandate of DREE for regional development, has also meant that federal officials tend to stress longer-term structural issues in their proposals and analysis of subagreements. Provincial officials, in contrast, tend to stress short-term, or more immediate development projects such as the attraction of a single major investment to the province. In Manitoba and British Columbia, provincial officials frequently complained that they did not have the staff or time to conduct the thorough macroeconomic analysis that was available to DREE officials. They also noted that federal officials concerned themselves too deeply with long-term issues. DREE officials, on the other hand, thought that too much provincial attention was focussed on industrial promotion and new investment and not enough on long-term issues. In Manitoba, this contention was reinforced by the fact that macroeconomic analysis is conducted in the finance department and not in the Department of Economic Development and Tourism, the ministry responsible for industrial affairs, a not uncommon practice in smaller provincial governments. Thus, a considerable gap remains between the two governments' officials in terms of their approach to economic development questions – a gap derived from different roles and different analytical perspectives. This tension will always be present, even if there are few overriding disputes between the two governments on the form and nature of economic development in Manitoba.

A more fundamental issue with respect to Enterprise Manitoba concerns the degree to which such a joint exercise in industrial policy making leads to one government having undue influence over another. This issue may be of no concern to some observers who feel that the coherence of industrial policy is increased if one level of government alone predominates. But from a political perspective, the question is important. If one assumes that provincial and federal governments represent important, but different constituencies that should be represented in any policy-making exercise with respect to industry, then balancing federal and provincial influence is necessary. Certainly in the Manitoba case, and in instances where other provincial governments need federal financial assistance, subagreements tend to become a crucial source of funds and heavily influence provincial spending in the policy area covered by the agreement. For example, the Enterprise Manitoba subagreement now encompasses virtually all the provincial Economic Development Department's industrial programs.

Despite this, it is difficult to say that either government has dominated the policy formulation process with respect to the subagreement. Both governments have made significant contributions to the overall shape of the subagreement, and in all cases the resulting proposals were the product of joint decision making. If there was any inherent bias in terms of the types of programs each government wished to encourage, it was that DREE was more in favour of stressing specific growth sectors of the economy and in providing industrial infrastructure to municipalities which could not otherwise afford it. The province, in contrast, was interested in establishing technology and enterprise development centres and programs to support industrial promotion activities. Naturally, the province would have preferred a block transfer of funds for industrial development on an unconditional basis. Both Manitoba and British Columbia (where DREE also has a significant industrial development subagreement), expressed concern that DREE was influencing provincial priorities.

Whether provincial priorities have in fact been interfered with, and whether this is always a bad thing, is open to question. There is evidence on both sides. One recently published study of the effects of GDAs on the Maritime provinces indicates they caused significant changes in both the way provincial programs are structured and the political roles which provincial governments play.[46] Internal DREE reviews of the GDA system, however, suggest the reverse – provincial policies are not influenced sufficiently by the GDAs and their sub-agreements and they do not sufficiently stress national economic development objectives, particularly the promotion of selected growth centres or sectors. Recent announcements on economic policy indicate that the federal government will move away from the GDA's for exactly those reasons (see chapter X).

The Manitoba case clearly lies somewhere between these two extremes. Provincial priorities have obviously been influenced by the federal government, but much of Enterprise Manitoba's program content originates in the province. Indeed, it is doubtful if Manitoba's development policies would have their present stature without the federal financial resources made available through DREE. The result, it would seem, has been a genuine compromise based on an agreed view of the problems facing the provincial economy. And that compromise has allowed the two governments to take a joint initiative which addresses, in a coherent manner, many of the structural problems of the province's manufacturing sector.

The Enterprise Manitoba model is obviously a limited one, and does not encompass all the issues which would be associated with a major intergovernmental effort to rebuild a provincial economy. But it certainly demonstrates the potential for bilateral cooperation on industrial policy issues.

IX. Can Intergovernmental Coordination Work?

The previous case studies show that intergovernmental coordination of industrial policy issues is, to say the least, uneven and varied. However, the reason intergovernmental relations are under-developed seems to be due to an underlying conflict between the nature of the decisions required in industrial policy and the kinds of substantive collaboration possible within the intergovernmental framework.

Industrial policy decisions *should* be based on an economic rationale that determines what resources are allocated, or which industry is assisted. Ideally, the objective is to favour the most efficient producers or to encourage the concentration of scarce resources in a particular sector, or firm, where opportunities may lie in the future. This is true whether a government uses market-based criteria for industrial policy or relies on some form of national strategy in which firms or sectors are "picked" by government. Of course, this ideal of economic efficiency is never entirely realized because industrial policy is also heavily influenced by social concerns. For example, policies are frequently set in place to maintain or rationalize firms in declining industrial sectors simply to preserve jobs.

The intergovernmental process, on the other hand, is not concerned with the functional efficiency of industrial policy so much as with equitable regional distribution of industrial activity and benefits. As already mentioned, from an intergovernmental perspective, industrial policy is very often seen as a zero-sum game. Inevitably, the decision to encourage a particular type of industrial activity has implications for specific regional interest groups; in a country such as Canada, with industries unique to different regions, one area will be favoured over another. The fact that provincial governments represent relatively homogenous economic interests only tends to heighten this inherent conflict.

In the analysis of the preceding case studies of intergovernmental collaboration on industrial policy, we attempted to determine if the *manner* in which intergovernmental relations are structured has any impact on reducing the degree to which industrial policy is seen in such contentious terms. This problem was seen most clearly in the discussion of the 1978 First Ministers' Meetings on the Economy when the inability to generate meaningful action on industrial-policy issues was in large measure due to the conferences' structure which exacerbated the inherent tendency for industrial policy discussions to produce adversity. A combination of a large number of participants representing many divergent regional economic interests, and a conference agenda that attempted to deal with a variety of subjects on which the participants' views differed greatly with respect to their importance and their need for a solution, resulted in a rather limited level of cooperation. The conferences thus presented the fundamental problem facing industrial policy and intergovernmental relations: how to get all regions to agree on the tremendous variety of issues which necessarily compose an industrial strategy.

A number of attempts have been made to overcome this problem. One solution is to limit geographically the participants in the intergovernmental process in the hope that through similar, or shared, regional interests, common strategies could be worked out. As seen in the case of CMP and WPC, this solution has met with limited success. While both organizations have been able to generate cooperation at a practical level in a diverse number of areas, neither was capable of addressing broader questions relating to the economic development of their regions. This is partly attributable to the still significant differences among the provincial economies within each region, a fact which tends to limit cooperative action on industrial questions to issues concerning common external problems faced by the regional members. But such difficulties in initiating intraregional cooperative action are also due to the lack of a regional political community which would benefit from joint projects that, in the short term at least, may not distribute benefits equally in each member province. At present, each premier is responsible to his own political constituency alone and, within that framework, a premier's political future rests on his ability to maximize the home province's benefits from any federal or interprovincial economic project. Until a regional political constituency appears, it is unlikely that regional collaboration will move much beyond what we have seen so far.

Another way of overcoming the hostility inherent in intergovernmental relations to industrial-policy decisions has been to limit the subject matter of discussions to those problems which all governments have a significant interest in solving. This strategy has been tried in the case of CCREM and the forest products initiative. In these situations, the presence of a common concern, or set of issues, allowed some indepth collaboration, although the presence of other factors also seems to be required. For example, there were, in both cases, existing professional commitments which helped to depoliticize the policy environment and encourage collaboration, and an institutional setting that created patterns of cooperation encouraging the pursuit of cooperative initiatives (in CCREM's case the existence of a permanent secretariat and in the forest products case, the FIDC and the DREE subagreement system).

A further strategy has rationalized the collaborative process by limiting the number of participating governments to as few as possible in order to avoid conflicting regional interests. This strategy can be seen most clearly in the DREE-GDA system: limiting the intergovernmental process to two major actors not only allows effective action, but expands the subject matter which such cooperation can address. As mentioned before, this is an important attribute when seeking mechanisms which can effectively formulate and implement an industrial policy.

There does, however, seem to be an inexorable logic to the whole nature of intergovernmental relations and industrial policy. That logic is simply that, to be effective, relations should *either* be based on specific issues where there is some acceptance of the need for a common policy, *or* be primarily bilateral in nature in order to simplify the negotiations and limit conflict. This is not to say that other forms of collaboration (for example, federal-provincial ministerial meetings) do not have their place. Indeed, they foster the communication that allows cooperation to develop, even though they often do not permit forceful and coherent action.

Attempts to structure intergovernmental relations are doomed to fail if they do not recognize the fundamental problems of reconciling regional economic differences. Such strategies as building up formal organizational structures or increasing the level of consultation can provide little benefit on their own. These procedural or organizational innovations only bear fruit when arrangements effectively reduce economic conflicts (for example, limiting the issues under consideration or the number of governments participating). This is why establishing permanent federal-provincial economic councils or committees will have little impact on improving federal-provincial economic cooperation. It would be hard to imagine, for example, how a permanent federal-provincial body to prepare agendas and present policy proposals to the 11 governments would have improved the results of the 1978 First Ministers' Meetings on the Economy. It might have ensured a more coherent and less contentious agenda, but would it have resulted in more substantive cooperation? A more complete knowledge of other governments' policy positions may enable governments to find a compromise, but it could also convince them of the futility of compromise and encourage independent action. The major advantage of such permanent organizations is their ability to keep governments thinking about cooperation, and their ability to isolate and promote cooperative actions not foreseen by individual governments. However, they fail to create the political constituency across a nation or region which allows government to take industrial policy initiatives which, of necessity, may not always distribute benefits in a regionally equitable manner.

A dilemma remains. At the intergovernmental level, effective action is elicited only by limiting the subject matter or the number of participants – clearly an insufficient basis for a national industrial strategy because it severely limits the range of policies which can be developed. Further, intergovernmental collaboration is very dependent on one level of government recognizing a particular problem or opportunity and seeking out intergovernmental collaboration to meet the challenge. Except in unusual circumstances, such initiatives are unlikely to come from provincial governments as they increasingly pursue their own economic interests. And intergovernmental organizations do not have the necessary scope or resources to tackle the problem of industrial policy on a broad front.

This opens up the question of what is the appropriate role for the federal government in industrial policy? Given the birth of provincial strategies and the mixed record of intergovernmental collaboration, to what extent should Ottawa seek independent action as a counterweight to provincial industrial strategies? To what extent should it play a role in promoting intergovernmental collaboration? It is to these questions that we now turn.

Part Four

Industrial Policy and the Federal Government

X. The Federal Government and Industrial Policy: Facing New Realities

Serious problems confront the implementors of a national industrial strategy. The provinces are now able, indeed anxious, to implement their own local strategies and naturally, these initiatives call the federal government's traditionally dominant role into question. Further, as we have seen, the usual mechanisms for encouraging interprovincial and federal-provincial cooperation have significant limitations. At a time when foreign governments are moving forcefully in industrial policy, Ottawa's legitimacy in the economic sphere is increasingly being questioned. At the *same* time, the instruments it has relied on primarily for economic management – Keynesian demand management, and recently, monetarism – are shopworn and discredited because of their failure to cope with the stagflation of the 1970s.

The Past Role

It is important to remember that the federal government has not always been seen as a weak or indecisive economic actor. Beginning with the National Policy in 1879, the federal government has played a key role in shaping the country's economic development. Indeed, many historians have claimed that Confederation was designed, in part, to unify the economies of British North America.[1] The federal government was given all the functions regarded as necessary for the development of industry and commerce, including responsibility to build a national railway.

147

Because of the physical structure of the country and its staples economy, government has always played a relatively large role in providing infrastructure. Originally, it was canals and railways; now it is telecommunications and airlines. However, new pressures have expanded the federal role in economic management. Some of these have been experienced by most western governments, particularly employment maintenance through Keynesian demand management. Others were unique to Canada. The weakness of our secondary manufacturing has, on occasion, encouraged the federal government to assume a more vigorous industrial-policy role than that taken in other developed countries. That role, for example, was bolstered by the impact of the two world wars and the reconstruction periods that followed.[2]

During World War II in particular, Ottawa's role in managing the country's economy was unsurpassed. Under the authority of the War Measures Act and the Munitions and Supply Act, the federal government assumed total control of the economy in 1940, including many functions normally exercised by provincial governments. The provinces surrendered their taxation powers to the federal government, for example, in return for support grants. In the industrial sector, the Munitions and Supply Act allowed the minister of Munitions and Supply to "compel manufacturers and construction contractors to do whatever the exigencies of war demanded, for such prices and on such terms and conditions as the Minister might consider to be fair and reasonable."[3] Through the Department of Munitions and Supply, a series of mechanisms, such as production boards, instituted to supervise the manufacture of war supplies, were established to facilitate the exercise of the minister's power. Many of these mechanisms were headed by a group of senior, private-sector executives (the "dollar a year" men) recruited by C.D. Howe.

It was testimony to Canada's underdeveloped industrial system that the government had to create a total of 28 Crown corporations to undertake activities in virtually every aspect of war production. The government also monitored war profits through the control section of the Department of Munitions and Supply and ensured that all the economy's resources were devoted to the war effort. Measures instituted by the federal government included export and import controls, commodity price fixing and, of course, rationing.

The cost was great: by the war's end the federal government had spent $800 million on industrial expansion, 75 per cent of that in the Crown corporation sector[4]; and government procurement on war supplies amounted to something in the order of $11 000 million. But, the effects on the economy were remarkable; by 1945 Canada was the fourth largest manufacturing country in the world.[5] Employment had risen by several orders of magnitude in many industries (employment in the aircraft industry, for example, increased 30 times), and exports jumped dramatically.[6]

Wartime industrial expansion was premised, of course, on exceptional circumstances not to prevail in the postwar period. Nevertheless, the wartime experience did provide the country with an augmented industrial base, particularly in many aspects of advanced manufacturing, and furnished the federal government with the necessary experience to play a significant role in industrial development after 1945.

Conversion to a peacetime economy also required a strong federal presence both to manage the physical transition and to provide the fiscal policies conducive to high growth and full employment. In addition, the outbreak of the Korean War and the general expansion of defence expenditure resulting from east-west tensions ensured a strong federal role in the first half of the 1950s. However, it was the content of federal industrial policy in the first postwar decade that later led to difficulties.

The government's postwar approach to industrial development was based on a rapid growth of the country's industrial base through tax incentives (for example, double depreciation) and, expansionary fiscal policy to encourage high demand and a rapid increase in capital investment. The idea was to reduce direct intervention and replace it with macroeconomic fiscal and monetary policy. In addition, traditional policies such as tariffs were used to protect expansion in secondary manufacturing, and on one occasion, import controls were used to ensure that such expansion was accomplished without draining exchange reserves. These policies were accompanied by a massive sale of federal war production assets (for example, factories, machine tools, etc.), frequently to foreign subsidiaries. In fact, these assets formed the backbone of such new industries as aircraft manufacture and electronics.[7]

The emphasis on tariff-protected domestic manufacturing was parallelled by an attempt to encourage resource exports and improve the country's sagging current account position. This was accomplished through investment tax credits and a trade policy which sought, through GATT negotiations, to open up foreign markets for resource products. These initiatives also meshed well with US policy during the 1950s which identified Canada as a primary, and secure, source of strategic resources.[8]

The approach was reminiscent of the National Policy:[9] the country's resources were to be its primary source of export earnings and domestic employment was maintained by manufacturing for import substitution. However, given the overwhelming strength of the US economy, it is hardly surprising that such policies also dramatically increased direct US investment in Canada's manufacturing and resource sectors.[10] High tariffs on imported consumer goods, lower tariffs on capital equipment, extremely attractive fiscal incentives to capital investment and administrative programs designed to encourage foreign investment all worked to this end.

Unfortunately, this approach to industrial development became more and more tenuous by the 1960s because of changes in the structure of the Canadian economy and the international economic system. Industrialization by branch plants and import substitution had become increasingly impractical because the relatively closed, trading environment of the early 1950s had given way to a more open, international economic system. The inability of many branch plants to exploit foreign markets while remaining heavily dependent on imported components led to increasing import penetration in the manufacturing sector.[11] But the approach had other problems. Its emphasis on branch-plant industrialization reinforced regional antagonisms by forcing western Canada and the Atlantic provinces to purchase expensive tariff-protected manufactured goods rather than cheaper foreign-produced ones. While all Canadians had to pay higher prices, it seemed, once again, that central Canada was being helped at the regions' expense. Perhaps even more important for the long-term structure of the economy (and its tendency to promote regional differences), was that the massive inflow of foreign, direct investment in manufacturing increased the concentration of secondary industry in Ontario and Quebec. As subsequent studies have shown, branch plants are more likely to be located in central Canada than domestically owned manufacturing plants, thus adding to the problem of diversifying industrial development and generating employment outside central Canada.[12]

Even the emphasis on resource development, which did benefit western Canada, again helped central Canada because many of these developments, particularly those which supplied the American market, were located in the central provinces (for example, aluminum and iron ore in Quebec, uranium and nonferrous minerals in Ontario). Thus, while the international political and economic circumstances of the 1940s and 1950s encouraged a prominent federal role in industrial development, the approach that emerged not only weakened the economy, but was also regionally disruptive.

The Present Dilemma

More recent changes in Canada's economic and political structure have undermined the federal government's role in industrial policy. The increasing bureaucratic and political competence of provincial governments, along with the growing importance of social issues during the 1960s, increased the provinces' importance in policy questions. In the 1970s, a burst of regional self-awareness over resource questions in the west and economic dependency in the Atlantic provinces shifted public attention away from national policy issues, and encouraged a more regional perspective, particularly on questions of economic development. As well, due to the nature of the electoral system, the federal governments of the 1970s did not effectively represent regional interests; this failure called into question the political legitimacy of the federal government when acting on economic issues characterized by significant regional differences of interest. Finally, Ottawa's declining share of total government expenditures in the 1970s demonstrated, in rather stark terms, that it was playing a less central role in the Canadian political scene. By the end of the decade, therefore, the federal government was suffering from an identity and legitimacy crisis.

Concern about decreased financial, political and constitutional power has been reflected in recent attempts by the federal government to free itself from some funding commitments to the provinces in the social-policy area. The objective here is to reduce the federal deficit and increase the government's direct, and discretionary expenditure on economic development including secondary industry.[13] A similar trend can be seen in Ottawa's move to provide itself with more defined economic powers under the Constitution.

But, just how serious is this decline of federal power in economic policy making? To answer this question it is necessary to look at several aspects of the federal role in industrial policy: the discretionary financial resources it can devote to industrial development; the question of its present constitutional authority on matters relating to the management of the economy; the political problems it faces in industrial policy; its existing approach to the development and implementation of industrial policy; and, finally, its capacity to deal with federal-provincial relations on industrial-policy questions.

Financial Resources

The government's ability to influence corporate decision making through taxation and expenditure policies has long been a central element of industrial policy. Traditionally, the federal government has dominated the taxation system in Canada, particularly during the postwar period. Throughout the 1960s and 1970s, it transferred tax "points" to the provinces in lieu of direct grants to assist with the costs of social programs which were established, in part, through federal initiatives (for example, medicare and postsecondary education). Most of these transfers have been on personal income tax, but corporate income tax points have been transferred as well.[14] In consequence, the proportion of total government revenue collected by Ottawa declined to a low of 45 per cent in 1978 from about 58 per cent in 1958.[15]

Despite this decline, the federal government still controls the taxation system because of its ability to define the corporate-tax base upon which both itself and the provinces collect taxes. By defining the tax base, Ottawa has been able to influence fiscal policy beyond the level of the corporate tax it levied (for example, by determining what corporate expenditures qualify as tax deductions). However, this ability has been seriously undermined in recent years. Ontario, Quebec and Alberta have established corporate-tax collection systems in which each province determines the tax base for its share of the corporate tax independently of the federal government. Apart from complicating the administration of tax collection, this system weakens the federal government's control and reduces the influence it can exert on corporate behaviour through the tax system.

While these defections from the federal tax system are important, it is difficult to know if they have seriously weakened the federal government's taxation power. In the first place, corporate tax is declining in importance as a revenue source for all governments. And in the future, it may be of decreasing importance to the implementation of industrial policy because of the difficulty involved in effectively targeting tax-based incentives to specific firms of possible interest to policy makers. As well, tax incentives offer less control,

Figure X.1 – Federal and Provincial Government Spending on Trade and Industry, 1956–1980 in 1971 dollars, 3-year Rolling Average

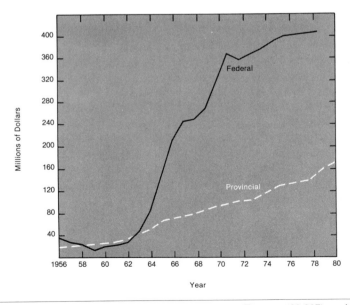

Source: Statistics Canada, *Provincial Government Finance* (68-207) various issues, *Federal Government Finance* (68-211) various issues.

and/or influence, over the specific form of corporate activity being encouraged. In addition, despite the establishment of separate provincial corporate tax systems, to date the manner in which the tax is levied has not varied significantly from the federal system.

In the area of direct expenditure on industrial development, including transfers (that is, grants) to industry, the federal government still retains the undisputed lead. It is very difficult to make comparisons between federal and provincial expenditures on industrial development because of differences in reporting conventions. Nevertheless, the available data seems to indicate that the federal government spends, on the average, about three times more on trade and industry than the 10 provinces combined (see Figure X.1). For example, in 1979-80, federal expenditure on trade and industry amounted to $865 million compared to a provincial total of $333 million.[16] In addition, a significant proportion of federal expenditure in this area has gone to the provinces on a transfer basis. In 1970-71, of $360 million of federal expenditure on trade and industry, about $98 million was transferred to the provinces; by 1977-78 this had grown to about $300 million out of a total federal expenditure of $767 million.[17] Such figures indicate the degree to which provincial spending on trade and industry itself depends on federal funding. Even removing the sums transferred to the provinces, federal industrial expenditures are still over twice as large as the provincial total. It is important to note as well that, at all levels of government, the percentage of expenditure devoted to industrial development rose during the 1970s, although in all cases it remained a small element of direct government expenditure.

Table X.1 – Federal and Provincial Expenditures on R&D, 1981

Funding Sector	Performing Sector					
	Federal Govt.	Prov. Govt.	Industry	University	Other	Total
Federal						
($ million)	827	2	150	274	1	1254
%	66	–	12	22	–	100
Provincial						
($ million)	—	114	35	60	8	217
%	—	52	16	28	4	100

Source: Statistics Canada, *Annual Review of Science Statistics 1981*, Cat. No. 13-212, May 1982, p. 7.

In the important area of support for R&D, the federal government is also dominant. As can be seen in Table X.1, overall expenditure by the provinces on R&D is less than a fifth of Ottawa's. Further, their support for private sector R&D is also considerably less in absolute terms. Because provincial expenditure is spread over 10 governments rather than one, it tends to be more diffuse in its impact. And when it comes to large, strategically important R&D projects, virtually no provincial government (with the possible exception of Alberta and its Heritage Fund) can match Ottawa's resources. In addition, recent commitments by the federal cabinet to increase the share of government expenditure on economic development indicate that the federal government's role in direct R&D assistance to industry is likely to increase.

One defect of the federal role, however, has been its tendency to reinforce the regional concentration of industrial activity (especially manufacturing) in central Canada. A large proportion of federal industrial assistance (exclusive of regional development assistance funded by DREE) is provided mainly on a passive basis – that is, the government relies on firms coming forward with proposals or requests for assistance. It should come as no surprise, therefore, to see that during the period 1975-1980, 72 to 83 per cent of IT&C's program expenditure on trade and industry went to Ontario and Quebec.[18] In R&D funding, the department's science-related expenditures were even more heavily concentrated in central Canada – Ontario and Quebec accounting for 87 per cent of total expenditure in 1978-79.[19] To some extent, DREE broke this pattern, especially in the Atlantic region; but the statistics point up the traditional problem of federal industrial policy. When the federal government attempts to channel funds to the existing industrial structure, regional inequities emerge that undermine the legitimacy of federal policy. It was not for lack of provocation that the regions often referred to IT&C and its industrial policies as "central Canada's DREE."

Constitutional Powers
The increasing challenge to federal constitutional authority on economic matters seems, at least on the surface, to be a far more serious problem. Concern over this issue has focussed almost entirely on the federal government's inability to prevent the provinces from hindering the operation of a functioning common market in Canada. This has led, as well, to an examination of provincial economic practices that create barriers to the movement of goods, services and people in Canada, as discussed in chapter V. However, the present limitations to the federal government's economic powers are due less to resurgent provincial economic protectionism than to a history of successive judicial decisions limiting or circumscribing the federal government's economic role.

The original BNA Act gave the federal government virtually all the powers considered important in economic management (for example, control over money and banking, tariffs, etc.) as well as a general responsibility to manage trade and commerce. The provinces, by contrast, were left with such limited powers as jurisdiction over property and civil rights, the ownership and mangagement of provincial lands and a number of social functions such as education. Since Confederation, however, a series of court interpretations have limited federal economic powers while giving a much broader interpretation to the provinces' "property and civil rights' " power, extending it to encompass the regulation of much business activity, including labour relations. The courts interpreted even the federal trade and commerce power, intended to give Ottawa a supervisory economic role, as applying only to interprovincial and international trade and commerce, rather than to activity within a single province. This has particular significance because many provincial jurisdictions are so physically large that much economic activity can be considered intraprovincial. Indeed, Ottawa may be correct in claiming that of all the federal governments in developed countries, Canada's probably has the least comprehensive economic powers. In most other federations, the central government has been given, either constitutionally or as a result of judicial interpretation, overall responsibility for trade and commerce.[20]

Given increasing regional tensions, a case may be made for expanding, or strengthening federal economic powers. However, as we have seen, most economic reform proposals have been directed at the federal government's ability to ensure a common market rather than widening the *scope* of its economic powers. Thus, federal proposals tabled in the summer of 1980 at the Continuing Committee of Ministers on the Constitution aimed to strengthen Section 121 of the Constitution Act which prohibits restrictions on the free movement of goods and persons by the provinces.[21] Rather than expand its power over trade and commerce, the federal government chose the ostensibly less contentious position of simply prohibiting the provinces from erecting economic barriers. And even this proposal met with considerable provincial opposition. This is hardly surprising, given that a simple reinforcement of the Canadian common market is unlikely to be attractive to any province other than Ontario, and possibly Quebec, because it limits a provincial government's ability to control the negative effects of the common market on the provincial economy.

If preservation of the common market creates division, the only strategy left to the federal government is to expand, or strengthen, its own powers. Then, two questions arise: Are such initiatives necessary? Or, are existing federal powers adequate to implement an industrial strategy?

These are very difficult questions. As has been pointed out, many important economic functions, such as the regulation of business activity and labour relations, are predominantly provincial. In addition, the growing importance of resource developments to the Canadian economy, especially in the energy sector, and the fact that the provinces in the main own and are responsible for supervising the development of those resources, has considerably increased the importance of the provincial economic jurisdictions. Despite these changes, however, the federal government still retains a wide variety of economic powers. Even in the energy sector, it was able to go ahead with the NEP, thanks to its control of interprovincial and export trade, corporate income tax and its ownership of a major oil company.

In fact, in spite of its limitations in relation to the provinces, the federal government's economic powers are still formidable. They include: the regulation of federally incorporated businesses; predominant control of the tax system; control of international and interprovincial trade and commerce; management of the money supply; credit and banking; weights and measures; and absolute jurisdiction over certain industrial activities as a result of its ability to declare that they are for "the general advantage of Canada" or that they are required for it to carry out its responsibility for "Peace, Order and Good Government" under the Constitution Act. These activities have included canals, atomic energy, aeronautics, railways, broadcasting and the wheat trade. In addition, in those industries or businesses under federal jurisdiction, many of the provinces' traditional areas of responsibility (for example, labour relations) are governed by federal legislation. Perhaps most important over the past few years, are Supreme Court rulings on the constitutionality of federal legislation on economic affairs which have extended (although in a tenuous fashion) the federal government's jurisdiction by expanding the interpretation of the federal "trade and commerce" power and allowing the use of the federal emergency power in peacetime for economic purposes (for example, wage and price controls).[22]

The federal government also has at its disposal another useful mechanism which can extend the range of its policy instruments, namely to use a constitutionally entrenched economic or regulatory power to achieve an industrial-policy objective in an indirect manner. For example, the ability to regulate interprovincial trade, and hence to regulate the construction of the northern pipeline, has allowed the federal government to lay down Canadian content requirements covering the procurement operations of the companies building the Alaska Highway gas pipeline. This enabled the federal government to create a new market for a growing number of Canadian firms supplying the international oil and gas industry and to provide those firms with a significant domestic market in which they could build an export capability.

However, such formal legislative powers, which usually involve some right to regulate an industry, are only part of the tool kit a gov-

156

ernment requires to implement an industrial policy. Other mechanisms at the federal government's disposal can be used to alter industrial behaviour and structure. Much industrial policy, in fact, relies on the power of the purse which, in turn, affects the federal government's ability to:

- offer financial incentives to encourage certain forms of corporate behaviour;
- provide certain services or infrastructure which can encourage selective forms of industrial activity;
- purchase or create an industrial enterprise to serve some public purpose;
- place conditions on the procurement of public goods to elicit favourable responses on the part of firms; or
- provide tax exemptions for certain forms of industrial activity (that is, "tax expenditure").

Indeed, a good deal of the federal government's strengths in the industrial-policy field can be attributed to its ability to spend money for specific industrial purposes. Much of the federal government's role in manpower policy relies on its ability to finance manpower training programs and employment referral centres. Similarly, while the federal government has no constitutional authority to control the emerging microelectronics industry, federal funding for such firms and the provision of federally developed technology in the form of Telidon is encouraging the emergence of a new and independent industrial capability in Canada. In fact, most of the federal government's policies with respect to regional industrial location, R&D, improving productivity and expansion of exports rely on programs providing tax incentives, cash grants or loans to attain their ends and not on any specific regulatory authority granted in the Constitution.

Perhaps the most interesting use of federal expenditure powers to achieve industrial objectives has been the establishment of commercial Crown corporations. The most notable recent example was Petro-Canada, but the concept is not limited to energy. The federal government has invested in civil airframe manufacturers (deHavilland and Canadair) to ensure that promising aircraft designs are marketed. These nationalized firms have also guaranteed a continuing market for high-technology aerospace component suppliers. Telesat Canada, a joint public-private sector corporation was designed to establish a domestic satellite telecommunications facility in Canada. Through the corporation, and government R&D assistance to selected firms, our country now has a viable space communications capability.

Apart from their inherent attractiveness as industrial-policy instruments (they are able to act directly and nonbureaucratically in the market place to achieve goals that would be impossible either through regulation or direct financial assistance), Crown corporations have an added advantage. Because they can work in provincial areas when a province needs and wants assistance, they are a useful intermediary for federal-provincial collaboration. Although the only case of such intermediation to date is the creation of DEVCO in the mid-1960s (set up to help restructure the Cape Breton economy following coal mine closures),[23] it is conceivable that the federal government could use Crown corporations to achieve industrial-policy goals in traditional areas of provincial jurisdiction. Also, in situations in which the provinces may be unable to agree upon joint interprovincial action and where federal regulatory control may not be suitable, Crown corporations could intervene. For example, if the Maritime provinces were unable to cooperate on the development of technology to exploit offshore resources, Ottawa could create a federal oceans development corporation. Clearly, such an initiative would only be successful if it were created before an interprovincial conflict arose; but it could serve as a useful device, focussing national resources on a specific technology development program that could not be duplicated by simply establishing a grant program to support marine industrial research or by regulating the industry. It could even be used to encourage the provinces to pool their resources.

The point is that the federal government's capability to implement industrial policy really depends on its ability both to spend or invest creatively to influence the private sector, and to utilize its existing jurisdiction imaginatively. Admittedly, the current expenditure constraints suffered by the federal government limit its freedom and may force it to meet its industrial policy objectives through regulation. Because of the federal government's jurisdictional weaknesses in some areas relating to industry, this situation may cause future difficulties. However, the shift of federal spending priorities to industrial development and initiatives such as the NEP indicate that more limited financial resources need not be a significant barrier to innovative, federal industrial initiatives. What is needed is a political commitment to a strong industrial leadership role, and some coherent priorities concerning the objectives and content of a federal industrial policy.

If jurisdictional issues are not a substantial barrier, and if limited financial resources can be overcome, why isn't Ottawa a strong presence in the industrial-policy arena? At present, it would seem two significant barriers exist. The first is the federal political commitment, or lack of it, to address both the regional distribution and the interventionist implications of a strong, industrial-policy role. The second is Ottawa's institutional weakness which hinders its ability to develop and implement an industrial strategy.

Political Barriers

In many respects, Ottawa's political problems in developing an industrial strategy are intractable and multidimensional. As discussed a number of times already in this study, the federal government's regional legitimacy when acting on industrial-policy issues is in question. Briefly, in our highly regionalized economy, the federal government has difficulty when addressing specific aspects of industrial strategy, such as not being seen as favouring one section of the country over another – particularly when the manufacturing sector is involved. The inherent potential for conflict because of regionally specific economic interests is aggravated by the central government's need to be seen by the electorate as acting in the long-term interests of the country as a whole. The difficulty here is that our electoral system, and patterns of regional support for particular political parties, have prevented significant regions from participating in the federal government and its institutions.[24] The result has been a widespread bitterness towards the federal system, by those in the regions (especially western Canada) who feel that not only are they denied a place in government, but that the federal system is primarily designed to serve the interests of central Canada. Obviously, these problems will not be overcome without a significant change in the representational character of federal institutions. Given the long struggle to patriate the Constitution, it is unlikely that any such change will come either quickly or easily. Until such changes do occur, improving the regional legitimacy of the federal government will be an uphill battle.

The picture is not all black, however. While regional loyalties and dissatisfactions make the construction of a national consensus on industrial policy difficult, there is also recent evidence that Canadians are rather ambivalent about their regional and national identities. In a lengthy and detailed study of the growth of "provincialism," David Elkins and Richard Simeon concluded that, despite growing loyalties to provincial governments, similarities were increasing in both the policy preferences of provincial constituents and the problems they faced. Such developments may lead to increased political conflicts, but they may also be a force for the creation of a new national consensus on issues. The authors therefore caution:

"... we have seen that loyalties to region and country (not to mention, city, family or profession) are not necessarily incompatible. Canadians do have multiple loyalties – and this is one of the forces that sustain a federal system. Strong ties to a provincial government do not preclude support for a strong federal government. For many, if not most Canadians, a strong federal Canada *entails* or presumes a strong province, and vice versa.

This suggests the inadequacy of two extreme positions: on one hand that regionalism or provincialism is somehow the "problem" whose solution requires that it must be replaced by an overarching Canadian loyalty; and on the other hand, that we should fundamentally shift power to the provinces."[25]

Canadians, we might conclude, are not innately hostile towards a federal government, provided that government is able to demonstrate its regional sensitivity.

The more elusive political problems of federal industrial strategy relate, as Richard French has noted, to two problems: first, the political risks for a government when it proclaims goals for which it can be held accountable; and second, an ingrained hostility in the upper reaches of the federal bureaucracy to the concept of industrial strategy. French argues that most political systems are averse to risk. Faced with a policy that has uncertain prospects, but which creates high public expectations, politicians will lose their resolve without significant outside support or pressure. The shrinking away from commitments to industrial strategy by the federal government in the early 1970s make this clear.[26] According to French, this withdrawal has been compounded by a hostility to the more positive, or dirigiste, proposals for industrial strategy centred in the Department of Finance and in senior levels of the IT&C.[27]

Opposition was partly ideological and partly policy oriented; in the case of the Finance Department, it was an objection to the interventionist nature of industrial-strategy proposals which originated in the PCO in the early 1970s. The Finance Department, in keeping with its role as the chief exponent, until recently, of Keynesian economic orthodoxy, preferred a mainly tax-based system which relied on the market and was largely neutral in its effects on individual firms. IT&C, on the other hand, opposed interventionism because the PCO's emphasis on a coherent and rational selection of priority sectors and firms ran against its traditional policy-making approach which was largely incrementalist and designed to support industry evenly on a sectoral basis. This position also largely supported the status quo in terms of both the location of industry and the process of industrial adjustment.

The result of the opposition was an approach to industrial policy that was, in French's view, incrementalist, centralist and continentalist. Incrementalist in its reluctance to pick particular sectors or firms for special attention, centralist in its status quo approach to industrial location which inevitably favoured the further concentration of industry in central Canada, and continentalist in its continued reliance on primary markets which de facto accepted Canada's heavy dependence on US trade and investment.[28]

Conflicting Approaches to Industrial Policy

Ideological and political problems at the federal level were also reflected in the development of institutions for industrial policy making. During the late 1960s and early 1970s the policy-making process for economic and industrial issues gradually spread out from Finance and IT&C to a whole series of agencies including DREE, Employment and Immigration Canada (EIC), Ministry of State for Science and Technology (MOSST), the Department of Indian Affairs and Northern Development (DIAND), and EMR.[29] Not only did the policy-making process become more fragmented, but also more diverse as many of these departments held very different views about the objectives of industrial policy and the appropriate instruments for implementing such policies. The most notable examples of conflicting approaches were those of IT&C and DREE. IT&C has favoured support for industries showing the best commercial performance, whereas DREE has preferred industrial policies that seek to help modernize and expand industries (often weaker ones) in developing regions, or to attract new investment into such regions.

These conflicts were not only a product of interdepartmental differences; IT&C itself encapsulated a number of divergent industrial interests, as it was the result of a merger in the late 1960s of the Department of Trade and Commerce and the Department of Industry. The former, was a senior member of the bureaucratic establishment and the latter, a new department which had emerged from the institutional innovation of the mid-1960s.[30] Not surprisingly, these two departments had very different views on the content of industrial policy; Trade and Commerce saw trade relations, export promotion and access to the international trading system as the cornerstones of industrial policy; the Department of Industry, on the other hand, was more directly concerned with the health of domestic industry generally and with the fate of the individual industrial sectors in particular. As Richard French has stated:

> "The formation of Industry, Trade and Commerce, brought together in a single entity instruments for structural intervention informed by an intellectual position which ultimately led to technological sovereignty, and instruments for trade promotion premised on assumptions largely consistent with those for free trade."[31]

In the late 1970s, partly as a result of the need to cope with the problems of managing wage and price controls and the readjustment period following the removal of controls, the government attempted to increase industrial coordination in the federal system. After experimenting with a number of informal civil service committees,[32] the government created BEDM in November 1978 to act as a central coordinating mechanism for economic policy. With two changes of government in the following three years, BEDM evolved into a cabinet committee on economic development serviced by a secretariat known as the Ministry of State for Economic Development (MSED).

Unfortunately, the role of coordinator assigned to both BEDM and MSED[33] did not lead, in and of itself, to any profound elaboration of industrial strategy. MSED's role was largely that of a mini-Treasury Board for the economic development expenditure envelope and its policy capacity was very limited. Considering its status as a small, new ministry, MSED's senior management chose a role which focussed on harmonizing departmental initiatives in the economic development area. The ministry reacted to initiatives from senior departments rather than developing its own economic and industrial policy.[34] Existing as a mechanism to lessen the divergent approaches of the various economic policy departments, MSED had not taken on a positive role with respect to developing overall economic strategies.

Regional Awareness and Federal-Provincial Relations
Perhaps just as important as the weaknesses of the federal apparatus was the limited integration of regional issues into federal-industrial policy making, and the low-key nature of federal-provincial relations management. With the exception of DREE, none of the federal economic departments had significant regional input into their policy making.

With its regional development mandate and its obvious need to be in contact with the provinces, DREE had a highly decentralized policy-development mechanism. As observed in the DREE-Manitoba case study in chapter VIII, program proposals were often developed between the provincial office of DREE and provincial economic or industrial development departments. Further, much of the department's regional economic analysis and monitoring was conducted at four regional headquarters, each headed by an assistant deputy minister. The national headquarters in Ottawa was mainly concerned with assuring the coherence of regional programs, and with processing and assessing the subagreement program proposals and the larger requests for regional, industrial-development grants. Consequently, national headquarters had only about 40 per cent of the department's staff, and programs funded under the GDAs (that is, programs which involved a substantial level of consultation between DREE and the individual provincial governments) consumed the largest part of the department's program expenditures.[35]

IT&C, on the other hand, had a highly centralized structure even though it was the main industrial development agency. Until recently, the department did not even have an adviser on federal-provincial relations and virtually all of its policy development work was done in Ottawa. The department did have a network of provincial offices; however, these offices, performing a program delivery and promotional function, had little input into the policy-making process. IT&C attempted in its most recent major program initiative, the Enterprise Development Program (EDP), to increase the input from provincial government departments. Provincial officials were regularly consulted on funding applications and provincial departments cooperated with IT&C in making the program known in the local business community.[36] EDP also had a system of provincial boards, the members of which included local businesspeople and provincial officials (as observers), to assess applicants up to a specified limit of loan and grant assistance. However, apart from the informal day-to-day contacts of IT&C and provincial officials, and a limited number of federal-provincial working parties, the EDP represented the department's most significant attempt to regionalize its policy development and implementation. It was not a strong record.

It would, however, be wrong to blame IT&C for deliberately seeking to ignore provincial input. Unlike some federal departments that share jurisdiction with the provinces (for example, Agriculture and Labour) or have close relations with the provinces as an operational necessity (for example, DREE), IT&C had no pressing need to cooperate with the provinces. The department's traditional organization along industry branch lines did not encourage a regional or provincial approach to industrial policy questions. In some ways, this relative isolation from the provinces was useful to the federal government. It provided an opportunity to work out a totally independent federal position on industrial development and obviated the problem, which the DREE policy-making process raised, of the diminished control that the federal government perceives it has over policy development when a provincial government is intimately involved in a project. However, as was made clear earlier, the growing importance of the provinces in the industrial-policy field meant that federal approaches dealing with specific sectors were more likely to result in program conflicts with the provinces. Such a situation can lead to serious political resentments as one province, or many, feel that their regional interests are not being reflected in federal industrial policy.

This problem was compounded by the fact that, until recently, Ottawa had no central agency either to coordinate the planning of industrial policy *or* to determine its federal-provincial priorities in this area. Despite the establishment of MSED, there was still no central, policy agency to deal with *industrial strategy* as such. A parallel problem existed in federal-provincial relations. The federal apparatus which dealt with federal-provincial relations was highly decentralized compared with provincial intergovernmental affairs' administrations. Some federal departments have quite elaborate federal-provincial relations' mechanisms, but many do not. At present, most federal departments have taken the fashionable route of

establishing federal-provincial relations divisions to inform departmental policy makers of provincial policy positions and the likely response to departmental initiatives. In many cases, the influence of
these sections is quite limited, particularly in departments where
technical or professional considerations weigh heavily in policy formulation or where jurisdictional authority and tradition have dic-
tated a unilateral federal approach.

Further, Ottawa's ability to coordinate each department's relations with the provinces was very limited. Unlike many provinces,
the federal government does not really have a central intergovernmental affairs agency. The Federal-Provincial Relations Office
(FPRO), which is now effectively the secretariat to the prime minister
on federal-provincial affairs and the Constitution, does have a coordinating role. It ensures that the departments take federal-
provincial relations considerations into account in the formulation
of policy papers for cabinet; it also helps to arrange first ministers'
meetings and attempts to act as an information clearing house on intergovernmental activities in a number of key areas of federal government policy. However, on a day-to-day basis, the departments are
really free to act on their own. For example, FPRO does not have the
same control over intergovernmental negotiations, or even agreements undertaken by departments, that its counterparts in Alberta
and Quebec do.

A New Federal Initiative

Not long after the November 1981 budget, the federal government
acted on the above concerns. In January 1982, the prime minister
announced a major change in the federal government's departmental organization for economic and regional development.[37] In an attempt to dramatically increase attention to regional development
questions, IT&C and DREE were combined into a new Department of
Regional Industrial Expansion (DRIE) (see Figure X.2). Trade promotion and trade policy were removed from IT&C and placed within a
newly expanded Department of External Affairs. Finally, in keeping
with the renewed emphasis on policy coordination, MSED was re-
named and expanded into a Ministry of State for Economic and Regional Development (MSERD) with a network of provincial offices each
headed by a federal economic development coordinator.[38] The ministry would also have a special responsibility for managing large resource or industrial development projects.

The impetus for this change arose, it would seem, from a widespread concern within the federal government that the public perception in the regions of its economic policies was poor. Federal
policy makers also felt that in areas of regional collaboration (for example, in DREE's GDA's), too much credit for federal funding and

Figure X.2 – Structure of Department of Regional Industrial Expansion (DRIE), 1982

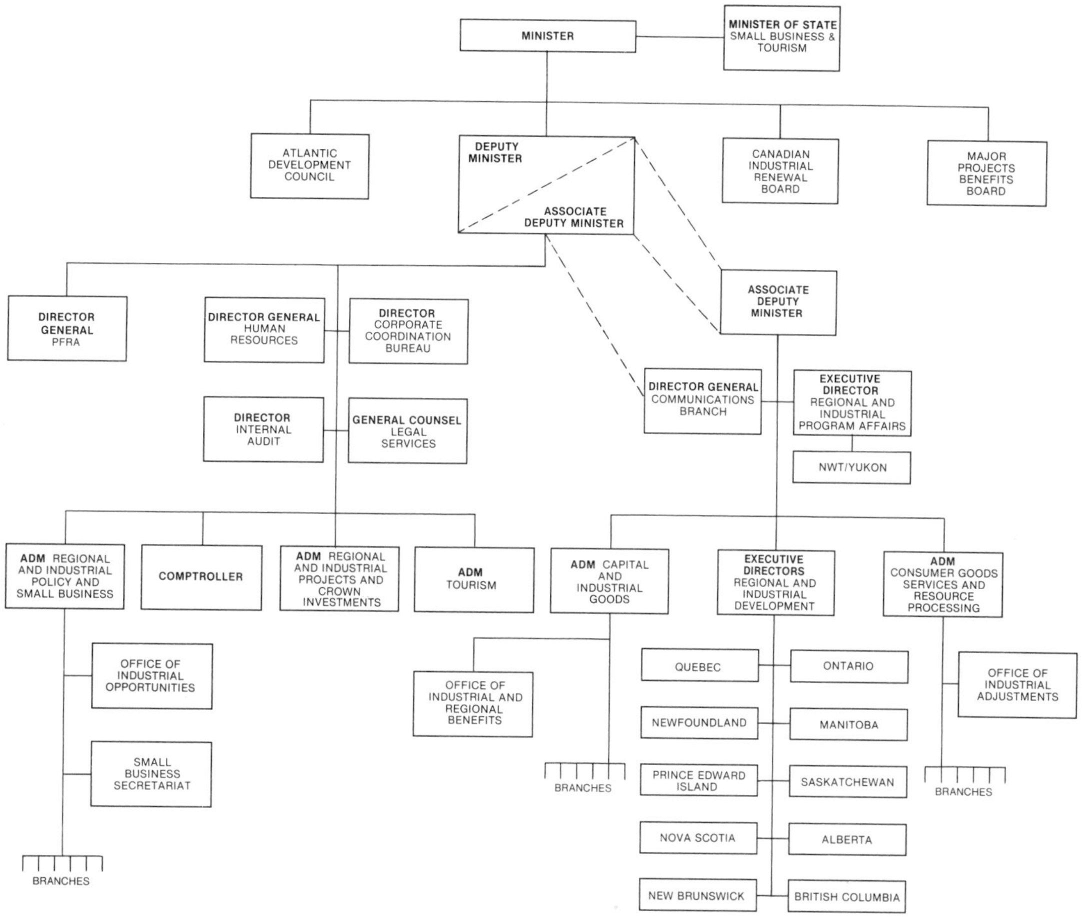

Source : Department of Regional Industrial Expansion, 1982.

initiatives went to provincial governments. The reorganization attempted not only to make industrial policy more regionally sensitive, but also to create a direct link between regional economic actors and federal departments.

The changes also reflected federal dissatisfaction with DREE's ability to impact significantly on regional disparities. In the economic development white paper[39] released with the November 1981 budget, and the January 1982 reorganization, the federal government indicated that regional development could now be contained more effectively in a general drive for economic development based on resource exploitation outside central Canada. There was less need, therefore, for a specific regional development department.[40] In future, all federal departments would be required to organize both their policy development and program delivery functions to reflect the government's new emphasis on regional development.

It is too early to know how the reorganization will fulfill the government's stated objectives, let alone solve the broader federal policy problems. There are already indications that the resource-based economic development policy contained in the November 1981 budget is not working. This is partly due to the recession and high interest rates making large-scale, capital-intensive projects such as Alsands too expensive and risky, and partly because of uncertainties about the long-term trend in resource prices. These problems, of course, question the validity of federal strategy assumptions, namely, that in the 1980s, resource products will increase in value relative to manufactured goods and provide Canada with a comparative advantage internationally.

However, other concerns remain about the logic of the reorganization. The first, centres on the manner in which responsibility for industrial policy has been divided among the various departments. There has always been some uncertainty within the federal government over the relationship between trade and industrial policy. By placing these two important aspects of economic policy in two very different departments, conflict seems certain. DRIE is now concerned almost entirely with regional, resource and industrial development - in short, with internal domestic industrial policies. On the other hand, External Affairs, primarily responsible for the smooth functioning of Canada's international relations, will be mainly interested in the implications of trade policy on those relations. With these two very different perspectives, there are bound to be continuing differences. In fact, completely independent and mutually exclusive policies may evolve.

There is also some confusion about how DRIE will effectively combine its regional and industrial development roles. Frequently, the process of encouraging certain types of industrial activity is seriously weakened by a parallel effort to ensure a balanced regional distribution of that activity – this dual effort leads to difficult and potentially impossible policy trade-offs. In its reorganization, the department has attempted to give greater priority to regional development by increasing the number of its regional offices and allowing the regions to administer programs. It also hopes to increase the involvement of the regional offices in the policy-making process. However, in large measure, IT&C's industrial sector branch organizational structure has been maintained as well as its emphasis on the functional, as distinct from the regional, dimension of industrial policy (see p. 165, Figure X.2). It is far from clear how the two dimensions will be merged. At present, it seems as if its primary emphasis on specific industrial sectors will remain, although softened by a more regionally decentralized method of administering programs.

The second area of concern surrounds MSERD's place in the new structure. There seem to be a number of contradictory signals about the ministry's true role. In its previous form, MSERD was primarily responsible for coordinating departmental expenditures, eliminating overlapping or contradictory programs or policies, and helping to bring the collective resources of a number of departments together to deal with specific, large, economic development issues (for example, the development of the Alsands project). It had, however, little policy-making capability of its own and lacked the incentives to gain it, if for no other reason than, as a central agency, it lacked the hands-on knowledge of the operation of specific industries and industrial programs, typical of a line department such as IT&C or DREE.

In its new form, MSERD gains a policy branch transferred from DREE, the greater part of which is located in the regions and is concerned with gathering information on regional economic trends and conditions. The ministry also has established a series of provincial offices headed by a federal economic development coordinator who serves as a focal point for the coordination of the federal departments' regional economic development activities. This reorganization will allow MSERD to be well informed on regional economic developments; however, whether it will have enough experience in the development and delivery of regional and industrial programs to assume a leadership role in initiating policy is difficult to discern. Significantly, DRIE has maintained a large regional and industrial policy capability under an assistant deputy minister. Its objectives are to increase regional contributions to decision making and strengthen "the department's role as the principal centre in government for industrial policy, industrial intelligence and relations between industry and government."[41] Because of this, it is less than clear whether MSERD or DRIE will have overall responsibility for industrial policy.

This lack of clarity is most obvious when the implications of the reorganization for federal-provincial relations are examined. Both DRIE and MSERD will now have greatly expanded regional offices. In

DRIE's case, not only will it have an office in each province, but in some cases several offices in the larger provinces. As mentioned earlier, the intent of both decentralization moves was to make federal policy more responsive to regional interests, but not necessarily to provincial governments. When the reorganization was announced, the government stated that instruments such as the federal-provincial GDAs would be phased out. In their place, the federal government would attempt to make its own policies more regionally appropriate, guided by regional economic strategies drafted by MSERD's regional offices and implemented by *all* federal departments. Such a policy of using a bureaucracy to inject regional sensitivity into federal policies, and, in effect, attempting to "end run" the provinces while dealing with regional economic interests, almost guarantees continued intergovernmental conflict.

In summary, the federal response to the problems of an incoherent industrial policy and the need to integrate regional interests into the policy-making process may be seriously misdirected. The federal government still lacks an institutional mechanism capable of addressing industrial strategy questions. The attempt to construct such a policy, contained in *Economic Development for Canada in the 1980s*, already seems to be coming to grief, primarily as a result of its outdated assumptions about world economic trends. Furthermore, the institutions which have been created have the potential for real conflict and confusion. The greater attention to independent federal action, combined with the attempt to create stronger linkages with regional economic actors, seems likely to provoke hostility among the provinces and could well intensify federal-provincial conflict.

XI. A Time For Change

The Canadian economy faces a very trying and uncertain future. The issues we must confront in the coming decade go far beyond the daunting problems of the current recession with its high rates of unemployment and low economic growth. Over the next decade, the challenge for Canadians will be to transform the economy structurally in order to compete effectively in what can only be called a radically altered, world-trade environment. There is no alternative to significant structural change. Our continued reliance on staple exports, combined with the weakness of much of our manufacturing sector, and our relatively underdeveloped capacity to innovate successfully, places us in a highly vulnerable position. We are unlikely to benefit from even the current, let alone future shifts, in the pattern of international trade.[1]

To face this new challenge, most governments in the industrially advanced countries are intervening substantially in their economies in order to promote and hasten the necessary structural changes. This is being done, almost without exception, in close collaboration with industry (and frequently labour). Industrialized countries all face considerable difficulties in this transition process, and confront obviously significant domestic political differences as to what are the appropriate measures to take. However, their commitment to change is undeniable, as is seen in the concrete actions they are taking at present to prepare themselves for a more difficult future.

By contrast, Canada's situation could hardly be more disturbing. As discussed earlier, at the very time when Canada needs effective leadership on national economic policy questions, our governments seem to be moving in opposite directions. At the federal level, leadership has been lacking for a variety of complex reasons outlined in the previous chapter, not the least of which has been the difficulty of implementing industrial policies in an economy that is highly differentiated from region to region, and where political consciousness of those regional differences is growing. At the same time, in large measure in response to the vacuum created by weak federal leadership, the provinces have become more aggressive and expert at promoting the industrial expansion of their own economies. The result has been a form of paralysis, an inability to forge a *national* effort to restructure industry at a crucial time in the country's economic development. It is a situation Canada can hardly afford at this stage in the evolution of the international economic system.

We are at a crossroads. What role will Canada's 11 governments play in promoting structural change? Industry's central role in most industrially advanced countries in shaping the content of national, industrial policy is largely premised on a significant and coherent commitment by government to the process of structural change. As we have seen, this commitment is the missing element in Canada and is why this study has concentrated so heavily on the role of government. Indeed, a good part of this study has been directed to determining just how decentralized, and directionless, economic policy making in Canada has become.

Clearly the provinces are key actors in industrial policy today. They do not possess all of the industrial-policy instruments at the disposal of the federal government, particularly the macroeconomic levers to manage the economy. However, they are building up a significant level of experience in many of the types of firm-specific and microeconomic industrial policies that are becoming the hallmark of the leading edge of industrial policy as practised elsewhere in the world. The provinces are also becoming increasingly aware of their own regional economic interests, an awareness that has found expression in their attempts to establish provincial industrial strategies.

Further, there has been a growth in recent years of a number of barriers to interprovincial trade and the movement of capital and workers. These barriers, along with provincial incentive schemes for industry and the increased perception by the provinces of their own territorial economic interests, pose a potential threat to the future of the Canadian economy as an integrated whole. The successful attempt by British Columbia to prevent the takeover of Macmillan-Bloedel by Canadian Pacific, the bidding wars between Ontario and Quebec for new industrial capacity in the automotive sector, and disputes between Ontario and Alberta over petrochemical plant expansion, all illustrate the potential severity of the situation.

The extent to which we do not have wholesale economic warfare between the provinces probably has more to do with their limited financial resources than to any commitment on their part to national economic harmony. As we have seen in chapter V, there is also reason to suspect that the high degree of regional specialization in economic activity, characteristic of each provincial economy, has to some extent limited the scope for competitive provincial industrial policies, as has the high level of integration which exists in the national economy in some important sectors (for example, the banking, transportation and retail systems). To date, it seems that the provinces have been diverging from one another, creating policies that essentially reinforce their existing, and very different, economic specializations, rather than seeking to directly compete with one another in a systematic manner.

In light of the international imperative facing the Canadian economy, however, this is not an encouraging situation. Even if nothing but the current state of affairs continues to exist, with diffuse leadership at the federal level and a gradual divergence in provincial industrial policies, we will be unable to address creatively the problem of structural change in the Canadian economy. Indeed, the current trends could mean that neither level of government will have the financial, technical or political resources required to promote such change.

Moreover, it is dangerous to assume that this drifting apart of economic interests will remain a benign process. In a contracting economy facing severe foreign competition, conflicts could become fierce. On the one hand, we have a manufacturing centre demanding public money and a protective trade policy to help restructure its industry, and, on the other, a staples-based periphery needing sizable government assistance to provide a transportation infrastructure for resource exports and advocating a trade policy favourable to the importation of inexpensive manufactured goods, as an alternative to its present reliance upon more costly domestic producers. Further, the state of the art in federal-provincial relations indicates that we can expect very little from the current structure of intergovernmental cooperative arrangements to help solve these difficulties.

We are – it bears repeating – at a crossroads. To survive or adapt to the new international imperatives, we *must* take stronger collective action. Without a fundamental change in the direction of federal-provincial decision making on industrial questions, however, that action will be seriously compromised. Harnessing the energies of our two levels of government to focus on the problem of industrial change in a more coherent and mutually reinforcing manner than is at present the case will be the linchpin of success for an industrial policy in Canada.

Finally, there is the role of the federal government. In the past, it has been able to provide strong economic leadership for the country: first, by creating a continent-wide economic system in the last century; and second, in this century, by ensuring the successful transition from a wartime to a peacetime industrialized economy. Since the early 1960s, its leadership role has atrophied – for reasons already explained. However, as events have recently demonstrated (for example, the case of the NEP), Ottawa can move swiftly and effectively to meet national economic objectives if it has the political will. *As we have seen, there need be no jurisdictional, or really any financial, barrier to a stronger federal presence in the industrial policy field.*

The primary challenge facing the federal government is to develop policies and instruments capable of correcting the structural problems of the Canadian economy, and to do this in a way that garners political support by demonstrating that such policies serve the interests of all Canadians. Undeniably, a strong federal role is required. The process of structural change is a long and difficult one, and a harnessing of provincial or even regional energies will not be enough to effect this change. Provinces on their own, or working together, cannot provide a national focus for industrial policy; they will miss opportunities which may be out of their own individual or joint areas of economic interest. Even if they do act collectively, they often lack the resources, or capacity, to act quickly or forcefully enough to seize an opportunity. Only the federal government can answer these needs and provide the required national leadership.

The solution to these problems will not be reached overnight; but some action must be taken *now* if it is to be effective. The following proposals could provide a basic point of departure. Although not a complete answer to the problem, they may form the basis for future and more substantial initiatives. The proposals relate to the three principal issues addressed in this study: the rise of provincial industrial strategies; the promotion of intergovernmental collaboration; and finally the role of the federal government.

Some Proposals for Change

Provincial Industrial Strategies
A great deal has been written about the rise of the provinces as aggressive advocates of regional self-interest. Terms such as "province building" have been coined to describe the increasingly explicit linkage now emerging between provincial governments and independent, regional economic strategies. While some of the rhetoric is overblown, during the past decade the industrial-policy capabilities of the provinces and their willingness to act in the industrial policy area to achieve provincial objectives have considerably expanded.

Perhaps the best way to deal with the more active industrial-policy role played by the provinces is to view provincial industrial strategies as an opportunity rather than a liability in the creation of a stronger and more aggressive response to restructuring the national economy. As we have seen, most provincial strategies are highly specialized and some are being implemented with considerable vigour. Indeed, there are very good political reasons why provinces should be considered effective in this area. The relatively homogeneous economy of each leaves less potential for conflicting demands that would dissipate their financial and policy resources. Alberta, for example, is in a good position to develop an industrial policy based on hydrocarbon developments – as indicated by its aggressive moves in the petrochemical industry and in energy technologies (for example, AOSTRA). Quebec, on the other hand, with the problems of a declining, and labour-intensive, manufacturing sector, has a greater political incentive than, say, the federal government, to concentrate on the problems of such a declining sector. Provincial governments, in other words, will be among the primary agents for ensuring structural change in Canada, especially if the federal government finds it impolitic to act on more than one regionally contentious policy area at a time.

It is clear, however, that this approach cannot constitute the sum total of an industrial strategy. First, there have to be mechanisms to help resolve the nascent problems of interprovincial conflict over industrial policy and to encourage intergovernmental collaboration. Second, as mentioned above, often cases arise where provinces are unable to take advantage of industrial development opportunities because these opportunities emerge outside their individual areas of interest, or if the provinces share an interest, cooperation cannot be arranged quickly enough, or on a sufficiently large scale to ensure success.

Intergovernmental Collaboration
Canada needs consistent and coherent industrial policies to adapt successfully to a radically changed international economic system; but, with 11 separate governments, the potential for inconsistent actions is great. Unfortunately, the intergovernmental process offers limited opportunities for the development and implementation of industrial policy. The interprovincial environment tends to turn questions of industrial policy into a zero-sum game in which the benefits are seen on a case-by-case basis and in highly regional terms – one province wins, another loses. At the federal-provincial level, a contest to see which level of government will gain control over a specific area often tends to frustrate cooperative action, making intergovernmental collaboration on industrial policy modest and slow. Indeed, the case studies indicate that the only way to overcome the problem of the zero sum game is either to limit the number of governments involved in collaboration, or confine the industrial-policy objectives under consideration to areas of common interest. Only in these circumstances will the provinces and the federal government

cooperate satisfactorily. It would seem, therefore, that intergovernmental collaboration will probably play a limited role in industrial policy making given the fact that a national approach is required and a wide variety of issues must be dealt with.

Further, these problems are likely to be compounded by the evolution of industrial policy itself.[2] Because of the increasing failure of traditional macroeconomic policies, industrialized countries have shifted gradually to policy instruments that seek to directly modify the activities of firms and industries.[3] In addition, there is a growing awareness by governments of the need to act decisively and quickly in industrial restructuring because of rapid changes in technologies and international comparative advantage. The trend in policy instruments towards more directed and specific action (for example, isolating a particular firm or industrial sector for attention), indicates that the territorial implications of any particular policy are likely to be more evident, and hence more difficult to cope with, in interprovincial or federal-provincial bargaining given the regionally specialized nature of the Canadian economy. Further, the speed and forcefulness required by governments when acting on industrial-development questions make it unlikely that the intergovernmental arena, with its slow and generally diffuse decision-making process, will provide a suitable environment for the development of effective national, or even regional, industrial policies.

This is not to say, however, that intergovernmental collaboration will be unimportant in the development of an industrial policy. At the very least, it will allow politicians and civil servants in different governments to communicate effectively – a necessary first step towards avoiding conflicts and duplication of policies. It is, therefore, unfortunate that even the most elementary institution of intergovernmental cooperation, the federal-provincial industry ministers' meeting, has been allowed to atrophy in recent years. Such conferences are incapable of producing industrial strategies, but their decline is an indication of how poorly equipped we are to deal, even in a very elementary way, with some of our industrial policy differences.

We should be concerned at the lack of a continuing mechanism to encourage consultation on industrial-policy issues for another important reason. A decentralized federation such as ours needs *some* form of organizational structure to encourage officials from different governments to collaborate. When governments meet infrequently – and then usually to deal with a specific problem or crisis – there is little incentive to seek broader cooperation. Simply then, intergovernmental consultation on industrial policy has to be much more regular.

A number of proposals have been made in recent years to create permanent organizations that could improve specific aspects of intergovernmental collaboration.[4] Ontario, for example, has proposed creating a Canadian domestic market development agency to help foster cooperation on government purchasing.[5] Unfortunately, these and other attempts at interprovincial or federal-provincial cooperation have met with resistance. Some provinces fear that such cooperative ventures will do little for them, and simply reinforce the existing distribution of economic activity in Canada. This suspicion is unfortunate, as it is just this type of project or subject-specific cooperation that can, with good will, build the necessary trust and experience to allow larger and more comprehensive forms of industrial-policy cooperation.

While the track record is not strong, two areas where the provinces and the federal government should try to cooperate are government procurement and R&D policy. Conflicting provincial initiatives can be especially damaging in these areas because, of all forms of government industrial assistance, R&D and procurement policy can be made almost totally ineffective when there are competing government initiatives in the same country. One area for practical cooperation could be major resource projects where both levels of government exercise some leverage over a developer's procurement policies. Cooperative action in steering developers' procurement to Canadian suppliers could provide an excellent opportunity to expand a national, industrial capacity in resource extraction equipment and technology. But initiatives such as these must be taken *now* before potentially competing procurement and technology policies are embedded in the industrial strategies of our various governments.

To guard against such unproductive competition, the federal government and the provinces should move rapidly to re-establish regular meetings of industry ministers and senior officials responsible for industry. Collectively they could be known as the Canadian Council of Industry and Technology Ministers. If possible, this group should have a small, permanent and independent secretariat providing a basic organizational capability for the council and acting as a resource group to explore possible areas of intergovernmental collaboration on industrial policy. The secretariat need only consist of a handful of senior civil servants seconded from various federal and provincial departments and the appropriate support staff. The council would provide the necessary infrastructure to pursue intergovernmental initiatives and ensure that some administrative pressure is brought to bear on the governments to pursue cooperation.

All too often, proposals for collaboration in this area whither and die for want of long-term bureaucratic resources. Sadly, the priority assigned to such activity within individual government departments is usually quite low given the pace of day-to-day issue management. Such an intergovernmental agency would help to solve this problem and make an important start in expanding and regularizing intergovernmental collaboration.

The Role of the Federal Government

Ottawa will carry the heaviest burden of adaptation in our more decentralized federal system. In the future, it will be called upon to play a difficult and sophisticated role. The federal government will have to be the effective leader in industrial policy making, but of necessity this role will require a great deal more regional sensitivity than before. At the same time, many of the problems resulting from decentralized decision making, such as the growing potential for contradictory or divergent policies, will be left for the federal government to solve.

In this new environment, the federal government's industrial-policy role will have to expand beyond its traditional concern with macroeconomic policies to embrace much more specific, and highly targeted, industrial programs capable of addressing individual regional problems or opportunities. At the same time, the government must cope effectively with the problem of fostering structural change in the economy to meet an increasingly competitive international environment in which highly targeted, national industrial policies play a large role. Indeed, given the realities of a decentralized political and economic system, and the requirement that policies in such an environment be highly specialized, the federal government will have to take on a dual role. *Many of the industrial policies it develops and implements will have to be carefully tailored to meet the diverse strengths of a highly regionalized economy. At the same time, it must act in the context of an overall national strategy addressing Canada's international competitive position. Thus, the federal government will have to be more activist, both in seeking out opportunities for regional cooperation, and in anticipating structural change in the economy.* At times this may require unilateral federal action. Indeed, external threats to the Canadian economy and the emergence of increasingly assertive provincial regimes will sometimes make this unilateral federal action mandatory – though Ottawa will have to be cognizant of regional needs and politic enough to recognize the important economic and political role the provinces now play in the industrial-policy process.

These imperatives imply that some major innovations will be required if the federal government is to deal effectively with decentralization in economic policy making. Such innovations would relate to two aspects of federal industrial policy: first, regional perspectives must be integrated into both the making and implementing of policy; and second, industrial planning needs a new institutional base so that it can be much more activist – capable of identifying federal industrial priorities and ensuring coherence in the formation and implementation of a wide variety of national and regional programs.

Integrating Regional Perspectives

To date, only one federal department, DREE, dealt extensively with the dual problem of integrating provincial input into its policies and implementing those policies in conjunction with the provinces. Other departments, such as Agriculture Canada, have well-developed informal working relationships with the provinces, partly because of shared jurisdiction. Unfortunately, in the industrial policy area, and, in particular, in the case of IT&C, the federal government tended to act alone and to collaborate with the provinces only when immediate problems emerged in the implementation of policy. Clearly, this was an unrealistic way to proceed.

DREE's "provincialist" approach may have been inappropriate to the more national orientation required of industrial policy today. However, the new department, DRIE, will have to be much more aware than IT&C of the need to seek policies and instruments appropriate for the regions. There may also be room for provincial input into the implementation of DRIE's other programs in addition to what informally existed for EDP.[6] More important, when creating new programs to assist industry, the department will have to seriously consider mechanisms which build in a greater level of consultation and collaboration with the provinces. An example of this form of collaboration can be seen in the Enterprise Manitoba project where DREE and the Manitoba Department of Economic Development jointly designed and implemented a coherent approach to the province's industrial problems. Significantly, IT&C played a minor, if reluctant, role in this project.

Based on the evidence of intergovernmental cooperation presented in Part Three, there is good reason to believe that bilateral approaches to industrial policy by the federal government offer the greatest opportunity for harmonious cooperation. They allow the federal government to tailor its policies to the needs of a specific province and to avoid introducing potentially conflicting objectives into a program – a danger when a number of provinces are involved. Bilateral approaches also allow the federal government to encourage only those aspects of provincial industrial policies which are most supportive of national industrial development objectives. Such an approach can allow the federal government to have a much more direct influence over the content and direction of provincial industrial strategies. This implies, therefore, that the federal government's approach to the formulation of industrial policy in the future should be highly specialized. For example, Ottawa would have industrial policy instruments designed specifically for Alberta which would focus on resource-extraction technology; in Nova Scotia, by contrast, federal support might be directed to marine industries and offshore technology.

There are some indications that the creation of DRIE reflects a greater interest by the federal government in integrating regional concerns into the policy-making process. However, it is not yet certain how the regional and industrial sector approaches to policy represented in DREE and IT&C will be integrated in the new department. Further, as noted in chapter X, the rationale for the reorganization – to ensure a presence in the regions which would allow the federal government to more accurately assess the needs of the economic interest groups in each province and directly deliver programs to meet those needs – does not adequately address the problem of dealing with provincial governments and their industrial development policies.

The attempt to make federal policy responsive to economic constituencies within each province seems designed more to increase federal bargaining power with provincial governments than to foster genuine collaboration with them. While both MSERD and DRIE will have an extensive network of provincial offices, it is far from clear that they will engage in joint policy development with provincial governments. Indeed, in a recent report on governmental policy and regional development, the Senate National Finance Committee was so concerned at the direction the new federal reorganization was taking that it recommended that both DRIE and MSERD be given a specific, regional development mandate. This committee also recommended that the federal government reconsider its stated intention to phase out the GDA system in light of the fact that such agreements offered a significant opportunity to assist in the coordination of federal and provincial economic policy making.[7]

Perhaps the new regional planning frameworks to be designed by MSERD's regional offices will provide an opportunity for solving the problem of regionalizing the federal government's industrial-policy planning process. The planning frameworks were originally designed to provide the analytical basis for new economic development agreements with the provinces which would supersede the GDAs. It was hoped that this planning process would act more as a device to tailor federal policy to regional interests, as distinct from simply provincial government interests. *There are now indications, however, that the new economic development agreements may be used by the federal government to discuss and develop industrial policy on a bilateral basis with individual provincial governments. It is recommended that they, in fact, be used in this way.*

In many cases, of course, it may not be possible to obtain provincial cooperation for industrial development, either because the province may not be interested, or because of interprovincial conflicts. In these situations, unilateral federal action will obviously be required and should be pursued with vigour. To be effective in any case, therefore, the federal role must be increasingly activist, focussed and selective. However, the current federal structures for intergovernmental relations and industrial policy making are unsuitable to this approach.

New Institutions

In essence, what is required is an institutional mechanism which can combine a more regionally tailored set of industrial-development programs with an integrated and coherent approach to national, industrial development. Given the federal government's present departmental organization, it would mean charging an existing department with overall responsibility for *both* industrial policy *and* an accompanying federal-provincial relations strategy. Ideally, such a positive role could be assumed by MSERD. However, the ministry's role as manager of the economic development expenditure envelope has meant that it has focussed on budget allocation and program coordination rather than on proposing new economic-development initiatives. This latter task has been largely left to the existing line departments in the field. It is hard to determine whether the addition of a regional policy unit from DREE and a series of representational offices in each province headed by a federal economic-development coordinator will make MSERD more effective in the development of an industrial policy. If it means, as seems likely, that MSERD will concentrate more on injecting regional perspectives into policies of the departments in the economic-development expenditure envelope, rather than developing an industrial policy, then we may only have half the solution to the integration of industry and regional policy. Indeed, MSERD's involvement in the broad range of economic policy from energy and mineral development to agriculture means that its ability to concentrate on explicitly industrial policy questions is, of necessity, limited. To be an effective industrial policy ministry today, it is essential to combine both an appreciation of the detailed workings of industry *and* an ability to plan at the macrolevel for industrial restructuring. Without both of these elements, such a department is unlikely to succeed.[8]

What is needed at the federal level is just such an integrated department, whether it is fashioned out of existing departments (for example, DRIE), or is an entirely new body. The department, whatever form it assumes, will have to pioneer methods of devising and implementing industrial policies that will integrate regional perspectives into individual programs and policies. At the same time, it must also build a strong central policy-planning mechanism to ensure that the initiatives taken by the department fit into a broader industrial strategy. More than a think tank or policy ministry, it will need to have administrative and budgetary control over a significant share of the federal government's industrial development programs and be in a position to make the necessary policy trade-offs among its various programs. The department would also require a well-developed, in-house, federal-provincial relations capability, which will have to be embedded both in its policy apparatus and in the branches concerned with program implementation. This feature would be essential as many of its programs could involve significant levels of federal-provincial collaboration.

We must be realistic, however, about the possibility of such a new department being able to promote both regional and industrial development. It should be clear that what is being advocated here is *not* a fusion of regional and industrial development policy, but rather an institutional device which could more effectively tailor industrial policy to regional specializations without losing sight of the overall national strategy. It is probably more sensible to rely on a traditional regional development agency such as DREE to overcome the structural difficulties caused by uneven regional development. The result may be some overlap in the provision of industrial assistance (as was the case between IT&C and DREE), but at least such an arrangement could help to avoid a situation in which one department attempts to carry out the impossible task of making tradeoffs between the regional equity/industrial efficiency aspects of policy proposals – a situation which would result from any attempt to combine industrial and regional policy in a single agency or department.

To be effective, this new or restructured industry department would be required to seek out imaginatively opportunities for industrial development and cooperation. This would involve the federal government in a catalytic role with the private sector and/or with one, or several, provincial governments. This implies not only that the policy-making capability of the department would have to be well developed, but also that a more *entrepreneurial* and *anticipatory* attitude to the development and implementation of industrial policy will be required. In short, to be successful the department would have to take a leadership role in framing and implementing industrial policy, both with industry and the provinces. As the evidence from this study indicates, if the federal government is to make a serious effort to solve the twin problems of industrial decline and regionalism, it cannot base its industrial policy on reactive or passive policies and instruments. Unless it assumes an activist role, it will be doomed to irrelevance.

Objections to this integrated department will, of course, be forthcoming. For example, there would be reservations that, after a major reorganization of the federal government's economic development departments, another reshuffling would be wasteful. However, the changes could be accomplished primarily through some modification to the existing structure of DRIE to incorporate a strengthened federal-provincial relations and industrial planning capability.

It is important to remember that to be successful, the changes proposed rely not so much on institutional reform per se, but more on a change in the attitude towards the development and implementation of industrial policy in the federal government - an attitude that is both activist and sympathetic to regional and provincial ambitions. For national policy to be successful, however, the provinces must also become more aware of the negative consequences of a tireless pursuit of regional self-interest for our future industrial viability as a nation. In short, both sides need to re-examine their attitudes and actions.

The first step towards the improvement of industrial policy making in Canada is to understand the problems generated by the regional differences arising from our staples economy. Action based on this understanding is next. However, as in all problems based on fundamental differences in economic interest, progress will be slow. Indeed, without some form of political commitment to overcome our difficulties, no amount of tinkering with the machinery of government or sophisticated approaches to policy making will solve our problems.

We must come to terms with the problems of effectively ensuring a positive and creative solution to industrial restructuring. And that solution will have to satisfy our ambition to remain an industrially advanced country with a reasonable level of regional equity. If we do not, we will be in grave danger not only of condoning the decline of the Canadian economy, but also of contributing to the demise of its underlying rationale.

Notes

Part One - Introduction

I. The International Imperative and Canadian Industrial Policy

1. See for example, Economic Council of Canada, *Fifteenth Annual Review: A Time for Reason*, Supply and Services Canada, Ottawa, 1978, esp. chap. 2; J. Maxwell, ed., *Policy Review and Outlook 1978: A Time for Realism*, C.D. Howe Research Institute, Montreal, 1978; *Policy Review and Outlook, 1979: Anticipating the Unexpected*, C.D. Howe Research Institute, Montreal, 1979; Michael Hudson, *Canada in the New Monetary Order: Borrow? Devalue? Restructure!*, Institute for Research on Public Policy, Montreal, 1978; and B.W. Wilkinson, *Canada in the Changing World Economy*, C.D. Howe Research Institute, Montreal, 1980.

2. See, for example, Canada, Senate Standing Committee on Foreign Affairs, *Canada-United States Relations: Canada's Trade Relations With the United States*, Queen's Printer, Ottawa, 1980; and Economic Council of Canada, *Looking Outward: A New Trade Strategy for Canada*, Information Canada, Ottawa, 1975.

3. Science Council of Canada, Report 29, *Forging the Links: A Technology Policy for Canada*, Supply and Services Canada, Ottawa, 1979; Canadian Institute for Economic Policy, *Out of Joint With the Times*, Ottawa, 1979.

4. For a review of some of these issues see Steven J. Warnecke ed., *International Trade and Industrial Policies: Government Intervention and an Open World Economy*, Macmillan, London, 1978; *Protectionism or Industrial Adjustment?* Atlantic Papers No. 39, Atlantic Institute for International Affairs, Paris, April 1980; and J. Pinder ed., "Industrial Policy and the International Economy," *National Industrial Strategies and the World Economy*, Croom Helm, London, 1982.

5. Richard N. Cooper, "U.S. Policies and Practices on Subsidies in International Trade," in S.J. Warnecke ed. *op. cit.*; and Stephen D. Krasner "United States Commercial and Monetary Policy: Unravelling the Paradox of External Strength and International Weakness," in *Between Power and Plenty: Foreign Economic Policies of Advanced Industrial States*, P.J. Katzenstein ed., University of Wisconsin Press, Madison, 1978, esp. pp. 81-85; and F. Lazar, *The New Protectionism: Non-Tariff Barriers and Their Effects on Canada*, Canadian Institute for Economic Policy, Ottawa, 1981, pp. 23-45.

6. For a more recent study of the French situation see, John Zysman, *Political Strategies for Industrial Order: State, Market and Industry in France*, University of California Press, Berkeley, 1977, chap. 1.

7. On America's particular view of the postwar economic situation see Krasner, *op. cit.*, pp. 72-81; and Charles S. Maier, "The Policies of Produc-

tivity: Foundations of American International Economic Policy After World War II," in Katzenstein ed., *op. cit.*

8. See S.J. Warnecke, "Introduction," *Industrial Policies in Western Europe*, S.J. Warnecke and E.N. Suleiman eds., Praeger, New York, 1975.

9. Keith Pavitt, "Technical Innovation and Industrial Development: The New Causality," *Futures*, December 1979; and "Technical Innovation and Industrial Development: The Dangers of Divergence," *Futures*, February 1980.

10. Lower-cost producers do not always come from the new industrializing countries (NICS); frequently, they result from technology being applied to production processes which lower the costs. The NICS are a growing element in international trade and are often able to dominate trade in certain commodities characterized by conventional technology and volume production where the advanced industrialized countries have high-cost producers. However, because of the growth in trade *among* advanced industrial countries, they have not yet captured a significant proportion of the overall trade of OECD member countries. See, *The Impact of the Newly Industrializing Countries on Production and Trade in Manufacturers*, OECD, Paris, 1979.

11. For a review of some of these policy instruments, see, *Selected Industrial Policy Instruments: Objectives and Scope*, OECD, Paris, 1978; *Agencies for Industrial Adaptation and Development*, OECD, Paris, 1978; *The Aims and Instruments of Industrial Policy: A Comparative Study*, OECD, Paris, 1975.

12. On this see, J. Hayward and M. Watson eds., *Planning Politics and Public Policy: The British, French and Italian Experience*, Cambridge University Press, London, 1975; M. Shanks, *Planning and Politics: The British Experience 1960-76*, Allen and Unwin, London, 1977; J. Hayward and Olga A. Narkiewicz, eds., *Planning in Europe*, Croom Helm, London, 1978.

13. S. Young with A.V. Lowe, *Intervention in the Mixed Economy*, Croom Helm, London, 1974, pp. 173-183; 198-210; see also W. Grant, *The Political Economy of Industrial Policy*, Butterworths, London, 1982, esp. chap. 3.

14. M. Jenkin, *British Industry and the North Sea: State Intervention in a Developing Industrial Sector*, Macmillan, London, 1981, pp. 6-9.

15. For a recent review of some of these issues see, Charles Carter ed., *Industrial Policy and Innovation*, Heinemann, London, 1981.

16. See, Ira C. Magaziner and Thomas M. Hout, *Japanese Industrial Policy*, Policy Studies Institute, London, 1980. For a recent review of the structure of Japanese industry see Kazno Sato ed., *Industry and Business in Japan*, M.E. Sharpe, White Plains, N.Y., 1980.

17. See Paul Malles, *Economic Consultative Bodies: Their Origins and Institutional Characteristics*, Economic Council of Canada Staff Study, Information Canada, Ottawa, 1970; Hans Gunter, "Trade Unions and Industrial Policies in Western Europe," Warnecke ed., *op. cit.*

18. See, Wilkinson, *op. cit.*, esp. pp. 126-132; 158-170.

19. J.N.H. Britton, "Locational Perspectives on Free Trade for Canada," *Canadian Public Policy*, 1978, vol. IV, no. 1, pp. 8-12.

20. See, G.B. Doern and R.W. Phidd, *The Politics and Management of Canadian Economic Policy*, Macmillan, Toronto, 1978, pp. 300-307.

21. International comparative statistics on financial assistance to industry are difficult to compile due to differences in reporting conventions. For a comparison with two of our trading partners see A. Peacock *et al.*, *Structural Economic Policies in West Germany and the United Kingdom*, Anglo-German Foundation, London, 1980, chap. 4.

22. On this, see, T. Naylor's *The History of Canadian Business*, 2 vols., James Lorimer and Company, Toronto, 1975; and T. Traves, *The State and*

Enterprise: Canadian Manufacturers and the Federal Government 1917-1931, University of Toronto Press, Toronto, 1979.

23. See, for example, Glen Williams, "The National Policy Tariffs: Industrial Underdevelopment Through Import Substitution," *Canadian Journal of Political Science*, June 1979, vol. XII, no. 2.

24. See Hugh G.J. Aitken, "Defensive Expansionism: The State and Economic Growth in Canada," in *The State and Economic Growth*, H.G.J. Aitkin ed., Social Science Research Council, New York, 1959.

25. This position was, of course, pioneered by the work of Harold Innis.

26. At its peak in 1950, manufacturing activity amounted to about 25 per cent of GDP.

27. The 1926 figure is from Canada, Task Force on the Structure of Canadian Industry, M. Watkins, Chairman, *Report*, Privy Council Office, Ottawa, 1968, and the 1970 figure from Statistics Canada, *Canada's International Investment Position*, Cat. No. 67-202.

II. Canada's Centre - Periphery Economy

1. See H.A. Innis, *The Fur Trade in Canada*, University of Toronto Press, Toronto, 1930, and *The Cod Fisheries*, University of Toronto Press, Toronto, 1940. On timber and wheat see A.R.M. Lower, *The Settlement of the Forest Frontier in Eastern Canada*, Macmillan, Toronto, 1936; and V.C. Fowke, *The National Policy and the Wheat Economy*, University of Toronto Press, Toronto, 1957.

2. Only about 32 per cent of Canada's 1979 exports were finished, end products. See Statistics Canada, *Survey of External Trade*, Cat. No. 65-001.

3. See for example K.H. Norrie, "Some Comments on Prairie Economic Alienation," *Canadian Public Policy*, Spring 1976, vol. II, no. 2; and J.M.S. Careless, "The Myth of the Downtrodden West," *Saturday Night*, May 1981, vol. 96, no. 5, pp. 30-36.

4. International comparisons are difficult to obtain, but among the industrialized countries, Canada, on a per capita basis, has a level of central government expenditure on regional development that is exceeded only by Italy. See *Re-appraisal of Regional Policies in OECD Countries*, OECD, Paris, 1974, pp. 118-122.

5. Per capita income is not a particularly satisfactory measure of regional inequality. For instance, it does not take into account differences in the cost of living between regions, or the average number of dependents in a family group over which a wage earner's taxable income may be spread. See, D.M. Cameron, "Regional Economic Disparities: The Challenge to Federalism and Public Policy," *Canadian Public Policy*, Autumn 1981, vol. VII, no. 4.

6. J. Maxwell and C. Pestieau, *Economic Realities of Contemporary Confederation*, C.D. Howe Research Institute, Montreal, 1980, p. 71.

7. Data previous to 1946 are not readily attainable on a regional basis, although decennial census data do give some idea of overall unemployment rates for the population. The 1931 census data for unemployment indicate that Ontario, and to a lesser extent Quebec, had a lower overall rate of unemployment than any other province and that, unlike in the postwar period, western Canada had the country's highest unemployment rate. See, Dominion Bureau of Statistics, *Seventh Census of Canada, 1931*, King's Printer, Ottawa, 1942, vol. 13, pp. 242-5.

8. Of course, in the last few years it has become obvious that Ontario's economy is not growing as rapidly as its western counterparts, especially Al-

berta and British Columbia. Per capita income levels are higher, and unemployment levels lower in western Canada compared with Ontario.

9. For example, in 1977 the Economic Council of Canada (ECC) found that Ontario had some of the best housing conditions, the lowest rate of infant mortality and the second highest level of persons in postsecondary education. Interestingly, while the western provinces did well in areas such as housing, life expectancy and postsecondary education, they had much higher than average rates for such statistics as divorce, legal offences and suicides. See, Economic Council of Canada, *Living Together: A Study of Regional Disparities*, Supply and Services Canada, Ottawa, 1977, pp. 56-9.

10. S.M. Lipset, *Agrarian Socialism: The Co-operative Commonwealth Federation in Saskatchewan, A Study in Political Sociology*, University of California Press, Berkeley, 1950, pp. 28; 93-7. Lipset paints a vivid and concise picture of the scale and scope of the economic disaster which hit Saskatchewan in the 1930s and the political consequences it incurred. See especially his chapter V, "The Economic Consequences of the Depression."

11. See S.A. Saunders, *The Economic History of the Maritime Provinces*, prepared for the Royal Commission on Dominion-Provincial Relations, King's Printer, Ottawa, 1939, pp. 1-22; 92-5; 100-101. The growth of the technology of steam power, both in ships and railways, not only eliminated the linkage between lumbering, shipbuilding and marine services, but also severely altered the locational advantages which the Maritime ports possessed in exploiting trade both internationally, and on a coastal basis.

12. On this conservationist aspect of Alberta policy see, Larry Pratt, "The State and Province Building: Alberta's Development Strategy," *The Canadian State: Political Economy and Political Power*, L. Panitch ed., University of Toronto Press, Toronto, 1977.

13. For a review of some of Alberta's industrial development objectives see Premier Lougheed's speech to the Calgary Chamber of Commerce, 6 September 1974, "Alberta's Industrial Strategies."

14. For a more detailed discussion of Quebec's exports see Carmine Nappi, *The Structure of Quebec's Exports*, C.D. Howe Research Institute, Montreal, 1978.

15. Statistics Canada, *Destination of Shipments of Manufacturers, 1979*, Supply and Services Canada, Ottawa, January 1983.

16. See Maxwell and Pestieau, *op. cit.*, pp. 61-2, note 4. Recent research on interregional service flows indicates, at least in the case of Quebec, that they are very regionally concentrated and tend to reflect traditional centre-periphery relations. See M. Polese, 'Interregional Service Flows, Economic Integration and Regional Policy: Some Considerations Based on Canadian Survey Data," paper presented at the Greek Regional Science Association meetings, Athens, September 1981, INRS, UQUAM, Montreal.

17. This is not a situation limited solely to Canada. Many advanced industrial nations have experienced pronounced differences in economic well-being between their centres and their peripheries. Indeed, the relationship has been of such a long-lasting nature and has remained despite considerable levels of national economic development and integration, that some analysts have come to believe that such situations represent a structured attempt to maintain the periphery in a dependent position – a situation which has been termed internal colonialism. See Michael Hechter, *Internal Colonialism: The Celtic Fringe in British National Development, 1536-1966*, University of California Press, Berkeley, 1975, esp. pp. 30-34.

18. See, W.H. Morton, *The Progressive Party in Canada*, University of Toronto Press, Toronto, 1950.

19. For a review of the attempts during the 1930s by the Social Credit government to change the nature of the credit system in Alberta see, C.B. MacPherson, *Democracy in Alberta: Social Credit and the Party System*, University of Toronto Press, Toronto, 1953, chaps. 6 & 7; and J.R. Mallory, *Social Credit and the Federal Power in Canada*, University of Toronto Press, Toronto, 1954, chaps. 5 & 6.

20. See, J. Richards and L. Pratt, *Prairie Capitalism: Power and Influence in the New West*, McClelland and Stewart, Toronto, 1979, chap. 5.

21. See, *Western Trade Objectives*, Western Premiers' Conference Position Paper, Yorkton, Saskatchewan, April 1978.

22. Nova Scotia, for example, elected candidates both at the provincial and federal level in 1867, who ran on a secession platform, and in 1886 the Nova Scotia legislature passed a resolution demanding secession from the Dominion for the three Maritime provinces.

23. See E.R. Forbes, *The Maritime Rights Movement 1919-1927: A Study in Canadian Regionalism*, McGill-Queen's University Press, Montreal, 1979, pp. 73-6. Tariffs, while an issue, caused dissension within the movement, with urban areas in favour of protection and rural areas in favour of reciprocity with the United States.

24. A. Careless, *Initiative and Response: Adaptation of Canadian Federalism to Regional Economic Development*, McGill-Queen's University Press, Montreal, 1977.

25. G. Veilleux, "Intergovernmental Canada: Government by Conference? A Fiscal and Economic Perspective," *Canadian Public Administration*, Spring 1980, vol. 23, no. 1, p. 37.

26. Richards and Pratt, *op. cit.*, chap. 7, esp. pp. 166-174.

27. K. McRoberts and D. Postgate, *Quebec: Social Change and Political Crisis*, McClelland and Stewart, Toronto, 1976.

28. Since the mid-1970s, Quebec's unemployment rate has been steadily growing, and in 1979 was second only to the Atlantic region which has Canada's worst unemployment levels. See, DREE, *Economic Development Prospects in Quebec*, Ottawa, December 1979, pp. 11-12.

29. For an analysis of how our present electoral system encourages such regional representation see, William P. Irvine, *Does Canada Need a New Electoral System?*, Institute of Intergovernmental Relations, Queen's University, Kingston, 1979, esp. pp. 11-14. For an alternative view, see, J.C. Courtney, "Reflections on Reforming the Canadian Electoral System," *Canadian Public Administration*, Autumn 1980, vol. 23, no. 3, esp. pp. 443-453.

Part Two - The Rise of Provincial Industrial Strategies

III. Policies on the Periphery: Industrial Strength Through Resources

1. Richard Simeon with Robert Miller, "Regional Variations in Public Policy," in *Small Worlds: Provinces and Parties in Canadian Political Life*, David Elkins and Richard Simeon eds., Methuen Publications, Agincourt, 1980. Recently, expenditures for industrial development have started to rise considerably.

2. *Ibid.*

3. In *Canadian Industrial Policy*, Ministry of Economic Development, Victoria, February 1978.

4. See Ministry of Economic Development, *Annual Report 1977*, Victoria, 1979, p. 19.

5. Interviews with provincial officials, Victoria, January 1980.

6. The Ministry of Universities, Communications and Science.

7. Science Council of British Columbia, *First Annual Report*, 1979, pp. 7-9. See also, H.W. Monks, "B.C. Government Forms Own Science Council to Stimulate Provinces' R&D Efforts," *Canadian Research*, vol. 12, no. 6, October/November 1979, pp. 23-25.

8. W.R. Bennett, "Towards an Economic Strategy for Canada: The British Columbia Position," speech given at the Conference of First Ministers, Ottawa, 13 February 1978.

9. Peter Lougheed, "Alberta's Industrial Strategy," speech to the Calgary Chamber of Commerce, 6 September 1974. Also quoted in John Richards and Larry Pratt, *Prairie Capitalism: Power and Influence in the New West*, McClelland and Stewart, Toronto, 1979, p. 168.

10. Richards and Pratt, *op. cit.*, pp. 162-174.

11. Peter Lougheed, speech to Calgary Chamber of Commerce, *op. cit.*

12. Interview, senior Alberta official.

13. Alberta Economic Development Department, *Annual Report 1981-82*; Alberta Opportunity Company Ltd., *Annual Report 1982*.

14. Alberta Opportunity Company Ltd., *Annual Report 1982*.

15. Interview with Alberta official; the program is officially known as "Alberta-Canada Subsidiary Agreement on Nutritive Processing Assistance"; the program was funded to a total of $17 million over the 1975-80 period.

16. Financial Post, *Survey of Mines and Energy Resources 1980*, p. 330. For a review of the company's activities see, D. Best, "Nova Corp.: It's more than an Alberta Corporation," *The Financial Post*, 27 December 1980, pp. 1-2.

17. AGTL, *Annual Report 1978*.

18. *Ibid.*

19. The Financial Post, *Survey of Mines & Energy Resources 1981*, p. 12.

20. AHSTF, *Annual Report 1980-81*; and Andrew G. Kniewasser, "The Effect of the AHSTF on Capital Markets," *Canadian Public Policy*, vol. VI, supplement Feb. 1980.

21. This is an estimate by Professor F. Helliwell of the University of British Columbia. See *Canadian Public Policy*, vol. VI, supplement, February 1980, pp. 179-80.

22. L. Hyndman, Speech to the conference of AHSTF, Edmonton, October 1979.

23. AHSTF, *Annual Report 1980-81*.

24. A.F. Collins, Deputy Treasurer of Alberta, "The AHSTF: An Overview of the Issues," *Canadian Public Policy*, vol. VI, supplement, February 1980; and I. Brown, "The $7 Billion Strategy," *Saturday Night*, December 1980, pp. 54, 56.

25. Alberta Oil Sands Technology and Research Authority, *Fifth Annual Report and Five Year Review*, Edmonton, 1980, pp. 56-58.

26. The strategy is outlined in detail in Alberta Research Council, *Long Range Plan*, Edmonton, December 1979.

27. This policy is outlined in the pamphlet, "A Policy Statement by the Government of Alberta," Department of Economic Development, Edmonton, 1 July 1980.

28. T.J. Courchene and J.C. Melvin, "Energy Revenues: The Consequences for the Rest of Canada," *Canadian Public Policy*, vol. VI, supplement, February 1980.

29. Crown corporations were established in such areas as shoe and brick manufacture. Unfortunately, many of them failed.

30. Statistics Canada, *Manufacturing Industries of Canada: National and Provincial Areas, 1975*, Cat. No. 31-203 and Statistics Canada, *Survey of Production 1976*, Cat. No. 61-202.

31. The following are the two companies' lending activities:

	SEDCO ($million)	AOC
1976	25.1	28.0
1977	31.3	17.5
1978	18.9	34.3

32. Canada, DREE, and the Government of Saskatchewan, *Canada-Saskatchewan Subsidiary Agreement on Iron and Steel*, Ottawa, July 1974.

33. Saskatchewan, Department of Industry and Commerce, *An Industrial Development Strategy for Saskatchewan*, Regina, 1976, p. 5.

34. Since 1969, manufacturing value added has grown by over 300 per cent in the province; it now accounts for 14.7 per cent of value added in Saskatchewan compared to 12.3 per cent in 1969.

35. SEDCO is currently building a research park at the University of Saskatchewan to encourage high-technology industries in the province, based on the successful experience of SED systems.

36. See "Sask-Tel bids for dominance in fibre optics," *Financial Times*, 19 May 1980; "Fibre Optics Plant, First Big Commercial System, Both for Saskatchewan," *The Electronics Communicator*, 9 April 1980, p. 4.

37. The province has a smaller version of Alberta's Heritage Fund, but to date much of its revenues have been used for current expenditure and investment projects, mostly on the social development side.

38. See Premier Devine's speech, "Saskatchewan: An Industrial Pact," in *Saskatchewan - Open for Business*, Conference Proceedings, Saskatchewan Industry and Commerce, Regina, 1982.

39. Canada, DREE, *Economic Development Prospects in Manitoba*, Ottawa, December 1979.

40. See Canada, DREE and Manitoba Department of Industry and Commerce, *Canada-Manitoba Subsidiary Agreement on Industrial Development*, Ottawa, April 21, 1978.

41. Canada, DREE, *Economic Development Prospects in the Atlantic Region*, Ottawa, 1979, p. 6.

42. *Ibid.*, p. 16. In terms of GDP growth, the region has lagged slightly compared to the Canadian average because of a poor performance in the service sector. The goods-producing sector has experienced above average growth rates. *Ibid.*, pp. 10-11.

43. Atlantic Development Council, *The Atlantic Region of Canada: Economic Development Strategies for the Eighties*, St. John's, 1978, p. 26.

44. New Brunswick, Department of Commerce and Development, *Manufacturing in New Brunswick: An Industrial Development Strategy*, Fredericton, March 1982.

45. DREE, *Economic Development Prospects in Nova Scotia*, Ottawa, 1979, pp. 21-24.

46. The province has about 10 development subagreements with DREE covering topics ranging from agriculture to R&D which represent commitments by both levels of government of about $290 million.

47. On the Nova Scotia government's attempts at industrialization during the 1960s see, Garth Hopkins, *Clairtone*, McClelland and Stewart, Toronto, 1978; and R.E. George, *The Life and Times of Industrial Estates Ltd.*, Institute of Public Affairs, Dalhousie University, Halifax, 1974.

48. Nova Scotia, Department of Development, *Toward An Economic Development Strategy For Nova Scotia: A Green Paper*, Halifax, May 1980.

49. *Ibid.*

50. See also, Nova Scotia, Department of Development, Task Force on Research and Technological Innovation, *Report*, Halifax, June 1981.

51. Prince Edward Island, Department of Tourism, Industry and Energy, "Prince Edward Island Industrial Development: Direction for the 80s," Charlottetown, April, 1982, mimeo.

52. Government of Newfoundland and Labrador, *Managing All Our Resources*, Newfoundland Information Services, St. John's, 1980, p. 11.

53. Minerals, forest products and fish comprise over 90 per cent of Newfoundland's exports. Many countries pose significant entry barriers on the import of more highly processed forms of these resource products.

54. See, Economic Council of Canada, *Newfoundland: From Dependency to Self-Reliance*, Supply & Services Canada, Ottawa, 1981; DREE, *Economic Development Prospects in Newfoundland*, Ottawa, 1979; and *Managing All Our Resources, op. cit.*

55. *Managing All Our Resources, op. cit.*, p. 44.

56. See, Government of Newfoundland and Labrador, *Towards A Science Policy for Newfoundland*, St. John's, November 1981.

57. J.D. House, "Premier Peckford, Petroleum Policy, and Popular Politics in Newfoundland and Labrador," *Journal of Canadian Studies*, vol. 17, no. 2, Summer 1982.

IV. A Troubled Heartland

1. Tom Traves, "Provincial Industrial Strategies," a report Prepared for the Science Council, March 1980.

2. Canada, DREE, *Economic Development Prospects in Ontario*, December 1979, pp. 7-11.

3. *Ibid.*

4. D.D. Purvis and F.F. Flatters, "Ontario, Policies and Problems of Adjustment in the Eighties," *Developments Abroad and the Domestic Economy*, vol. 1, Ontario Economic Council, Toronto, 1980.

5. On this see J.N.H. Britton, "Locational Perspectives on Free Trade for Canada," *Canadian Public Policy*, 1978, vol. iv, no. 1, pp. 8-12.

6. This is being realized increasingly by branch-plant managers; see J.K. Carman, "Technology Transfer Within a Multinational: The Case of Westinghouse Canada Ltd.," in *The Adoption of Foreign Technology by Canadian Industry*, proceedings of a workshop sponsored by the Science Council of Canada, Ottawa, 1981.

7. Science Council of Canada, *Forging the Links: A Technology Policy for Canada*, Supply and Services Canada, Ottawa, 1979, pp. 33-34.

8. K. Pavitt, "Technical Innovation and Industrial Development," *Futures*, vol. 11(6), December 1979; and W.H. Davidson, "Trends in the Transfer of US Technology to Canada," *The Adoption of Foreign Technology by Canadian Industry, op. cit.*

9. Some aspects of microelectronics technology may give production advantages back to the advanced industrial countries. See, K. Hoffman and H. Rush, "Microelectronics, Industry and the Third World," *Futures*, August 1980.

10. See notes for the use of the Hon. Wm. G. Davis, "Powers Over the Economy," Conference of First Ministers on the Constitution, Ottawa, 8-12 September 1980, Doc. 800-14/079; and Mr. Davis' "Concluding Statement," 13 September 1980, pp. 8-9.

11. Larry Grossman (Ontario Minister of Industry and Tourism), "Redefining Government's Role in Our Economic Future," *The Business Quarterly*, Summer 1979, p. 79.

12. See Canada, Senate, *Proceedings of the Senate Standing Committee on Foreign Affairs: Canadian Relations with the United States*, no. 22, 7 April 1981, pp. 15-25; 36-39.

13. L. Grossman, "Redefining Government's Role," *op. cit.*, p. 80.

14. See, for example, Larry Grossman, "Notes for an Address to the Board of Trade of Metropolitan Toronto," 21 February 1979; and Government of Ontario, *Towards An Economic Policy for Canada*, presentation to the First Ministers' Conference on the Economy, 1978.

15. See Mr. Grossman's speech to the Ontario legislature's Estimates Committee, Legislature of Ontario, *Debates*, 20 November 1979, and Ontario, Ministry of Treasury and Economics, "Supplementary Measures to Stimulate the Ontario Economy," Toronto, 13 November 1980.

16. Ontario has made a number of proposals designed to increase interprovincial cooperation on procurement. See Ontario, Ministry of Industry and Tourism, *Interprovincial Economic Cooperation: Towards the Development of a Canadian Common Market*, Toronto, January 1981.

17. In addition, the EDF has disbursed over $17 million in grants to a miscellaneous group of manufacturing firms.

18. Larry Grossman, speech to Metropolitan Toronto Board of Trade, 21 February 1979.

19. Ministry of Treasury and Economics, "Supplementary Measures to Stimulate the Ontario Economy," Toronto, 13 November 1980.

20. Ontario, Board of Industrial Leadership and Development, *Building Ontario in the 1980s*, Toronto, January 1981.

21. See, Ontario, Ministry of Industry and Tourism, *The Report of the Advisory Committee on Global Product Mandating*, Toronto, 1981; and Ontario, Ministry of Industry and Tourism, *Microelectronics: Report of the Task Force to the Government of Ontario*, Toronto, October 1981.

22. See, for example, R. Speirs, "BILD's Spending Plan is a Mix of Innovations and Old Programs," *Globe and Mail*, 27 January 1982, p. 5 and "Davis Asked to Explain How BILD Assists Jobless," *Globe and Mail*, 24 November 1981, p. CL7.

23. See, Britton, *op. cit.*; and J.T. Davis, "Some Implications of Recent Trends in the Provincial Distribution of Income and Industrial Product in Canada," *Canadian Geographer*, vol. XXIV, no. 3, 1980.

24. Canada, DREE, *Economic Development Prospects in Quebec*, December 1979.

25. *Ibid.*, p. 20.

26. Government of Quebec, Minister of State for Economic Development, *Challenges for Quebec: A Statement on Economic Policy*, Éditeur officiel, Quebec, 1979, p. 61.

27. *Ibid.*, p. 78.

28. *Ibid.*, pp. 14; 39-41; 137.

29. See, for example, Albert Breton, "The Economics of Nationalism," *Journal of Political Economy*, LXXII, no. 4., 1964.

30. An alternative, cultural explanation pointing out the limitations of the purely economic argument is Charles Taylor's "Nationalism and the Political Intelligentsia: A Case Study," *Queen's Quarterly*, vol. LXII, no. 1, 1965. For a discussion of the Breton and Taylor theses see, Kenneth McRoberts and Dale Postgate, *Quebec: Social Change and Political Crisis*, McClelland and Stewart, Toronto, 1976, pp. 103-109.

31. Government of Quebec, *Bâtir le Québec: Énoncé politique économique*, Éditeur officiel, Quebec, 1979, p. 37.

32. An assessment of Bill 101 on the province's industrial community has been provided in Yvon Allaire and Roger Miller's *L'entreprise canadienne et la loi sur la francisation du milieu de travail*, C.D. Howe Research Institute, Montreal, 1980.

33. Published in an English abridgement by the Quebec government as *Challenges for Quebec: A Statement on Economic Policy*, Éditeur officiel, Quebec, 1979.

34. *Challenges for Quebec, op. cit.*, p. 127.

35. The SNA accounts for about 25 per cent of the province's production of asbestos fibre in volume terms and about 40 per cent in terms of value.

36. *Challenges for Quebec, op. cit.*, pp. 161-164.

37. SGF, *Rapport annuel*, 1981. The SGF's mandate includes assisting with the structural adjustment of the Quebec economy. In the forest products sector, its investment in the Donohue/Saint-Félicien project indicates that it is also attempting to meet government policy objectives for the sector which include, increased forward processing of resources and domestic participation in the industry. See, *Challenges for Quebec: A Statement on Economic Policy, op. cit.*, p. 111.

38. P. Fournier, *Les Sociétes d'État et les Objectifs Économiques du Québec: Une Évaluation Préliminaire*, Éditeur officiel, Quebec, 1979, pp. 73-75.

39. Quebec, Ministry of State for Economic Development, *The Technology Conversion: Challenge for Quebec, Phase 2*, Éditeur officiel, Quebec, 1982, pp. 53; 198-99; 201; 203.

40. Caisse de depôt et de placement, *Rapport annuel 1978*.

41. Fournier, *op. cit.*, pp. 34-8.

42. For a review of some of these tensions see, A.D. Gray, "Politicization of the Caisse," *Financial Times of Canada*, 26 January 1981, p. 11; and Wendie Kerr, "Policy Shift Revives Row Over Caisse's Role," *Globe and Mail*, 11 April 1981, p. B.1 and, "Rate Policy Change Stirs Caisse Controversy in Quebec," *Globe and Mail*, 13 April, 1981, p. B.6.

43. See A.H. Wilson, *Research Councils in the Provinces: A Canadian Resource*, Science Council Background Study 19, Information Canada, Ottawa, 1971.

44. Government of Quebec, *A Collective Project: Statement of Policy Objectives and Plan for the Implementation of a Research Policy for Quebec*, Éditeur officiel, Quebec, 1980.

45. Quebec, Ministry of State for Economic Development, *The Technology Conversion: Challenges for Quebec Phase 2*, Éditeur officiel, Quebec, 1982. The plan covers the period 1982-86.

46. For a review on the measures proposed in *The Technology Conversion*, see the series of articles entitled "Le virage technologique," in *Gestion*, février 1983, pp. 4-18.

47. *The Technology Conversion, op. cit.*, p. 52.

48. See, for example, Governments of British Columbia, Alberta, Saskatchewan and Manitoba, *Western Trade Objectives*, Western Premiers' Conference Position Paper, Yorkton, Saskatchewan, 13-14 April 1978.

49. See chapt. V, fn. 5, p. 264

50. "No Trespassing in Ontario," *The Economist*, 13 March 1982, pp. 79-80.

51. Witness, for example, the placement of a province-wide urban transit bus order with General Motors rather than Bombardier Ltd. because of GM's promise to build additional new assembly facilities at Ste Thérèse. In the words of the premier, "Especially in this period of economic sluggish-

ness, the purchasing policy does not allow us therefore to consider General Motors as an external competitor, unless one establishes a criterion of pure 'cultural preference', which would soon lead us to the creation of a genuine economic ghetto." Quoted in *Le Devoir*, 14 January 1978.

V. Provincial Industrial Policies - Ten or One?

1. For a review of the effectiveness of one attempt at provincial counter-cyclical policy see, Peter Gusen, *The Role of the Provinces in Economic Stabilization: The Case of Ontario's Auto Sales Tax Rebate*, Conference Board of Canada, Ottawa, 1978. For a summary of the arguments in favour of a provincial role in countercyclical policy, see, British Columbia, Ministry of Economic Development, *The Role of the Provinces in Stabilization*, Victoria, February 1978, pp. 3-19.

2. See, for example, the R&D objectives of the Alberta Research Council's *Long Range Plan*, Edmonton, December 1979; of the Science Council of British Columbia, *First Annual Report*, 1979; and statements contained in Newfoundland's economic development plan, *Managing All Our Resources*, Newfoundland Information Services, St. John's, 1980.

3. See, for example, "In Alberta's Petrochemical Hopes, Petrosar - the Cloud on the Horizon," *Canadian Petroleum*, May 1977, pp. 14-17.

4. Another area of competitive research is oceanography, with Newfoundland, British Columbia and Nova Scotia pursuing oceanic research, although many of these projects are being funded, at least in part, with federal funds. See J. Maxwell and C. Pestieau, *Economic Realities of Contemporary Confederation*, C.D. Howe Research Institute, Montreal, 1980, p. 85.

5. For example, from 1 July 1969 to 31 December 1979 Quebec received $167 337 000 in regional development incentives for industry compared to $47 911 000 for Ontario from DREE. In terms of direct transfers to industry from IT&C, Quebec firms received $333.8 million compared to $383.6 million for Ontario. On a per capita basis, using 1980 population estimates, this works out to $50.17 per capita for Ontario and $78.30 for Quebec. Sources: DREE, *Report on Regional Development Incentives*, Ottawa, 1980, p. 11; and IT & C, unpublished data.

6. See, for example, the position paper published by the four western provincial governments, *Western Trade Objectives*, Western Premiers' Conference Position Paper, Yorkton, Saskatchewan, April 1978.

7. See, for example, A.E. Safarian, *Canadian Federalism and Economic Integration*, Information Canada, Ottawa, 1974 and *Ten Markets or One? Regional Barriers to Economic Activity in Canada*, Ontario Economic Council, Toronto, 1980; Pestieau and Maxwell, *op. cit.*, chap. 6; A. Breton, *Discriminating Government Policies in Federal Countries*, Private Planning Association of Canada, Montreal, 1967; and I. Bernier, "Le concept d'union économique dans la Constitution canadienne: de l'intégration commerciale à l'intégration des facteurs de production," *Cahiers de Droit*, vol. 20, 1979, pp. 177ff.

8. Restrictions usually have a great deal more to do with limiting the numbers of professionals or trades people practising in a province in order to prevent the flooding of a market, and less frequently, with ensuring that persons qualifying for a licenced occupation are knowledgeable of local circumstances affecting their jobs.

9. Safarian, *Ten Markets or One?*, *op. cit.*, pp. 4-6. Provinces also sometimes restrict provincial civil service employment to local residents, although skill shortages in the provinces, particularly the smaller ones, mean

that for the more specialized occupations provinces often have to recruit nationally.

10. Newfoundland claims, for example, that its offshore labour regulations parallell federal regulations concerning the employment of local residents in the Northern Pipeline project and that the regulations have displaced 750 foreign workers in offshore jobs, not other Canadians. See the text of Premier Peckford's telex to Prime Minister Trudeau made public in a Newfoundland Information Service press release dated 7 July 1980.

11. See M.J. Trebilcock, G. Kaiser and J.R.S. Prichard, "Restrictions on the Interprovincial Mobility of Resources, Goods, Capital and Labour," *Intergovernmental Relations*, Ontario Economic Council, Toronto, 1977.

12. Agriculture Canada, *Directory of Agricultural Marketing Boards in Canada*, Ottawa, June 1980.

13. For a description of the background see, Safarian, *Canadian Federalism, op. cit.*, pp. 51-54.

14. P.W. Hogg, "Freedom of Movement of Goods, Persons, Services and Capital: Canadian Case Law," Osgood Hall Law School, York University, paper presented at McGill University, Montreal, 22 September 1979, pp. 4-5.

15. For a review of the creation of the national marketing boards see, Grace Skogstad, "The Farm Products Marketing Agencies Act: A Case Study of Agricultural Policy," *Canadian Public Policy*, vol. VI, no. 1, 1980.

16. However, the courts have not allowed a province to use its regulatory power in such matters as labour or product standards, in a way to prevent goods entering into its territory from another province.

17. Hogg, *op. cit.*, pp. 5-6.

18. Recent attempts in late 1980 by Ontario's Industry Minister Larry Grossman to convince Alberta of the need to more effectively consider Ontario's capacity for Alberta's major resource development projects fell on deaf ears. However, Ontario has been able to get consideration for joint provincial action on medical purchases. See, Ontario, Ministry of Industry and Tourism, *Interprovincial Economic Co-operation: Towards the Development of a Canadian Common Market*, Toronto, January 1981, pp. 11-12.

19. One recent study of procurement in the electrical industry showed that provincial hydro companies generally showed a preference for *provincial* suppliers, but with little or no procurement preference being given to out-of-province *Canadian* suppliers. This policy contrasts sharply with foreign practice where national suppliers of equipment are given absolute preference and where governments subsidize significantly power generation equipment exports. See, B. Beale, *Energy and Industry: The Potential of Energy Development Projects for Canadian Industries in the Eighties*, Canadian Institute for Economic Policy, Ottawa, 1980, esp. pp. 71-73.

20. Government of Canada, "Powers over the Economy: Securing the Canadian Economic Union in the Constitution," Continuing Committee of Ministers on the Constitution, Doc. 830-81/036, July 1980.

21. *Ibid.*

22. For example, the Ontario Small Business Development Corporation. British Columbia has also proposed tax advantages to provincial investors in local firms.

23. Based on distributions obtained from 1975-76 and 1976-77 accounts in Statistics Canada, *Provincial Government Finance*, Cat. 68-207. There are wide disparities in the proportion of provincial spending on trade and industry which is transferred to business, both between individual provinces and between annual reports.

24. Data supplied by Statistics Canada.

25. For a fuller discussion of some of these attempts between the provinces to compete for industry see, Allan Tupper, *Public Money in the Private Sector: Industrial Assistance Policy and Canadian Federalism*, Queens University, Institute for Intergovernmental Relations, Kingston, 1982, esp. chap. 5.

26. *Ibid.*, pp. 62-63.

Part Three - Intergovernmental Coordination and Industrial Policy

VI. A Nation of Governments

1. For a good compendium of the literature in this area see, *Federalism and Intergovernmental Relations in Australia, Canada, the United States and Other Countries: A Bibliography*, Institute of Intergovernmental Relations, Queen's University, Kingston, 1967; and, *Supplements* published in 1976 and 1979.

2. FPRO officials have estimated the number as being nearer to 1000 today.

3. Alberta intergovernmental affairs' figures indicated 782 meetings in 1975. See G. Veilleux, "L'évolution des mechanismes de liaison intergouvernementale," in *Confrontation and Collaboration: Intergovernmental Relations in Canada Today*, R. Simeon ed., Institute of Public Administration of Canada, Toronto, 1979, p. 38. Some of Veilleux's figures for federal-provincial meetings differ from those published by the Alberta Department of Federal and Intergovernmental Affairs in its Annual Reports.

4. Canada, Federal-Provincial Relations Office, *Federal-Provincial Programs and Activities: A Descriptive Inventory*, Supply and Services Canada, Ottawa, 1982, pp. iii; 266-272. If transfer payments and tax transfers are included this figure rises to over $15 billion.

5. Since 1980, FPRO has not had its own minister in the federal cabinet, but is represented by the prime minister.

6. Veilleux, *op. cit.*, pp. 64-77.

7. H.A. Stevenson, "The Federal Presence in Education 1939-80," and S. Hargraves, "Federal Intervention in Canadian Education," *Federal Provincial Relations: Education Canada*, J.W.G. Ivany and M.E. Manley-Casimir eds., OISE Press, Toronto, 1981, pp. 15-18; 28-32.

8. For example, R. Simeon, *Federal-Provincial Diplomacy: The Making of Recent Policy in Canada*, University of Toronto Press, Toronto 1972; J.S. Dupré *et al.*, *Federalism and Policy Development: The Case of Adult Occupational Training in Ontario*, University of Toronto Press, Toronto, 1973; A. Careless, *Initiative and Response: The Adaptation of Canadian Federalism to Regional Economic Development*, McGill-Queen's University Press, Montreal, 1977; R.M. Burns, *Intergovernmental Liaison on Fiscal and Economic Matters*, Queen's Printer, Ottawa, 1969; Rand Dyck, "The Canada Assistance Plan: The Ultimate in Co-operative Federalism," *Canadian Public Administration*, vol. 17, no. 4, 1974; V. Seymour Wilson, "Federal-Provincial Relations and Federal Policy Processes," in *Public Policy in Canada: Organisation, Process and Management*, G.B. Doern and P. Aucoin eds., Macmillan, Toronto, 1979; M. Westmacott, "The National Transportation Act and Western Canada: A Case Study in Co-operative Federalism," *Canadian Public Administration*, vol. 16, no. 3, 1973; D.V. Smiley, "Federal-Provincial Conflict in Canada," *Publius*, vol. 4, Summer 1974; and R.J. Schultz, *Feder-*

alism, Bureaucracy, and Public Policy: The Politics of Highway Transport Regulation, McGill-Queen's University Press, Montreal, 1980.

9. Dyck, *op. cit.*; Smiley *op. cit.*

10. D.V. Smiley, *Canada in Question: Federalism in the Eighties*, 3rd ed., McGraw-Hill Ryerson, Toronto, 1980, p. 111-113.

11. *Ibid.*, p. 113.

12. Gordon Robertson, "The Role of Interministerial Conferences in the Decision-Making Process," in Simeon ed., *Confrontation and Collaboration, op. cit.*, pp. 87-88.

VII. Intergovernmental Collaboration in Action

1. A review of the scope of the provinces' relations with American states is available in R.H. Leach, D.E. Walker and T.A. Levy, "Province-State Trans-border Relations: A Preliminary Assessment," *Canadian Public Administration*, vol. 16, no. 3, Fall 1973.

2. Alberta, Department of Federal and Intergovernmental Affairs, *Fifth Annual Report*, Edmonton, March 1978, p. 14.

3. *Ibid.*, p. 15.

4. Governments of Nova Scotia, New Brunswick and Prince Edward Island, *Report on Maritime Union*, (Deustch Report), Queen's Printer, Halifax, October 1971. The report was commissioned in 1968.

5. Alexander B. Campbell, Gerald A. Regan and Richard B. Hatfield, "The Move Toward Maritime Integration and the Role of the Council of Maritime Premiers," *Canadian Public Administration*, vol. 15, no. 4, Winter 1972, p. 601.

6. E.E. Fanjoy, "The Record of Co-operation in the Maritimes," Speech to IPAC Conference on Regional Cooperation in the Maritimes, Halifax, 21 April 1981.

7. For example, the council attempts to ensure that its agencies have representative offices in each province and a rough balance of employment between the provinces.

8. P. Grant, "Claiming the Prize Ends the Bickering," *Globe and Mail*, March 1981. A final agreement to build the college was signed in the early summer of 1983.

9. Atlantic Development Council, *The Atlantic Region of Canada: Economic Development Strategies for the Eighties*, St. John's, 1978, p. 26.

10. "Regional Preference in Provincial Purchasing and Tendering Policies," CMP Press Statement, March 1980.

11. See, A. Whittingham, "Why Atlantic Provinces Feel the Big Power Crunch," *Financial Post*, 12 June 1976. In the mid-1970s, for example, Nova Scotia derived 65 per cent of its electrical energy from oil-fired generating stations.

12. "Gillespie Boosts Maritime Energy," *Financial Post*, 4 February 1978; Council of Maritime Premiers, *Sixth Annual Report*, Halifax, 1978, p. 6.

13. The Maritime provinces were upset at what they regarded as the federal government's stalling over its financial commitments to the MEC. See, "Ottawa Holding Up MEC," *Chronicle Herald*, Halifax, 27 May 1978.

14. "Memorandum of Understanding Between Canada, New Brunswick, Nova Scotia and Prince Edward Island: Maritime Energy Corporation," Halifax, 16 February 1979. A copy of this memorandum was released in a press statement by EMR in Ottawa on 19 February 1979.

15. The federal government would purchase all the power output from Point Lepreau and immediately resell it to the three Maritime utilities. In

this way, the MEC would have a guaranteed market for its power and could obtain a good credit rating, thus lowering its borrowing costs.

16. See, "MEC: Must Start Over Again," *Modern Power and Engineering,* August 1979, p. 3; "Snags Hit Formation of Maritime Energy Corporation," *Modern Power and Engineering,* August 1979; and Interview, Council of Maritime Premiers' official, March 1981.

17. See, "Ottawa Has to Decide in One Year on Maritime Energy Corporation, Hatfield Says," *Globe and Mail,* 27 July 1979.

18. C. Wood, "Super-Utility Revived Under New Terms," *Canadian Renewable Energy News,* January 1980, p. 9.

19. "Maritime Energy Corpse Buried by Council of Maritime Premiers," *Energy Analects,* 3 October 1980, p. 4; "Premiers Agree to Pull Plug on Maritime Energy Corporation," *Globe and Mail,* 24 September 1980, p. 13.

20. Council of Maritime Premiers, "Press Communiqué," 42nd Session, Amherst, Nova Scotia, 8-9 December 1980.

21. See, L.F. Kirkpatrick, President, Nova Scotia Power Corp., "Regional Cooperation in Electrical Generation - A Review," Speech, Halifax, 21 April 1981.

22. Council of Maritime Premiers, *Sixth Annual Report, op. cit.,* p. 8.

23. Nova Scotia Research Foundation Corporation, *Marine Manufacturing: An Atlantic Opportunity,* Dartmouth, Nova Scotia, August 1979; and Council of Maritime Premiers' Committee on Research and Development, *Technological Innovation: An Industrial Imperative,* Halifax, October 1981.

24. *Report on Maritime Union, op. cit.,* p. 59.

25. A. Campbell, *et al., op. cit.,* p. 606.

26. *Ibid.,* pp. 606-607. A similar position was taken by the council's first secretary in his review of the CMP's first five years of activity. See, A.A. Lomas, "The Council of Maritime Premiers: Report and Evaluation After Five Years," in *Canadian Federalism: Myth or Reality?,* Peter J. Meekison, ed., Methuen, Toronto, 1977, p. 361.

27. A recent study of the nature of cooperative agreements in all areas (including economic) which have been developed through the CMP claimed that the results of such agreements demonstrates a low level of political integration in the region and hence little underlying political constituency for collaborative ventures. See, E.H.S. Holm, "The Council of Maritime Premiers: The Process of Political Integration in the Canadian Maritimes," Unpublished thesis, Tufts University, October 1977.

28. Details on the early evolution of the WPC and an evaluation of its work are contained in the following articles: M. Westmacott and P. Dore, "Intergovernmental Co-operation in Western Canada: The Western Economic Opportunities Conference," in P. Meekison ed., *op. cit.;* and G.T. Gartner, "A Review of Co-operation Among the Western Provinces," *Canadian Public Administration,* vol. 20, no. 1, 1977.

29. Westmacott and Dore, *op. cit.,* p. 343.

30. *Ibid.,* p. 345.

31. *Ibid.,* pp. 346-350.

32. The western provinces produced four position papers for the Western Economic Opportunities Conference (WEOC) on the following topics: transportation, economic and industrial development opportunities, agriculture, and capital financing and financial institutions. All the papers were critical of federal policy and the existing structure of the national economy. A complete record of the WEOC proceedings, including the documents tabled by the various governments, is contained in *Western Economic Opportunities Conference: Verbatim Record and Documents,* Supply and Services Canada, Ottawa, 1977.

33. A record of the achievements of the WPC is contained in the communiqués issued after each annual meeting. They have been issued since 1974 and provide a record of the decisions taken by the premiers.

34. Interview, Saskatchewan intergovernmental affairs official, Regina, March 1981.

35. The common position is contained in the document *Western Trade Objectives* issued by the WPC at Yorkton, Saskatchewan, in April 1978.

36. Western Premiers' Task Force on Constitutional Trends, *Reports*. To date, three reports have been published: the first in 1977, a second, in April 1978, and a third, in March 1979.

37. See Communiqué No. 3, "Third Report of the Premiers' Task Force on Constitutional Trends," Western Premiers' Conference, Prince George, British Columbia, March 1979.

38. A review of the communiqués from the years 1974 and 1976-80 indicates that of the issues discussed by the premiers, 27 concerned some aspect of federal government policy that affected the region, eight concerned joint provincial action on a matter of provincial jurisdiction, and four involved both.

39. See Communiqué, Western Premiers' Conference, Vancouver, 27-28 September 1974.

40. Gartner, *op. cit.*

41. Communiqué No. 1, "The Economy," Western Premiers' Conference, Prince George, British Columbia, March 1979.

VIII. Federal-Provincial Collaboration over Industrial Policy

1. The council was established as a corporation with share capital under Part II of the *Canada Corporations Act*. Its name was changed to the Canadian Council of Resource and Environment Ministers in 1971.

2. The portfolios varied from province to province and on occasion representation was from outside the environment or resource portfolios; for example, Ontario was represented for a time by the Minister of Municipal Affairs, and Nova Scotia has been represented by a Minister of Highways.

3. Apart from its annual report, CCREM produced a monthly *Resources-Environment Bulletin* which was circulated to over 8000 individuals, a limited circulation publication, *References*, which was primarily bibliographical but also listed new legislation in the environmental field, and a number of individual reports, books and conference proceedings. In addition, CCREM also circulated to government members a series of "Inter-Committee Letters" which reported on decisions taken at the council's various committee meetings and by the council itself.

4. M.S. Whittington, "CCREM: An Experiment in Interjurisdictional Coordination," Paper prepared for the Science Council of Canada, May 1978.

5. Canadian Council of Resource and Environment Ministers, Task Force on Forest Policy, *Forest Policies in Canada*, 3 vols., Ottawa, June 1976.

6. Interview, CCREM official, November 1981.

7. See, Douglas Brown and Julia Eastman, *The Limits of Consultation: Ottawa, the Provinces and the Private Sector Debate Industrial Strategy*, Science Council of Canada, Ottawa, 1981, Part B.

8. *Ibid.*, pp. 66-72.

9. About 80 position and background papers were tabled during the February First Ministers' Conference.

10. Brown and Eastman, *op. cit.*, pp. 36-37; 71.

11. *Ibid.*, p. 71.

12. Government of British Columbia, "Towards an Economic Strategy for Canada: the British Columbia Position," February 1978, esp. pp. 13-16.

13. Government of Ontario, "An Economic Development Strategy for Canada," Federal-Provincial First Ministers' Conference on the Economy, February 13-15, 1978; and William G. Davis, "Notes for Remarks on Commercial Policy," Ottawa, 14 February 1978.

14. The Montreal Star commented "Motherhood Looms Large," in Brown and Eastman, *op. cit.*, p. 40.

15. A working group of federal-provincial officials was established after the First Ministers' Conferences to look at opportunities for collective procurement by all 11 governments of selected products. A number of studies was carried out, but initiatives resulted from the working group of officials.

16. Brown and Eastman, *op. cit.*, p. 49.

17. *Ibid.*, pp. 62-63.

18. *Ibid.*, p. 63.

19. F.L.C. Reed & Associates Ltd. and Forest Management Institute (Canada), *Forest Management in Canada*, vol. 1, Canadian Forestry Service, Ottawa, January 1978, pp. 131-132.

20. Statistics Canada, *Summary of External Trade*, data for 1980, Cat. No. 65-001,

21. Reed & Associates, *op. cit.*, p. 132.

22. See, for example, Reed & Associates, *op. cit.*; Canadian Council of Resource and Environment Ministers, Task Force on Forest Policy, *op. cit.*, vol. I; and, *Report of the Special Task Force on Ontario's Pulp and Paper Industry*, Ministry of Industry and Tourism, Toronto, November 1978.

23. Reed & Associates, *op. cit.*, pp. 23-24.

24. For an evaluation of Ontario's pulp and paper mills see, *Report of The Special Task Force, op. cit.*, Appendix III.

25. These roles are in large part assumed by the Canadian Forestry Service of Environment Canada although, recently, responsibility for forest products research has been turned over to the private sector. For a review of federal forestry policies during the 1960s and early 1970s see, J.H.G. Smith and G. Lessard, *Forest Resources Research in Canada: Current Status, Adequacy, Desirability and Future Development*, Science Council of Canada Background Study 14, Information Canada, Ottawa, 1971.

26. Canada, Industry, Trade and Commerce, *Sector Profile: The Canadian Forest Products Industry*, Ottawa, 1978, pp. 2-3.

27. Reed & Associates, *op. cit.*, chap. 4 for a review of historic practices; and also CCREM, *op. cit.*, vol. II. Ontario recently revised its regulations. See, "Forests are Forever (II)," *Globe and Mail*, 3 March 1980, p. 6.

28. Canada, DREE, *Annual Report 1979-80*.

29. Details of the early part of the development of forestry policy come from interviews with officials in DREE, ITC and the Ontario Ministry of Northern Affairs.

30. IT&C, *Sector Profile, op. cit.*, p. 13.

31. Board of Economic Development Ministers, press release, 1 February 1979. The grant program was increased to $276 million in July 1980.

32. DREE, *Annual Report 1979-80*.

33. DREE, press release, "Canada and New Brunswick Sign $42 Million Pulp & Paper Agreement," 27 August 1980.

34. Interview, Ontario official.

35. Calculated from DREE press releases.

36. See, Nicholas Sidor, "Forest Industry Development Policies: Industrial Strategy or Corporate Welfare?," Publication #3, Canadian Centre for Policy Alternatives, Ottawa, 1981; also F.C. Anderson and C. Bonsor, "The

Economic Future of the Forest Products Industry in Northern Ontario," (study for the Ontario Royal Commission on the Northern Environment), mimeo., 1980.

37. See DREE, press release, "De Bané Announces Forestry Assistance Program," 31 July 1980.

38. A number of modest, technology-development programs were initiated during the 1970s with several provinces. The most recent example, and indeed the most significant, is the joint Alberta-Canada agreement on energy resources research. Involving a federal commitment of $96 million to assist nonoil sands related energy research in Alberta, it was partly designed to compensate Alberta for holding down the wellhead price of oil for a fifteen month period in 1974. See Alberta/Canada Energy Resources Research Fund, *Fourth Annual Report*, 1 April 1979 to 31 March 1980.

39. The total refers to funds committed during the life of agreements which were still active during 1979-80 and not simply the money expended during that year. The total excludes subagreements covering the Yukon, Northwest Territories and Prince Edward Island. Prince Edward Island has a separate Comprehensive Development Plan with Ottawa which preceded the GDA system. The federal commitment is about $2.4 billion. Figures obtained from Canada, DREE, *Annual Report 1979-80*, pp. 52-54.

40. For a general description of the subagreement and its programming components see, Canada, DREE and Manitoba, Department of Industry and Commerce, *Canada/Manitoba Subsidiary Agreement on Industrial Development*, Ottawa, 21 April 1978.

41. *Ibid.*, p. 23.

42. See, COMEF, *Manitoba 1962-1975*, Winnipeg, 1963. In addition to the MDC, the Roblin government established a coordinating agency, the Manitoba Development Authority, a provincial design institute, and the Manitoba Research Council.

43. These views were obtained from interviews with senior officials in the Manitoba Department of Economic Development, Winnipeg, November 1979.

44. Interviews with officials, DREE, Manitoba Provincial Office, Winnipeg, November 1979.

45. Donald J. Savoie, "The General Development Agreement Approach and the Bureaucratization of Provincial Governments in the Atlantic Provinces," *Canadian Public Administration*, vol. 24, no. 1, Spring 1981, pp. 119-121.

46. *Ibid.*

Part Four - Industrial Policy and the Federal Government

X. The Federal Government and Industrial Policy: Facing New Realities

1. There is, of course, a considerable debate among historians concerning which economic interests were served by the Confederation agreement – the newly rising industrial establishment or the traditional commercial élite. See, Naylor, *The History of Canadian Business*, 2 vols., James Lorimer and Company, Toronto, 1975; and G. Williams, "The National Policy Tariffs: Industrial Underdevelopment Through Import Substitution," *Canadian Journal of Political Science*, vol XII, no. 2, June 1979.

2. For a perceptive analysis of the extent of federal industrial policy from World War I to the Depression, see Tom Traves, *The State and Enter-*

prise: Canadian Manufacturers and the Federal Government 1917-1931, University of Toronto Press, Toronto, 1979.

3. J.N. Kennedy, *History of the Department of Munitions and Supply,* vol. 1, King's Printer, Ottawa, 1950, p. 5.

4. *Ibid.,* vol. II, p. 9.

5. Leslie Roberts, *The Life and Times of Clarence Decatur Howe,* Clarke Irwin, Toronto, 1957, p. 119.

6. Wartime employment in the aircraft industry rose from 4000 to 116 000. In the auto industry, the import content of vehicles declined from 36 to 25.3 per cent by 1945, and in the electronics industry, it declined from 21 to 15 per cent, while exports grew from 76 to 95 per cent and 43.3 to 85 per cent of production, respectively, for the two industries. Kennedy, *op. cit.,* vol. I, pp. 25; 102; 208.

7. Virtually all of the wartime plants established by the federal government were turned over to the private sector at approximately a third of their replacement value in return for commitments from manufacturers that existing employment levels would be maintained for five years. Well over $100 million in assets were sold or leased in this way by 1947. See, Kennedy, *op. cit.,* vol. II, p. 481; D.A. Wolfe, "Economic Growth and Foreign Investment: A Perspective on Canadian Economic Policy 1945-1957," *Journal of Canadian Studies,* vol. 13, no. 1, Spring 1978, p. 5; and J.J. Brown, "Assets to Ashes," *Macleans,* vol. 59, 15 July 1946.

8. This description of postwar economic policy is drawn largely from Wolfe, *op. cit.*

9. *Ibid.,* p. 18.

10. Government of Canada, *Foreign Direct Investment in Canada,* Information Canada, Ottawa, 1972, pp. 14-15.

11. Science Council of Canada Industrial Policies Committee, *Uncertain Prospects: Canadian Manufacturing Industry 1971-77,* Minister of Supply and Services Canada, Ottawa, October 1977, pp. 16-19.

12. D.M. Ray, "The Location of U.S. Manufacturing Subsidiaries in Canada," *Economic Geography,* 1971; and D.M. Ray, "Dimensions of Canadian Regionalism," Department of Energy, Mines and Resources Geographical Paper 49, Ottawa, 1971. Even the expansion of industrial activity during World War II was concentrated in central Canada. For example, during the war Winnipeg, Edmonton and Regina lost industrial employment; over 50 per cent of industrial employment remained in Montreal and Toronto despite a dramatic increase in such employment during the war. Kennedy, *op. cit.,* vol. II, p. 503.

13. G.B. Doern, "Spending Priorities: The Liberal View," *How Ottawa Spends Your Tax Dollars, Federal Priorities 1981,* G.B. Doern ed., James Lorimer & Co., Toronto, 1981.

14. The standard federal corporate tax rate is 46 per cent; 10 per cent of this is rebated to the province in which the firm being taxed resides.

15. G. Veilleux, "L'évolution des mécanismes de liaison intergouvernementale," in *Confrontation and Collaboration: Intergovernmental Relations in Canada Today,* A. Simeon ed., Institute of Public Administration of Canada, Toronto, 1979, p. 37.

16. This, of course, excludes the significant sums involved in federal government loans and guarantees to business, both through departmental programs and such agencies as the Federal Business Development Bank and the Export Development Corporation.

17. The bulk of these transfers are in the form of DREE support for subagreements signed under federal-provincial general development agreements.

18. Statistics supplied by ITC; they exclude expenditures on tourism.

19. Ministry of State for Science and Technology, *Federal Science Activities, 1981/82*, Supply and Services, Ottawa, 1981, p. 94.

20. For a brief review of the history of judicial interpretation of the Constitution Act, see, Martha Fletcher, "Judicial Review and the Division of Powers in Canada," *Canadian Federalism: Myth or Reality*, Peter J. Meekison, ed., 3rd ed., Toronto, Methuen, 1977, pp. 100-123. In the United States, for example, the trade and commerce power has been interpreted by the courts in a broad manner such that a locally based firm can come under federal jurisdiction even if it only has a limited connection to an industry which is heavily involved in interstate trade. Further, the scope for such regulation is considerable, varying from product standards to occupational safety and health. Because the American states cover relatively small areas, and because of the high degree of economic integration in the United States, this extension of federal economic power to control interstate trade and commerce effectively means that few large American firms can escape federal regulation. See, Alexander Smith, *The Commerce Power in Canada and the United States*, Butterworths, Toronto, 1963.

21. "Powers Over the Economy: Options Submitted for Consideration by the Government of Canada to Safeguard the Canadian Economic Union in the Constitution," CCMC Document 830-83/007, Ottawa, 1980.

22. See Fletcher, *op. cit.*; and A. Paus-Jensen, "Resource Taxation and the Supreme Court of Canada: The Cigol Case," *Canadian Public Policy*, vol. 5, no. 1, Winter 1979; P.H. Russell, "The *Anti-Inflation* Case: The Anatomy of a Constitutional Decision," *Canadian Public Administration*, vol. 20, no. 4, Winter 1977; and S.I. Bushnell, "The Control of Natural Resources through the Trade and Commerce Power and Proprietary Rights," *Canadian Public Policy*, vol. 6, no. 2, Spring 1980. One author has argued that the Constitution Act is sufficiently flexible to allow the federal government legislative control in a wider number of economic and social areas than has been assumed traditionally. See, Barry Strayer, "The Flexibility of the BNA Act," in *Agenda 1970: Proposals for a Creative Politics*, T. Lloyd and J. McLeod eds., University of Toronto Press, Toronto, 1968.

23. For a description of DEVCO's development see, Allan Tupper, "Public Enterprise as Social Welfare: The Case of the Cape Breton Development Corporation," *Canadian Public Policy*, Autumn 1978, vol. IV, no. 4.

24. The Task Force on National Unity made a number of recommendations concerning the reform of our electoral system (that is, the adoption of proportional representation) and also the reform of a number of federal institutions including the Supreme Court, the Senate and regulatory agencies to ensure balanced regional representation. See, Report of the Task Force on National Unity (Pepin-Robarts Report), *A Future Together: Observations and Recommendations*, Supply and Services Canada, Ottawa, 1979.

25. R. Simeon and D. Elkins, "Conclusions: Province, Nation, Country and Confederation," *Small Worlds: Parties and Provinces in Canadian Political Life*, D.J. Elkins and Richard Simeon eds, Methuen, Toronto, 1980, p. 289.

26. Richard D. French, *How Ottawa Decides: Planning and Industrial Policy Making, 1968-1980*, Canadian Institute for Economic Policy, Ottawa, 1980, p. 131.

27. *Ibid.*, pp. 109-117.

28. *Ibid.*, p. 114.

29. The development of Consumer and Corporate Affairs, DREE, and EIC into economic policy departments is covered in R.W. Phidd and G.B. Doern, *The Politics and Management of Canadian Economic Policy*, Macmillan,

Toronto, 1978. MOSST's role is reviewed in R. French and P. Aucoin, *Knowledge, Power and Public Policy*, Science Council of Canada, Background Study 31, Information Canada, Ottawa, 1974.

30. For a review of the evolution of IT&C, see Doern and Phidd, *op. cit.*, pp. 269-273.

31. French, *op. cit.*, p. 110.

32. A committee of economic deputy ministers known as DM-10 was established in the mid-1970s to advise the cabinet on the removal of wage and price controls and economic policy for the postcontrols period. Shortly thereafter, an interdepartmental committee on industrial and trade policy was established to help coordinate the formulation of industrial policy with the government's involvement in the Multilateral Trade Negotiations.

33. MSED's functions as a Ministry of State were set out in Order-in-Council P.C. December 19, 1978-3803 and included: the development, coordination and evaluation of comprehensive economic policies; promotion of industry-government and federal-provincial consultations over economic issues; advising the Treasury Board on the allocation of manpower and financial resources supporting economic development; and improving and integrating the delivery of federal economic development programs in Canada. In fact, the ministry's advisory function to Treasury Board, that is, the allocation of resources in the economic development envelope, has become its major function.

34. Interview, former MSED official.

35. DREE, *Climate for Regional Development*, Ottawa, 1976.

36. In some provinces, for example in Ontario, the federal government is requested by the province to allow it to distribute material on federal industrial assistance programs to eliminate duplication of effort. In addition, in provinces with small industrial development budgets, clients are frequently asked to exhaust the federal assistance programs available before seeking provincial assistance. Sometimes large provinces are required to do this as well.

37. Office of the Prime Minister, press release, "Reorganization for Economic Development," 12 January 1982. A bill (C-123) was introduced for first reading on 30 June 1982 to provide the legal framework for the changes announced in January. When this study was in press, the bill had not been passed.

38. For a general overview of MSERD's structure and operation see, R.W. Crowley, "A New Power Focus in Ottawa: The Ministry of State for Economic and Regional Development," *Optimum*, vol. 13, no. 2, 1982.

39. Canada, Department of Finance, *Economic Development for Canada in the 1980s*, Ottawa, November 1981.

40. N.H. Lithwick, "Regional Policy: The Embodiment of Contradictions"; and G.B. Doern, "Liberal Priorities 1982: The Limits of Scheming Virtuously," in *How Ottawa Spends Your Tax Dollars: National Policy and Economic Development, 1982*, G.B. Doern ed., James Lorimer & Co., Toronto, 1982.

41. IT&C and DREE, "Reorganisation Bulletin," no. 10, 7 July 1982.

XI. A Time for Change

1. On this, see, Science Council of Canada, *Forging the Links: A Technology Policy for Canada*, Supply and Services Canada, Ottawa, 1979, pp. 30-34; and Science Council of Canada Industrial Policies Committee,

Hard Times, Hard Choices: Technology and the Balance of Payments, Supply and Services Canada, Ottawa, 1981.

2. See chapter I.

3. In large measure, this has been the result of the failure of traditional macroeconomic policy instruments to produce the kinds of structural adjustments in the economy demanded because of the changing nature of international economic relations. Not only do traditional policy instruments seem incapable either of addressing current problems (for example, the failure of Keynesian economic policy to deal with stagflation) or of providing politically acceptable results (for example, the increasingly unacceptable trade-off monetarism offers between unemployment and inflation), but many of the problems of adapting industry to changing economic circumstances are simply not addressed by such macroeconomic tools. For example, we seem to be reaching the limits to which our tax system can cope with virtually every type of industrial adjustment without imposing a deleterious impact both on the equity of the system and its ability to raise revenue.

4. See the proposal from the Deputy Minister of Intergovernmental Affairs of Ontario, in D. Stevenson, "The Role of Intergovernmental Conferences in the Decision-Making Process," *Confrontation and Collaboration - Intergovernmental Relations in Canada Today*, R. Simeon ed., Institute of Public Administration of Canada, Toronto, 1979, esp. pp. 96-98; and Albert Robinson, "How to Agree About Budgeting: An Intergovernmental Commission Might Do the Trick," *Policy Options*, vol. 2, no. 3, July/August 1981.

5. L. Grossman, *Interprovincial Economic Co-operation: Towards the Development of a Canadian Common Market*, Ministry of Industry and Tourism, Toronto, January 1981.

6. It should be noted that IT&C's Enterprise Development Program, which was established in the late 1970s, was a first attempt to devolve program administration to the regions and, through provincial boards, to involve not only local businessmen, but provincial officials as well.

7. Canada, Senate Standing Committee on National Finance, *Government Policy and Regional Development*, Supply and Services Canada, Ottawa, 1982, esp. chaps. 7 and 8.

8. Indeed, the experience with central policy ministries in general has not been a happy one. On Canada's experience with such ministries see, P. Aucoin and Richard French, *Knowledge, Power and Public Policy*, Science Council Background Study 31, Information Canada, Ottawa, 1974. In the mid-1960s, the United Kingdom experimented with a central policy ministry for economic planning which was also a failure; see Trevor Smith, "Britain," *Planning, Politics and Public Policy: The British, French and Italian Experience*, M. Watson and J. Hayward eds., Cambridge University Press, London, 1975; R. Opie, "Economic Planning and Growth," *op., cit.*, and A. Graham, "Industrial Policy," *The Labour Government's Economic Record 1964-70*, W. Beckerman ed., Duckworth, London, 1972; and M. Shanks, *Planning and Politics: The British Experience 1960-76*, Allan and Unwin, London, 1977.

Glossary

AEC	Alberta Energy Company
AGTL	Alberta Gas Trunk Lines
AHSTF	Alberta Heritage Savings Trust Fund
AOC	Alberta Opportunity Company
AOSTRA	Alberta Oil Sands Technology and Research Authority
BEDM	Board of Economic Development Ministers
BILD	Board of Industrial Leadership and Development
CAD/CAM	Computer-Aided Design/Computer-Aided Manufacturing
C-CORE	Centre for Cold Oceans Resources Engineering
CCREM	Canadian Council of Resource and Environment Ministers
CDP	Comprehensive Development Plan
CDP	La Caisse de dépôt et de placement
CMP	Council of Maritime Premiers
CRIQ	Centre de recherche industrielle du Québec
DEVCO	Cape Breton Development Corporation
DREE	Department of Regional Economic Expansion
DRIE	Department of Regional Industrial Expansion
EDF	Employment Development Fund
EDP	Enterprise Development Program
ECC	Economic Council of Canada
EIC	Employment and Immigration Canada
EMR	Energy, Mines and Resources Canada
FIDC	Forest Industry Development Committee
FPRO	Federal-Provincial Relations Office
GATT	General Agreement on Tariffs and Trade
GDA	General Development Agreement
IDEA Corporation	Innovation Development for Employment Advancement Corporation
IREQ	Institut de recherche d'Hydro-Québec
ISABs	Industrial Sector Advisory Boards
IT&C	(The Department of) Industry, Trade and Commerce
MEC	Maritime Energy Corporation

MOSST	Ministry of State for Science and Technology
MSED	Ministry of State for Economic Development
MSERD	Ministry of State for Economic and Regional Development
MTNs	Multilateral Trade Negotiations
NEP	National Energy Policy
NICs	Newly Industrializing Countries
NORDCO Ltd.	Newfoundland Oceans Research Development Corporation Ltd.
PEC	Prairie Economic Council
PCO	Privy Council Office
SDI	Société de développement industriel
SEDCO	Saskatchewan Economic Development Corporation
SGF	Société générale de financement
SODICC	Société de développement des industries de la culture et des communications
VACRED	Voluntary Advisory Committee on Regional Economic Development
WEOC	Western Economic Opportunities Conference
WPC	Western Premiers' Conference

Publications of the Science Council of Canada

Policy Reports

Report No. 1, **A Space Program for Canada,** July 1967 (SS22-1967/1, $0.75), 31 p.

Report No. 2, **The Proposal for an Intense Neutron Generator: Initial Assessment and Recommendation,** December 1967 (SS22-1967/2, $0.75), 12 p.

Report No. 3, **A Major Program of Water Resources Research in Canada,** September 1968 (SS22-1968/3, $0.75), 37 p.

Report No. 4, **Towards a National Science Policy in Canada,** October 1968 (SS22-1968/4, $1.00), 56 p.

Report No. 5, **University Research and the Federal Government,** September 1969 (SS22-1969/5, $0.75), 28 p.

Report No. 6, **A Policy for Scientific and Technical Information Dissemination,** September 1969 (SS22-1969/6, $0.75), 35 p.

Report No. 7, **Earth Sciences Serving the Nation – Recommendations,** April 1970 (SS22-1970/7, $0.75), 36 p.

Report No. 8, **Seeing the Forest and the Trees,** October 1970 (SS22-1970/8, $0.75), 22 p.

Report No. 9, **This Land is Their Land...,** October 1970 (SS22-1970/9, $0.75), 41 p.

Report No. 10, **Canada, Science and the Oceans,** November 1970 (SS22-1970/10, $0.75), 37 p.

Report No. 11, **A Canadian STOL Air Transport System – A Major Program,** December 1970 (SS22-1970/11, $0.75), 33 p.

Report No. 12, **Two Blades of Grass: The Challenge Facing Agriculture,** March 1971 (SS22-1971/12, $1.25), 61 p.

Report No. 13, **A Trans-Canada Computer Communications Network: Phase 1 of a Major Program on Computers,** August 1971 (SS22-1971/13, $0.75), 41 p.

Report No. 14, **Cities for Tomorrow: Some Applications of Science and Technology to Urban Development,** September 1971 (SS22-1971/14, $1.25), 67 p.

Report No. 15, **Innovation in a Cold Climate: The Dilemma of Canadian Manufacturing,** October 1971 (SS22-1971/15, $0.75), 49 p.

Report No. 16, **It is Not Too Late - Yet: A look at some pollution problems in Canada...,** June 1972 (SS22-1972/16, $1.00), 52 p.

Report No. 17, **Lifelines: Some Policies for a Basic Biology in Canada,** August 1972 (SS22-1972/17, $1.00), 73 p.

Report No. 18, **Policy Objectives for Basic Research in Canada,** September 1972 (SS22-1972/18, $1.00), 75 p.

Report No. 19, **Natural Resource Policy Issues in Canada,** January 1973 (SS22-1973/19, $1.25), 59 p.

Report No. 20, **Canada, Science and International Affairs,** April 1973 (SS22-1973/20, $1.25), 66 p.

Report No. 21, **Strategies of Development for the Canadian Computer Industry,** September 1973 (SS22-1973/21, $1.50), 80 p.

Report No. 22, **Science for Health Services,** October 1974 (SS22-1974/22, $2.00), 140 p.

Report No. 23, **Canada's Energy Opportunities,** March 1975 (SS22-1975/23, Canada: $4.95, other countries: $5.95), 135 p.

Report No. 24, **Technology Transfer: Government Laboratories to Manufacturing Industry,** December 1975 (SS22-1975/24, Canada: $1.00, other countries: $1.20), 61 p.

Report No. 25, **Population, Technology and Resources,** July 1976 (SS22-1976/25, Canada: $3.00, other countries: $3.60), 91 p.

Report No. 26, **Northward Looking: A Strategy and a Science Policy for Northern Development,** August 1977 (SS22-1977/26, Canada: $2.50, other countries: $3.00), 95 p.

Report No. 27, **Canada as a Conserver Society: Resource Uncertainties and the Need for New Technologies,** September 1977 (SS22-1977/27, Canada: $4.00, other countries: $4.80), 108 p.

Report No. 28, **Policies and Poisons: The Containment of Long-term Hazards to Human Health in the Environment and in the Workplace,** October 1977 (SS22-1977/28, Canada: $2.00, other countries: $2.40), 76 p.

Report No. 29, **Forging the Links: A Technology Policy for Canada,** February 1979 (SS22-1979/29, Canada: $2.25, other countries: $2.70), 72 p.

Report No. 30, **Roads to Energy Self-Reliance: The Necessary National Demonstrations,** June 1979 (SS22-1979/30, Canada: $4.50, other countries: $5.40), 200 p.

Report No. 31, **University Research in Jeopardy: The Threat of Declining Enrolment,** December 1979 (SS22-1979/31, Canada: $2.95, other countries: $3.55), 61 p.

Report No. 32, **Collaboration for Self-Reliance: Canada's Scientific and Technological Contribution to the Food Supply of Developing Countries,** March 1981 (SS22-1981/32, Canada: $3.95, other countries: $4.75), 112 p.

Report No. 33, **Tomorrow is Too Late: Planning Now for an Information Society,** April 1982 (SS22-1982/33, Canada: $4.50, other countries: $5.40), 77 p.

Report No. 34, **Transportation in a Resource-Conscious Future: Intercity Passenger Travel in Canada,** September 1982 (SS22-1982/34, Canada: $4.95, other countries: $5.95), 112 p.

Report No. 35, **Regulating the Regulators: Science, Values and Decisions,** October 1982 (SS22-1982/35, Canada: $4.95, other countries: $5.95), 106 p.

Statements of Council

Supporting Canadian Science: Time for Action, May 1978
Canada's Threatened Forests, March 1983

Statements of Council Committees

Toward a Conserver Society: A Statement of Concern, by the Committee on the Implications of a Conserver Society, 1976, 22 p.

Erosion of the Research Manpower Base in Canada: A Statement of Concern, by the Task Force on Research in Canada, 1976.

Uncertain Prospects: Canadian Manufacturing Industry 1971-1977, by the Industrial Policies Committee, 1977, 55 p.

Communications and Computers: Information and Canadian Society, by an ad hoc committee, 1978, 40 p.

A Scenario for the Implementation of Interactive Computer-Communications Systems in the Home, by the Committee on Computers and Communication, 1979, 40 p.

Multinationals and Industrial Strategy: The Role of World Product Mandates, by the Working Group on Industrial Policies, 1980, 77 p.

Hard Times, Hard Choices: A Statement, by the Industrial Policies Committee, 1981, 99 p.

The Science Education of Women in Canada: A Statement of Concern, by the Science and Education Committee, 1982.

Reports on Matters Referred by the Minister

Research and Development in Canada, a report of the Ad Hoc Advisory Committee to the Minister of State for Science and Technology, 1979, 32 p.

Public Awareness of Science and Technology in Canada, a staff report to the Minister of State for Science and Technology, 1981, 57 p.

Background Studies

Background Study No. 1,	**Upper Atmosphere and Space Programs in Canada,** by J.H. Chapman, P.A. Forsyth, P.A. Lapp, G.N. Patterson, February 1967 (SS21-1/1, $2.50), 258 p.
Background Study No. 2,	**Physics in Canada: Survey and Outlook, by a Study Group of the Canadian Association of Physicists,** headed by D.C. Rose, May 1967 (SS21-1/2, $2.50), 385 p.
Background Study No. 3,	**Psychology in Canada,** by M.H. Appley and Jean Rickwood, September 1967 (SS21-1/3, $2.50), 131 p.
Background Study No. 4,	**The Proposal for an Intense Neutron Generator: Scientific and Economic Evaluation,** by a Committee of the Science Council of Canada, December 1967 (SS21-1/4, $2.00), 181 p.
Background Study No. 5,	**Water Resources Research in Canada,** by J.P. Bruce and D.E.L. Maasland, July 1968 (SS21-1/5, $2.50), 169 p.
Background Study No. 6,	**Background Studies in Science Policy: Projections of R&D Manpower and Expenditure,** by R.W. Jackson, D.W. Henderson and B. Leung, 1969 (SS21-1/6, $1.25), 85 p.
Background Study No. 7,	**The Role of the Federal Government in Support of Research in Canadian Universities,** by John B. Macdonald, L.P. Dugal, J.S. Dupré, J.B. Marshall, J.G. Parr, E. Sirluck, and E. Vogt, 1969 (SS21-1/7, $3.75), 361 p.

Background Study No. 8,	**Scientific and Technical Information in Canada, Part I,** by J.P.I. Tyas, 1969 (SS21-1/8, $1.50), 62 p. Part II, Chapter 1, Government Departments and Agencies (SS21-1/8-2-1, $1.75), 168 p. Part II, Chapter 2, Industry (SS21-1/8-2-2, $1.25), 80 p. Part II, Chapter 3, Universities (SS21-1/8-2-3, $1.75), 115 p. Part II, Chapter 4, International Organizations and Foreign Countries (SS21-1/8-2-4, $1.00), 63 p. Part II, Chapter 5, Techniques and Sources (SS21-1/8-2-5, $1.15), 99 p. Part II, Chapter 6, Libraries (SS21-1/8-2-6, $1.00), 49 p. Part II, Chapter 7, Economics (SS21-1/8-2-7, $1.00), 63 p.
Background Study No. 9,	**Chemistry and Chemical Engineering: A Survey of Research and Development in Canada,** by a Study Group of the Chemical Institute of Canada, 1969 (SS21-1/9, $2.50), 102 p.
Background Study No. 10,	**Agricultural Science in Canada,** by B.N. Smallman, D.A. Chant, D.M. Connor, J.C. Gilson, A.E. Hannah, D.N. Huntley, E. Mercer, M. Shaw, 1970 (SS21-1/10, $2.00), 148 p.
Background Study No. 11,	**Background to Invention,** by Andrew H. Wilson, 1970 (SS21-1/11, $1.50), 77 p.
Background Study No. 12,	**Aeronautics - Highway to the Future,** by J.J. Green, 1970 (SS21-1/12, $2.50), 148 p.
Background Study No. 13,	**Earth Sciences Serving the Nation,** by Roger A. Blais, Charles H. Smith, J.E. Blanchard, J.T. Cawley, D.R. Derry, Y.O. Fortier, G.G.L. Henderson, J.R. Mackay, J.S. Scott, H.O. Seigel, R.B. Toombs, H.D.B. Wilson, 1971 (SS21-1/13, $4.50), 363 p.
Background Study No. 14,	**Forest Resources in Canada,** by J. Harry, G. Smith and Gilles Lessard, May 1971 (SS21-1/14, $3.50), 204 p.
Background Study No. 15,	**Scientific Activities in Fisheries and Wildlife Resources,** by D.H. Pimlott, C.J. Kerswill and J.R. Bider, June 1971 (SS21-1/15, $3.50), 191 p.
Background Study No. 16,	**Ad Mare: Canada Looks to the Sea,** by R.W. Stewart and L.M. Dickie, September 1971 (SS21-1/16, $2.50), 175 p.
Background Study No. 17,	**A Survey of Canadian Activity in Transportation R&D,** by C.B. Lewis, May 1971 (SS21-1/17, $0.75), 29 p.
Background Study No. 18,	**From Formalin to Fortran: Basic Biology in Canada,** by P.A. Larkin and W.J.D. Stephen, August 1971 (SS21-1/18, $2.50), 79 p.
Background Study No. 19,	**Research Councils in the Provinces: A Canadian Resource,** by Andrew H. Wilson, June 1971 (SS21-1/19, $1.50), 115 p.
Background Study No. 20,	**Prospects for Scientists and Engineers in Canada,** by Frank Kelly, March 1971 (SS21-1/20, $1.00), 61 p.
Background Study No. 21,	**Basic Research,** by P. Kruus, December 1971 (SS21-1/21, $1.50), 73 p.
Background Study No. 22,	**The Multinational Firm, Foreign Direct Investment, and Canadian Science Policy,** by Arthur J. Cordell, December 1971 (SS21-1/22, $1.50), 95 p.

Background Study No. 23,	**Innovation and the Structure of Canadian Industry,** by Pierre L. Bourgault, October 1972 (SS21-1/23, $4.00), 135 p.
Background Study No. 24,	**Air Quality - Local, Regional and Global Aspects,** by R.E. Munn, October 1972 (SS21-1/24, $0.75), 39 p.
Background Study No. 25,	**National Engineering, Scientific and Technological Societies of Canada,** by the Management Committee of SCITEC and Prof. Allen S. West, December 1971 (SS21-1/25, $2.50), 131 p.
Background Study No. 26,	**Governments and Innovation,** by Andrew H. Wilson, April 1973 (SS21-1/26, $3.75), 275 p.
Background Study No. 27,	**Essays on Aspects of Resource Policy,** by W.D. Bennett, A.D. Chambers, A.R. Thompson, H.R. Eddy, and A.J. Cordell, May 1973 (SS21-1/27, $2.50), 113 p.
Background Study No. 28,	**Education and Jobs: Career patterns among selected Canadian science graduates with international comparisons,** by A.D. Boyd and A.C. Gross, June 1973 (SS21-1/28, $2.25), 139 p.
Background Study No. 29,	**Health Care in Canada: A Commentary,** by H. Rocke Robertson, August 1973 (SS21-1/29, $2.75), 173 p.
Background Study No. 30,	**A Technology Assessment System: A Case Study of East Coast Offshore Petroleum Exploration,** by M. Gibbons and R. Voyer, March 1974 (SS21-1/30, $2.00), 114 p.
Background Study No. 31,	**Knowledge, Power and Public Policy,** by Peter Aucoin and Richard French, November 1974 (SS21-1/31, $2.00), 95 p.
Background Study No. 32,	**Technology Transfer in Construction,** by A.D. Boyd and A.H. Wilson, January 1975 (SS21-1/32, $3.50), 163 p.
Background Study No. 33,	**Energy Conservation,** by F.H. Knelman, July 1975 (SS21-1/33, Canada: $1.75, other countries: $2.10), 169 p.
Background Study No. 34,	**Northern Development and Technology Assessment Systems: A study of petroleum development programs in the Mackenzie Delta-Beaufort Sea Region and the Arctic Islands,** by Robert F. Keith, David W. Fischer, Colin E. De'Ath, Edward J. Farkas, George R. Francis, and Sally C. Lerner, January 1976 (SS21-1/34, Canada: $3.75, other countries: $4.50), 219 p.
Background Study No. 35,	**The Role and Function of Government Laboratories and the Transfer of Technology to the Manufacturing Sector,** by A.J. Cordell and J.M. Gilmour, April 1976 (SS21-1/35, Canada: $6.50, other countries: $7.80), 397 p.
Background Study No. 36,	**The Political Economy of Northern Development,** by K.J. Rea, April 1976 (SS21-1/36, Canada: $4.00, other countries: $4.80), 251 p.
Background Study No. 37,	**Mathematical Sciences in Canada,** by Klaus P. Beltzner, A. John Coleman, and Gordon D. Edwards, July 1976 (SS21-1/37, Canada: $6.50, other countries: $7.80), 339 p.
Background Study No. 38,	**Human Goals and Science Policy,** by R.W. Jackson, October 1976 (SS21-1/38, Canada: $4.00, other countries: $4.80), 134 p.

Background Study No. 39,	**Canadian Law and the Control of Exposure to Hazards,** by Robert T. Franson, Alastair R. Lucas, Lorne Giroux, and Patrick Kenniff, October 1977 (SS21-1/39, Canada: $4.00, other countries: $4.80), 152 p.
Background Study No. 40,	**Government Regulation of the Occupational and General Environments in the United Kingdom, United States and Sweden,** by Roger Williams, October 1977 (SS21-1/40, Canada: $5.00, other countries: $6.00), 155 p.
Background Study No. 41,	**Regulatory Processes and Jurisdictional Issues in the Regulation of Hazardous Products in Canada,** by G. Bruce Doern, October 1977 (SS21-1/41, Canada: $5.50, other countries: $6.00), 201 p.
Background Study No. 42,	**The Strathcona Sound Mining Project: A Case Study of Decision Making,** by Robert B. Gibson, February 1978 (SS21-1/42, Canada: $8.00, other countries: $9.60), 274 p.
Background Study No. 43,	**The Weakest Link: A Technological Perspective on Canadian Industry Underdevelopment,** by John N.H. Britton and James M. Gilmour, assisted by Mark G. Murphy, October 1978 (SS21-1/43, Canada: $5.00, other countries: $6.00), 216 p.
Background Study No. 44,	**Canadian Government Participation in International Science and Technology,** by Jocelyn Maynard Ghent, February 1979 (SS21-1/44, Canada: $4.50, other countries: $5.40), 136 p.
Background Study No. 45,	**Partnership in Development: Canadian Universities and World Food,** by William E. Tossell, August 1980 (SS21-1/45, Canada: $6.00, other countries: $7.20), 145 p.
Background Study No. 46,	**The Peripheral Nature of Scientific and Technological Controversy in Federal Policy Formation,** by G. Bruce Doern, July 1981 (SS21-1/46, Canada: $4.95, other countries: $5.95), 108 p.
Background Study No. 47,	**Public Inquiries in Canada,** by Liora Salter and Debra Slaco, with the assistance of Karin Konstantynowicz, September 1981, (SS21-1/47, Canada: $7.95, other countries: $9.55), 232 p.
Background Study No. 48,	**Threshold Firms: Backing Canada's Winners,** by Guy P.F. Steed, July 1982, (SS21-1/48, Canada: $6.95, other countries: $8.35), 173 p.
Background Study No. 49,	**Governments and Microelectronics: The European Experience,** by Dirk de Vos, March 1983, (SS21-1/49, Canada: $4.50, other countries: $5.40), 112 p.
Background Study No. 50,	**The Challenge of Diversity: Industrial Policy in the Canadian Federation,** by Michael Jenkin, July 1983, (SS21-1/50, Canada: $8.95, other countries: $10.75), 214 p.

Occasional Publications

1976
Energy Scenarios for the Future, by Hedlin, Menzies & Associates, 423 p.
Science and the North: An Essay on Aspirations, by Peter Larkin, 8 p.

A Nuclear Dialogue: Proceedings of a Workshop on Issues in Nuclear Power for Canada, 75 p.

1977
An Overview of the Canadian Mercury Problem, by Clarence T. Charlebois, 20 p.
An Overview of the Vinyl Chloride Hazard in Canada, by J. Basuk, 16 p.
Materials Recycling: History, Status, Potential, by F.T. Gerson Limited, 98 p.

The Workshop on Optimization of Age Distribution in University Research:
      – Proceedings
      – Papers for Discussion, 215 p.
      – Background Papers, 338 p.
Living with Climatic Change: A Proceedings, 90 p.
Proceedings of the Seminar on Natural Gas from the Arctic by Marine Mode: A Preliminary Assessment, 254 p.
Seminar on a National Transportation System for Optimum Service: A Proceedings, 73 p.

1978
A Northern Resource Centre: A First Step Toward a University of the North, by the Committee on Northern Development
An Overview of the Canadian Asbestos Problem, by Clarence T. Charlebois, 20 p.
An Overview of the Oxides of Nitrogren Problem in Canada, by J. Basuk, 48 p.
Federal Funding of Science in Canada: Apparent and Effective Levels, by J. Miedzinski and K.P. Beltzner, 78 p.

Appropriate Scale for Canadian Industry: A Proceedings, 211 p.
Proceedings of the Public Forum on Policies and Poisons, held in Toronto, 15 November 1977, 40 p.
Science Policies in Smaller Industrialized Northern Countries: A Proceedings, 93 p.

1979
A Canadian Context for Science Education, by James E. Page, 52 p.
An Overview of the Ionizing Radiation Hazard in Canada, by J. Basuk, 225 p.
Canadian Food and Agriculture: Sustainability and Self-Reliance: A Discussion Paper, by the Committee on Canada's Scientific and Technological Contribution to World Food Supply, 52 p.

From the Bottom Up - Involvement of Canadian NGOs in Food and Rural Development in the Third World: A Proceedings, 153 p.
Opportunities in Canadian Transportation
    Conference Proceedings: 1, 162 p.
    Auto Sub-Conference Proceedings: 2, 136 p.
    Bus/Rail Sub-Conference Proceedings: 3, 122 p.
    Air Sub-Conference Proceedings: 4, 131 p.
The Politics of an Industrial Strategy: A Proceedings, 115 p.

1980
Food for the Poor: The Role of CIDA in Agricultural, Fisheries and Rural Development, by Suteera Thomson, 194 p.
Science in Social Issues: Implications for Teaching, by Glen S. Aikenhead, 81 p.

Entropy and the Economic Process: A Proceedings, 107 p.

Opportunitites in Canadian Transportation Conference Proceedings: 5, 270 p.
Proceedings of the Seminar on University Research in Jeopardy, 83 p.
Social Issues in Human Genetics - Genetic Screening and Counselling: A Proceedings,
    110 p.
The Impact of the Microelectronics Revolution on Work and Working: A Proceedings,
    73 p.

1981
An Engineer's View of Science Education, by Donald A. George, 34 p.
**The Limits of Consultation: A Debate among Ottawa, the Provinces, and the
    Private Sector on an Industrial Strategy,** by D. Brown, J. Eastman, with
    I. Robinson, 195 p.

Biotechnology in Canada - Promises and Concerns, 62 p.
Challenge of the Research Complex:
        Volume 1: Proceedings, 116 p.
        Volume 2: Papers, 324 p.
The Adoption of Foreign Technology by Canadian Industry, 152 p.
The Impact of the Microelectronics Revolution on the Canadian Electronics Industry,
    109 p.
Policy Issues in Computer-Aided Learning, 51 p.

1982
What is Scientific Thinking? by Hugh Munby, 43 p.
Macroscole, A Holistic Approach to Science Teaching, by M. Risi, 61 p.

Québec Science Education - Which Directions?, 135 p.
Who turns the Wheel?, 136 p.

1983
Parliamentarians and Science, by Karen Fish, 49 p.
**Scientific Literacy: Towards Balance in Setting Goals for School Science
    Programs,** by Douglas A. Roberts, 43 p.
The Conserver Society Revisited, by Ted Schrecker, 50 p.